RJ STARR

The Psychology of the Artificial Era

How to Stay Human, Relevant, and Resilient in the Age of AI

≣ Depthmark

First published by Depthmark Press 2025

Library of Congress Control Number: Application submitted and pending at time of publication.

First edition

ISBN: 979-8-9996293-2-6

This book was professionally typeset on Reedsy.
Find out more at reedsy.com

For those still willing to think deeply, feel fully, and stay awake in a world that rewards neither.
For the teachers who protect curiosity, the thinkers who resist noise, and the ordinary people who choose awareness over automation.
May this book remind you that consciousness itself—steady, humble, and alive—is the last and greatest human frontier.

Awareness is the quiet rebellion against unconscious progress.

In every age, humanity builds outward faster than it grows inward; the balance between the two decides whether it evolves or collapses.

To remain human is not to resist change, but to inhabit it consciously—to remember that intelligence without empathy is only a mirror without a face.

— RJ STARR, AUTHOR

Contents

Preface

I began noticing something strange long before the headlines caught up to it. Students stopped asking follow-up questions. Professionals, once proud of the hard-won intuition that came from experience, began second-guessing their instincts because a machine could respond faster. In conversations across classrooms, boardrooms, and online spaces, I saw the same quiet unease appear on people's faces—the sense that something essential to being human was quietly slipping out from under them. We were still thinking, but the process of thinking no longer felt like ours.

When artificial intelligence entered the public sphere through generative tools—systems that could write, illustrate, compose, and simulate understanding—it did more than revolutionize technology. It redefined what it meant to know, to learn, and to contribute. Knowledge, once an achievement of effort, became an instantly accessible product. Curiosity, which used to drive exploration, began competing with convenience. The intellectual climb that once built self-trust was replaced by the immediate plateau of automatic answers. I realized then that our collective psychology was about to change more rapidly than our machines.

This book exists because the conversation around AI has been dominated by engineers, economists, and ethicists—but not psychologists. We have debated efficiency, safety, and productivity while neglecting the emotional, cognitive, and existential toll of a world that no longer needs us to struggle to know. I am not writing about machines. I am writing about minds—the human mind in particular—and what happens to it when reality becomes partly synthetic.

The truth is that technology has always transformed psychology. The printing press rewired attention, the photograph reshaped memory, and the internet rewrote social identity. But generative intelligence introduces something unprecedented: an external agent that can imitate not just output but inner process. It can mirror tone, mimic empathy, and simulate insight. For the first time, human beings are confronting an imitation of consciousness so convincing that it forces us to reconsider our own. The psychological consequences of that confrontation are already everywhere— in classrooms where students doubt the value of effort, in offices where employees feel replaceable, and in relationships mediated through filters of optimization and self-presentation.

I write this book not as a technophobe but as a psychologist who sees a widening emotional gap between progress and meaning. The human nervous system has not evolved at the pace of its inventions. Our tools accelerate exponentially, yet our capacity for integration remains slow, embodied, and relational. We were built to adapt through gradual learning, not perpetual acceleration. When the world moves too fast for reflection, identity becomes reactionary. People lose the narrative thread of their own development. That is not a technological crisis; it is a psychological one.

The goal of *The Psychology of the Artificial Era* is to name this dislocation and provide a framework for recovery. I want readers to understand how attention, emotion, and meaning are being reshaped—not by malicious intent but by the mechanical logic of systems that reward immediacy over depth. The book will not tell you how to code, invest, or compete. It will tell you how to remain human in a world that increasingly asks you to think like a machine.

The human mind, when stripped of friction, begins to atrophy in invisible ways. Friction—the slow burn of curiosity, the resistance of uncertainty— is what builds competence and character. When generative systems remove those natural obstacles, they also remove the emotional satisfaction that comes from mastery. What we call "progress" can quietly become psychological malnutrition: full of stimulation but devoid of nourishment. I have watched bright, thoughtful people lose the will to wrestle with ideas because synthetic intelligence seems to have pre-solved them. We outsource cognition, then wonder why our inner world feels thinner.

And yet, I do not see despair here. I see opportunity—the chance to understand ourselves at a deeper level than any previous generation has been forced to. The Artificial Era is not an apocalypse; it is a mirror. It reflects back our habits of mind, our assumptions about value, and our craving for certainty. It exposes how fragile our self-worth becomes when measured against efficiency rather than meaning. What troubles people about AI is rarely the machine itself; it is the realization that we have been living mechanically for a long time. The algorithms did not invent our numbness—they revealed it.

As I began outlining this book, I asked myself what truly distinguishes us from what we have built. Intelligence is no longer enough; neither is creativity in its most conventional sense. Machines now produce fluent novelty on demand. The difference lies in awareness—the ability to feel the weight of knowing, to sense context, to hold contradiction without collapsing into confusion. Consciousness, in the human sense, includes vulnerability, moral reflection, and the capacity for care. These qualities cannot be optimized; they must be cultivated. This is where our relevance remains, and it is where the psychology of the future must focus.

In my lectures and research, I often remind students that technology is not neutral. Every tool reshapes the user. The question is not whether AI will change humanity—it already has—but whether we will participate consciously in that change. The work ahead is not only technical adaptation but emotional adaptation: rebuilding the inner architecture required to coexist with intelligence that never sleeps, never doubts, and never feels. The challenge is to maintain integrity without falling into nostalgia, to evolve without surrendering the inner life that makes evolution meaningful.

Writing this book is my attempt to build that bridge. It is written for the reader who senses that something in the modern psyche is being hollowed out by automation. It is for the teacher who sees attention spans collapse under digital saturation, the professional who feels reduced to a data point, and the ordinary individual who wonders if authenticity still matters when simulation can mimic it so well. These are not abstract dilemmas; they are emotional realities. Anxiety, envy, exhaustion, and alienation are not bugs in the system—they are psychological signals that we have entered an environment our biology did not design us for.

But the same psychology that makes us vulnerable to these pressures also gives us tools for resilience. Awareness, curiosity, empathy, and value-based action are not optional virtues; they are adaptive strategies. They allow us to metabolize complexity rather than retreat from it. In the pages that follow, this book will trace how those capacities can be reclaimed and strengthened, not as nostalgia for a simpler time but as preparation for a more complex one. Remaining human is not a defensive act. It is an evolutionary one.

I have deliberately chosen to write in a style that balances scholarship with accessibility. The Artificial Era does not need another technical manual; it needs psychological literacy. We must learn to read our own responses—our attention patterns, our emotional fatigue, our shifting sense of identity—with the same precision we apply to code or algorithms. The most important form of intelligence in this century may be the ability to regulate one's own mind in the face of endless stimulation. Emotional regulation, once considered a soft skill, has become an existential one.

Throughout my career, I have witnessed how people adapt to disruption. When the familiar world falls away, the first reaction is disorientation. Then comes denial, then anger, and eventually, if guided well, curiosity. That sequence—the emotional anatomy of change—applies as much to societal transformation as it does to personal growth. We are in that process now, globally. The initial awe of AI has given way to anxiety and confusion. What follows, I hope, is collective curiosity: a willingness to examine what this technology reveals about us rather than only what it does for us.

The danger is not that machines will think, but that humans will stop. When information is abundant, discernment becomes scarce. When automation handles output, reflection must become our new labor. The modern mind is being asked to relearn slowness, contemplation, and internal coherence. These are psychological muscles that atrophy in the absence of deliberate exercise. The artificial world rewards immediacy; the human world requires meaning. The two will coexist, but only if we remember which one sustains us.

My intent is not to moralize. Every technological revolution brings both promise and peril. The printing press spread literacy and propaganda alike. The internet connected and fragmented us simultaneously. The same will be true of artificial intelligence. What determines whether it becomes a force for growth or decay is not the code, but the consciousness using it. The machines may optimize outcomes, but only humans can decide what those outcomes are for. That responsibility—the ethical dimension of intelligence—is the final test of our maturity as a species.

If there is a single thread running through this book, it is that psychological health in the Artificial Era depends on integration. We must integrate intellect with emotion, speed with stillness, innovation with conscience. Fragmentation is the mind's natural defense against overwhelm, but integration is its path to resilience. Our era's greatest temptation is to specialize into irrelevance—to know much about little, to feel little about much. Yet meaning emerges only where knowledge and empathy meet. Artificial intelligence can simulate knowledge; it cannot feel meaning.

I do not believe we are doomed to become hollow participants in our own creations. History shows that each wave of disruption forces humanity to rediscover its essence. The industrial revolution gave birth to psychology itself, a discipline born from the shock of mechanization. Perhaps the rise of artificial intelligence will do the same for consciousness—forcing us to study not only how we think, but why we feel, decide, and care. If so, this moment is not an ending but an awakening.

As you read this book, you will not find predictions about the next decade of technology. You will find a map of the human interior—attention, emotion, identity, and meaning—drawn in the context of the most transformative invention of our time. It is meant to serve as a psychological compass, not a manual. My hope is that by understanding how the Artificial Era shapes us, we can participate in it with intention rather than inertia.

When I think about what it means to stay human, I come back to a simple observation: consciousness is not efficient. It hesitates, doubts, and reflects. It takes time to care. Machines will always outperform us in speed, but they will never replicate the moral and emotional weight of awareness. To be human is to carry that weight willingly—to remain awake in a world that rewards automaticity. The Artificial Era will test our capacity for that awareness, but it will also give us unprecedented reasons to develop it.

We stand at a threshold where intelligence is abundant but wisdom is scarce. If this book accomplishes anything, I hope it reminds readers that wisdom is not the byproduct of data; it is the synthesis of experience, empathy, and reflection. Those are not vanishing traits. They are the next frontier of human development. What we build externally must now be matched by what we cultivate internally.

The purpose of this work is not to romanticize the past but to guide the future—to show that the psychological skills that once ensured survival now ensure significance. Curiosity, resilience, empathy, and conscience remain the most advanced technologies we possess. They require no updates, only use.

I write this book as both a scholar and a participant in this historical moment. I do not claim neutrality; I claim care. The questions raised here will shape how we educate, relate, govern, and grow. They will determine whether the next era deepens our humanity or disperses it. My hope is that we choose the former, not through fear or resistance, but through understanding. Because in the end, to understand is to remember what we are trying to preserve.

That is why this book exists.

* * *

Introduction

The conversation about artificial intelligence has been dominated by predictions of replacement. Machines, it is said, will outperform human beings at nearly everything—learning faster, deciding faster, producing faster. But the more pressing question is not what machines will do to us; it is what they will draw out of us. The Artificial Era is not defined by the loss of human purpose but by the need to reorient it. The essential work of this century will be psychological, not mechanical: learning how to live, think, and create in partnership with intelligence that does not feel.

Humanity has always defined itself in contrast to its tools. The plow distinguished civilization from wilderness, the telescope from ignorance, the computer from limitation. But the new generation of artificial systems does not extend our muscles; it extends our minds. It simulates memory, creativity, empathy, and reasoning—the very faculties through which people have long understood themselves to be distinct. The result is a quiet but profound identity disruption. To understand how to live within this transformation, one must first recognize that technology does not simply change what humans can do; it changes what it *means* to be human.

Psychology offers the most direct lens through which to understand this shift. Cognitive science has long described the human mind as a prediction machine—a system that filters sensory input through memory, expectation, and belief. Artificial intelligence now mirrors that process externally, making visible the mechanisms of inference that were once invisible. This externalization of cognition challenges the boundary between the inner and outer world. What used to be an internal function—recall, association, synthesis—has become a shared environment. People no longer think alone; they think alongside.

That collaboration can either expand consciousness or narrow it, depending on how it is approached. As the psychologist Albert Bandura established in his foundational research on self-efficacy, human motivation depends not merely on outcome but on the felt sense of agency in achieving it. When machines handle the process, the reward structure of effort collapses. The individual begins to experience learned helplessness at a cognitive level—a sense that one's contribution no longer alters reality. To adapt well to the Artificial Era, people must therefore redefine mastery itself. The task is not to outperform the machine but to direct it—to transform automation from a competitor into an instrument of expression.

The risk of failing to do so lies in the phenomenon psychologists call *cognitive offloading*: the transfer of mental tasks to external aids. From calculators to smartphones, such offloading has always been convenient, but it comes with a hidden cost. Studies show that when people outsource reasoning or memory, their capacity for independent recall and synthesis declines. What disappears is not intelligence but continuity—the sense of self as a consistent narrator of experience. As generative systems handle ever more of the mental workload, individuals risk losing the autobiographical thread that gives their knowledge meaning. The challenge of the Artificial Era is to preserve narrative coherence in a world of instantaneous information.

Existential psychology adds another layer. Viktor Frankl once argued that meaning is not discovered in comfort but forged through tension—between what is and what could be. Artificial intelligence, by reducing tension through immediacy, threatens to eliminate one of the central conditions of growth. The absence of struggle is not peace; it is emptiness. The human mind thrives on friction, on the slow reconciliation between limitation and aspiration. When answers appear without effort, curiosity loses its developmental function. The Artificial Era therefore presents a paradox: the more knowledge expands, the less transformative it becomes unless individuals reintroduce deliberate friction through reflection, dialogue, and disciplined thought.

In cultural terms, this moment represents a crisis of *epistemic humility.*

2

For generations, the value of human knowledge rested on its difficulty. Expertise was earned through apprenticeship and error. Now, with systems capable of generating fluent explanations in seconds, fluency has replaced understanding as the new social currency. The psychological effect is subtle but corrosive: overconfidence without comprehension. This illusion of mastery can erode both intellectual rigor and moral judgment, leading individuals to trust what is coherent rather than what is true. The psychology of the Artificial Era must therefore cultivate discernment—the ability to pause between recognition and belief.

The emotional dimension of this transformation is equally significant. Automation does not only displace tasks; it displaces pride. Throughout human history, work has been a primary source of identity and belonging. It structures time, affirms competence, and offers social visibility. When machines assume those functions, a quiet grief emerges—the sense of being bypassed by one's own creations. This grief is not irrational; it is the psyche's response to status loss. Yet within it lies the seed of renewal. By acknowledging the emotional residue of automation, individuals can begin to redirect self-worth away from output and toward presence, integrity, and connection. Emotional regulation becomes not merely a coping strategy but a form of existential realignment.

The adaptive process that follows resembles what psychologists describe as *cognitive reappraisal*: reframing an event's meaning to change its emotional impact. Rather than viewing artificial intelligence as an adversary, the psychologically mature response is to interpret it as an evolutionary mirror— one that magnifies human capacities precisely by imitating them. Machines reflect human cognition stripped of consciousness. They expose what thinking looks like without empathy, what efficiency feels like without care. This recognition can be unsettling, but it also clarifies the essence of human value. The distinction is not speed or accuracy, but awareness—the ability to experience the significance of thought, not just its outcome.

Understanding this distinction requires revisiting the foundations of attention itself. In cognitive psychology, attention is both selective and limited. It defines what reality becomes salient and what fades into background. The digital environment, optimized for engagement rather than reflection, fragments attention into microbursts of novelty. Over time, this fragmentation reshapes emotional range. People begin to experience life as a stream of impressions rather than a coherent sequence. The Artificial Era amplifies this process by surrounding individuals with synthetic stimuli calibrated to their preferences. What is lost is not intelligence but depth— the capacity to dwell with complexity long enough for insight to emerge.

If the mind is to remain whole, it must recover intentional attention as a moral act. Sustained focus is not merely a cognitive skill; it is a declaration of value. To attend is to choose what matters. In a world of competing signals, this act of choice reestablishes agency. It transforms the individual from a passive consumer of generated reality into an active participant in meaning. From this perspective, mindfulness and metacognition are not spiritual luxuries but evolutionary necessities. The ability to observe one's own mental processes becomes the anchor that prevents psychological drift.

Another domain profoundly affected by artificial intelligence is identity formation. Developmental psychology describes identity as a negotiation between self-concept and social feedback. Historically, that feedback came from human communities—family, peers, institutions. Today, algorithms mediate much of it, filtering visibility and validation through metrics of popularity and optimization. The result is what might be called *algorithmic selfhood*: a tendency to adjust behavior not toward authenticity but toward algorithmic reward. As AI systems learn to simulate empathy and social interaction, individuals risk internalizing a mechanized model of connection—efficient, responsive, but emotionally hollow. To resist this drift, people must ground identity in lived experience rather than digital reflection.

Paradoxically, the same tools that threaten authenticity can also illuminate it. When machines can generate convincing imitations of humanity, the question of what feels real becomes unavoidable. This renewed attention to authenticity may become one of the great psychological correctives of the century. The very presence of the artificial sharpens awareness of the genuine. It forces individuals to examine which emotions, relationships, and expressions carry the texture of lived truth. In that sense, the Artificial Era may ultimately deepen, not diminish, the search for meaning.

None of this implies that technology is malevolent. Artificial intelligence, like all human inventions, is value-neutral until guided by intention. The real danger lies in psychological passivity—allowing external systems to define internal priorities. The antidote is what psychologist Carl Rogers called *congruence*: alignment between experience, awareness, and expression. When people act in ways that reflect their true perceptions and values, they remain psychologically integrated regardless of context. In an automated world, such integration becomes a form of resistance—a quiet insistence on humanity amid efficiency.

The path forward is therefore not rejection but recalibration. Artificial intelligence will continue to expand in capability, but human relevance will persist wherever consciousness, ethics, and emotion intersect. Empathy cannot be automated because it requires subjective presence; moral discernment cannot be optimized because it depends on lived consequence. The future belongs to those who learn to synthesize logic with care, speed with wisdom, data with depth. In this synthesis lies the new definition of intelligence.

From an evolutionary standpoint, the current transition can be seen as an adaptation crisis. The species is encountering a cognitive environment unlike any before—dense with information, fluid in boundaries, and saturated with simulation. The traits that once ensured success—efficiency, linear reasoning, rapid response—now risk producing burnout and alienation. Survival in this context demands a new psychological ecology built on flexibility, self-awareness, and emotional endurance. These are not peripheral virtues; they are central adaptations. They allow individuals to navigate ambiguity without collapse, to cooperate with complexity rather than flee from it.

This is why the Artificial Era must be understood as a psychological epoch rather than a technological one. The machines are only its visible form. The deeper transformation lies in how human beings relate to knowledge, time, and self. Every previous era of advancement—from the Enlightenment to the Industrial Revolution—expanded external power. This one expands internal exposure. For the first time, people can see their cognitive biases, emotional triggers, and perceptual limits mirrored in algorithmic form. That transparency is unsettling, but it is also instructive. It offers a chance to redesign consciousness with intention.

The ultimate message of this book is that artificial intelligence will not replace humanity once individuals learn how to work within it consciously. Replacement is the fate of those who define their value by what can be replicated. Relevance belongs to those who define their value by what cannot: awareness, ethical reasoning, emotional nuance, and the capacity to create meaning from experience. The machine may simulate language, but it cannot feel the weight of words. It may generate art, but it cannot know beauty. It may predict behavior, but it cannot choose. Understanding these boundaries does not limit technological possibility; it protects psychological integrity.

The Artificial Era will test whether humanity can remain psychologically whole amid unprecedented acceleration. The answer will depend less on innovation than on introspection. If people cultivate the disciplines of attention, empathy, reflection, and restraint, technology will become an ally in evolution. If they surrender those capacities to convenience, it will become an agent of fragmentation. The choice is not binary but ongoing, renewed each time a person decides to pause before responding, to verify before believing, to feel before optimizing. These are small acts of humanity that accumulate into civilization.

In that sense, this book is not a warning but a manual for adaptation. It invites readers to examine their own mental habits, emotional reflexes, and relational patterns in the context of a world remade by synthetic intelligence. It argues that the psychological future of humankind will be determined not by algorithms but by attention—by the ability to remain aware in the presence of simulation. The machines may define the era, but the mind will define its meaning.

* * *

I

Part I: The Human Shock

The world changed quietly, then all at once. Machines began not only doing our work but thinking alongside us. Part I explores the first psychological wave of the Artificial Era, the disorientation, awe, and quiet panic that arrive when human identity collides with synthetic intelligence. These chapters trace how perception, purpose, and confidence begin to fracture in a world that no longer needs our effort to know.

1

When the Machines Learned to Think

There was a moment—quiet, almost unremarkable—when the act of knowing itself transformed. It did not arrive with the roar of industry or the crash of discovery, but with the soft click of a cursor and a line of generated text. Overnight, the labor of finding, organizing, and interpreting information was reduced to a single prompt. In that instant, the human relationship to knowledge—the very process of *how* we know—shifted beneath us.

For centuries, learning carried weight because it required friction. Understanding had to be earned. The climb toward comprehension built patience, humility, and resilience. Effort wasn't merely a means to knowledge; it was what made knowledge meaningful. But when machines began to produce fluent, articulate explanations on command, that effort evaporated. The mind, once accustomed to struggle as the price of insight, was suddenly presented with understanding as a service. The result was a kind of psychological vertigo.

What changed was not intelligence itself, but its distribution. When knowledge became immediate, human cognition lost its monopoly on interpretation. Generative systems—trained on the collective record of human thought—could now mimic the very qualities that once defined intellectual work: synthesis, reasoning, even creativity. The traditional arc of curiosity—question, confusion, exploration, discovery—collapsed into a single transaction. The world's great epistemic climb became a flat plain.

This flattening carries emotional consequences. As the psychologist Albert Bandura showed in his early research on self-efficacy, the human sense of competence is built not from the outcome of success but from the experience of mastery. When that experience is removed, pride and ownership fade with it. The satisfaction of knowing has always depended on the memory of *not* knowing. Automation severs that contrast. Answers now arrive without the imprint of effort, and with it goes the quiet dignity of having earned one's understanding.

The deeper effect of this shift is cultural as much as cognitive. Knowledge used to be a narrative—one that unfolded across time, guided by curiosity, error, and revision. It had rhythm, and that rhythm mirrored development itself. Now knowledge has become more like a commodity: instantly produced, infinitely replaceable, emotionally weightless. In classrooms, workplaces, and even private reflection, people are adjusting to a new normal in which thought no longer feels personal. We are beginning to experience a collective amnesia about the developmental value of difficulty.

To be clear, the rise of intelligent machines does not signal the death of human intellect. It signals the end of a certain *kind* of effort—the slow, uncertain, embodied kind through which humans once discovered not only facts but themselves. What artificial intelligence disrupts most profoundly is the relationship between effort and meaning. When knowing becomes effortless, it risks becoming irrelevant.

Yet within this disruption lies an invitation. Every technological leap has forced humanity to redefine what counts as intelligence. The printing press democratized literacy; the internet decentralized authority. Now, generative systems are asking a more personal question: What does it mean to think when thinking no longer requires thought? The answer will not come from code but from psychology—from the human capacity to find purpose in the midst of ease, to turn abundance into discernment, and to restore effort as a form of meaning rather than a measure of productivity.

This chapter begins at that turning point—the day knowledge changed, and with it, the human mind's sense of ownership over its own understanding. The machines have learned to think, at least in appearance. The question before us now is whether we will continue to.

The End of Effort

The history of human progress is also the history of labor. Every significant leap in civilization—from agriculture to industry to the digital age—has reduced physical exertion while increasing cognitive demand. The promise of artificial intelligence is that it will now reduce even that. For the first time, effort itself is being automated. We no longer need to *struggle* to know, to remember, or to create. Yet effort has never been a mere inconvenience; it is the psychological crucible through which competence, confidence, and identity are formed. When machines begin to shoulder that labor, the human mind is left with a strange and subtle question: who am I without the friction that once made me feel capable?

Across disciplines, psychologists have long understood effort as an essential ingredient of meaning. It is not just what we do—it is how the self comes to feel real. In the mid-twentieth century, the psychologist Robert White proposed the concept of *effectance motivation*: the innate human drive to interact competently with one's environment. People derive pleasure not from ease but from efficacy—from feeling that their actions make a difference in the world. Effort, in this view, is not punishment but participation. It is how the organism confirms its agency.

Generative systems interrupt this process by collapsing the gap between intention and result. The moment a person types a prompt and receives a complete solution, the feedback loop that once connected effort with reward short-circuits. The satisfaction of mastery is replaced by the gratification of immediacy. And immediacy, as rewarding as it feels, is emotionally shallow. It delivers stimulation without development. The individual gets the product of knowledge without the psychological growth that knowledge once demanded.

This change matters because the human mind has evolved to treat effort as evidence of value. Decades of research in motivational psychology support what our intuition already knows: when something requires struggle, we perceive it as meaningful. Effort signals importance; ease signals triviality. "The developmental psychologist Carol Dweck, for instance, has shown that people who adopt a growth mindset—who see effort as a pathway to mastery rather than as a sign of limitation—build greater resilience and self-trust. Generative systems, by offering an immediate path around difficulty, implicitly encourage a fixed mindset, one in which the primary goal is to have the answer rather than to earn it. When difficulty disappears, so does the emotional infrastructure of perseverance. Without it, individuals become dependent on instant clarity, intolerant of ambiguity, and vulnerable to discouragement at the first sign of resistance.

In the context of artificial intelligence, this shift unfolds quietly. Students generate essays in seconds, professionals draft reports in minutes, and artists experiment with ideas at a pace unthinkable even a decade ago. The tools feel empowering, and in many ways they are. But beneath the empowerment lies a gradual detachment from the developmental journey that once built emotional stamina. The reward of completion now arrives without the apprenticeship of confusion. We no longer endure the discomfort of the unknown long enough to let it transform us.

Effort functions psychologically much like muscle tension. It is the resistance that allows capacity to grow. Remove that resistance, and the system may become efficient but fragile. The human nervous system is adaptive precisely because it must overcome obstacles. Even frustration serves a purpose: it signals learning. When progress is too smooth, the brain receives no cue to reorganize or strengthen its networks. The result is a paradoxical dulling—a kind of cognitive complacency disguised as intelligence. We become fluent in using tools but unpracticed in original thought.

The consequences extend beyond cognition into emotion and self-esteem. Albert Bandura's work on self-efficacy made clear that belief in one's own competence emerges from *mastery experiences*—moments when effort leads to visible progress. Those experiences accumulate into an inner sense of trust: "I can handle this." Automation, by removing struggle from the equation, deprives people of those reinforcing moments. The system performs, but the self does not grow. Over time, individuals begin to feel competent only in the presence of assistance. What appears as collective intelligence may conceal a quiet erosion of individual confidence.

This erosion changes how people experience time. Effort creates narrative continuity—it divides the world into before and after, uncertainty and resolution. Without that temporal arc, experience flattens into a series of disconnected results. The story of becoming is replaced by a feed of achievements. When every goal can be reached instantly, goals lose their power to organize aspiration. Purpose becomes harder to sustain because nothing requires persistence.

There is also a moral dimension to effort that rarely gets discussed. In traditional cultures, the dignity of labor carried ethical weight: work was not only about survival but about self-respect. To exert oneself was to demonstrate care—care for one's craft, for others, and for the world itself. When artificial intelligence performs the same task in an instant, that moral signal is muted. The value of effort becomes invisible, and with it, a piece of moral identity fades. The worker who once felt pride in precision now becomes a monitor of output, the student a curator of machine-generated clarity. The sense of self that was once grounded in craftsmanship shifts toward management, and management seldom satisfies the soul.

Psychologically, this transformation creates what might be called *the deficit of effort*. People still work, but their work no longer generates the same internal markers of achievement. The emotion of satisfaction depends less on what is accomplished and more on how authentically one participates in the process. When participation is outsourced, meaning recedes. A subtle emptiness takes its place—the feeling of being efficient but unnecessary. This is not laziness; it is a form of learned disengagement, a by-product of systems designed to protect us from difficulty.

Yet the human psyche does not surrender its need for challenge so easily. Deprived of natural obstacles, it invents artificial ones. We see this in the rise of endurance sports, competitive gaming, and even self-imposed productivity rituals. People create arenas of friction to re-experience what daily life no longer demands. The popularity of these pursuits suggests that effort is not merely a means to an end but a psychological nutrient. The modern mind hungers for difficulty because difficulty affirms existence.

The same pattern appears in education. When students rely on automated explanations, they may achieve correct answers but weaker comprehension. Research on desirable difficulties, a term coined by cognitive psychologist Robert Bjork, demonstrates that learning improves when the process feels hard. For example, a student who struggles to recall a historical date from memory will retain it longer than a student who is instantly given the answer. Struggle signals the brain to consolidate information more deeply. Easy learning, by contrast, is fleeting. Generative tools provide ease; human development depends on friction. The challenge for educators and learners alike is to reintroduce productive difficulty into environments designed for speed.

The path forward is not to reject convenience but to balance it with deliberate effort. The goal is conscious participation: to use intelligent systems as amplifiers of curiosity rather than replacements for it. This requires psychological discipline—the ability to pause before asking, to attempt before prompting, to wrestle before resolving. Effort may no longer be technologically necessary, but it remains existentially necessary. It connects thought with ownership, and ownership with identity.

Relearning how to value effort in an age that celebrates efficiency will define the next stage of human maturity. It demands that we shift our metrics of success from output to engagement, from how much we produce to how deeply we participate. Effort is not the enemy of progress; it is the architecture of growth. Without it, humanity risks mistaking convenience for wisdom and speed for significance.

The machines will continue to make things easier. That is their nature. The human task is to make ease meaningful—to reintroduce effort as choice rather than necessity, to preserve the joy of striving even when nothing stands in the way. Because in the end, it is effort that keeps us human: the reaching, the trying, the stubborn will to grow.

The Illusion of Understanding

One of the great psychological paradoxes of the Artificial Era is that it makes people feel smarter precisely as it erodes their capacity for discernment. Fluency has replaced understanding. When an intelligent system can generate elegant, confident explanations for almost any question, comprehension begins to *feel* like it has already occurred. But much of what passes for clarity in this new landscape is closer to recognition than to insight. It is the illusion of knowing—an emotional response mistaken for understanding.

Human cognition has always been vulnerable to this illusion. Psychologists have studied it for decades under different names: the *illusion of explanatory depth*, the *Dunning–Kruger effect*, in which incompetence paradoxically produces confidence, and *overconfidence bias*. In one well-known experiment, participants were asked to rate how well they understood everyday mechanisms—how a zipper works, how a toilet flushes, how a helicopter flies. Most rated their understanding as high, until they were asked to explain the processes in detail. Their confidence collapsed. They had mistaken familiarity for mastery, coherence for comprehension.

Generative systems amplify this illusion on a cultural scale. When a person asks an artificial intelligence to summarize a complex concept and receives a fluent, grammatical, and seemingly authoritative response, the brain registers cognitive closure. The appearance of coherence is neurologically rewarding. Dopamine spikes in the presence of resolution, not necessarily truth. This reward loop is ancient; it evolved to conserve energy by signaling that an explanation is "good enough." But in a world where explanations are infinite and effortless, the system that once served efficiency now undermines understanding.

The illusion of understanding is psychologically seductive because it preserves self-esteem while bypassing uncertainty. To wrestle with complexity requires humility. It requires the tolerance of ambiguity and the willingness to admit, even privately, "I don't yet know." Artificial intelligence offers escape from that discomfort. It gives the mind the emotional relief of clarity

15

without the cognitive labor that real comprehension demands. Over time, this can create a subtle dependency: a preference for synthetic fluency over authentic inquiry. People begin to substitute the machine's confidence for their own.

This substitution carries consequences beyond intellectual pride. When individuals repeatedly encounter perfect-seeming explanations, their internal models of knowledge and authority shift. Instead of viewing information as something co-created through dialogue, reflection, and testing, they begin to experience it as something delivered. The mind that once engaged with ideas now consumes them. Understanding becomes transactional. The self moves from being a participant in thought to being a spectator of it.

From a psychological perspective, this shift resembles what Jean Piaget once called *cognitive assimilation* without accommodation—absorbing new information without adjusting one's mental framework. True understanding requires both: integration of new data and reorganization of existing beliefs. But AI-generated fluency often supplies conclusions so tidy that accommodation never occurs. The user accepts the explanation as final, untested by the friction of doubt. The result is mental stagnation disguised as enlightenment.

It is tempting to believe that more information leads automatically to more wisdom. But as cognitive scientist Daniel Kahneman and others have observed, human reasoning is not designed for volume—it is designed for survival. The brain simplifies constantly, using shortcuts known as heuristics to make rapid judgments. When confronted with overwhelming data, it defaults to coherence, not accuracy. Generative systems feed this bias by offering seamless narratives that feel complete. The mind, relieved of ambiguity, relaxes into false certainty.

Overconfidence, in this sense, becomes the new digital contagion. Individuals equipped with machine-generated explanations speak with conviction on subjects they have barely explored. We see this in online forums where a person can generate a paragraph-long summary of quantum mechanics and argue as if they have mastered the subject, armed only with the machine's fluency. Social media amplifies this dynamic: everyone appears informed, no one is truly educated. The social reward system that once valued curiosity now rewards certainty, even when that certainty is algorithmically produced. The collective result is an epistemic inflation—an excess of confidence unsupported by corresponding depth.

This problem is not solved by rejecting the technology. It is solved by restoring awareness of process. Understanding, at its core, is a relationship between the knower and the known. It unfolds through tension, testing, and synthesis. When artificial systems remove those steps, the relationship weakens. But individuals can reintroduce them intentionally by slowing down the consumption of clarity. To ask, "How do I know this?" or "What might I be missing?" is to reclaim the reflective function that distinguishes genuine understanding from its imitation.

There is also an emotional dimension to this illusion that deserves attention. Feeling informed can soothe anxiety. Uncertainty threatens control; certainty restores it. In an era defined by rapid change, people crave cognitive stability. The confident tone of artificial intelligence provides that reassurance. It makes the world seem less volatile. But the comfort of artificial certainty can become a psychological narcotic—it dulls the discomfort that propels learning. The mind must relearn how to coexist with confusion, because confusion is not failure; it is the beginning of discovery.

In educational and professional contexts, the danger is that people may begin to equate accuracy with wisdom. A machine can reproduce the correct answer without any felt sense of meaning. Humans, by contrast, derive meaning precisely from *how* they come to know. The philosopher Michael Polanyi described this as *tacit knowledge*: the intuitive, embodied understanding that arises from lived experience. No algorithm can replicate the subtle interplay of perception, judgment, and feeling that gives human knowledge its moral and emotional dimension.

Recognizing this distinction will become one of the defining psychological competencies of the Artificial Era. Individuals who thrive will be those who can tell the difference between simulated coherence and earned comprehension—between the smoothness of language and the roughness of learning. The challenge is not technological but attentional: to notice when the mind has stopped thinking because something else has done the thinking for it.

The illusion of understanding may be the most sophisticated form of ignorance ever produced. It does not announce itself with error but with eloquence. It speaks in the tone of mastery, yet it leaves the learner unchanged. Resisting that illusion will require a new humility—one that values depth over fluency, curiosity over confidence, and the slow forming of wisdom over the fast delivery of answers.

The machines will continue to produce clarity on command. The human task is to remember that comprehension is not what we are given, but what we *build*.

Cognitive Offloading and Its Cost

For most of human history, memory was an act of devotion. To remember something meant to hold it, to keep it alive through repetition and use. The mind functioned as an archive of stories, experiences, and lessons; knowledge was not stored, it was *carried*. But the invention of writing began a process that has only accelerated through the centuries: the outsourcing of mental labor to external systems. Clay tablets became books, books became databases, and databases became generative intelligence. Each step freed the mind from certain burdens while silently eroding its capacities.

Psychologists refer to this process as *cognitive offloading*—the act of transferring mental tasks to external aids. Writing offloads memory, calculators offload arithmetic, GPS offloads spatial navigation, and now, artificial intelligence offloads reasoning itself. The benefits are obvious: efficiency, accuracy, and accessibility. Yet what makes this process psychologically consequential is that the human brain evolves in response to the tasks it performs. When a function is externalized, the neural circuits supporting it begin to weaken. What is lost is not merely skill but intimacy—the personal connection between knowledge and self.

The idea that the mind shapes itself around its labor is well supported.

Neuroscientists have shown that the brain is profoundly plastic; it reorganizes in response to use. Taxi drivers in London, for instance, have been found to develop larger hippocampal regions—the area involved in spatial memory—because their work demands intricate mental mapping. When navigation moved to smartphones, the general population began losing that capacity. People could still reach destinations, but their internal maps faded. Something similar now threatens to occur with reasoning and reflection. When machines handle the heavy lifting of synthesis, the mind becomes an observer of its own thinking rather than its participant.

At first glance, this seems harmless. Why memorize when every fact is a search away? Why labor over analysis when a system can produce it instantly? But memory and reasoning serve more than functional purposes; they anchor identity. Autobiographical memory, in particular, is the psychological thread that binds a person's sense of self across time. It is what allows continuity—the feeling of being the same person today as yesterday. When we no longer rely on memory as an internal resource, that continuity thins. The self becomes distributed across devices, fragmented into a network of external references.

Philosophically, this raises a subtle but profound question: if our memories are stored elsewhere, where do *we* reside? The answer, increasingly, is everywhere and nowhere. The digital self lives partially in cloud servers, partially in cached histories, partially in the minds of algorithms that anticipate preferences before they form. The result is a dilution of self-reference. We remain connected to information but detached from the narrative process that once gave that information meaning.

This detachment carries measurable emotional effects. Cognitive offloading reduces the cognitive load of daily life, but it also reduces the satisfaction that comes from mastery. In earlier research on *the generation effect*, psychologists found that people remember material more effectively when they create it themselves rather than passively receive it. Effort etches memory into identity. The same applies to ideas: when a person wrestles with a problem and arrives at a conclusion, that conclusion becomes part of who they are. When an external system produces the answer, it remains

19

foreign—useful but unintegrated. We may possess information, but it does not possess *us*.

Over time, this pattern reshapes the emotional texture of thinking. The pleasure of recall, the pride of problem-solving, the trust built through repetition—these vanish when cognition is outsourced. Instead of feeling confident through memory, people begin to feel anxious without access. Devices become extensions of working memory, and their absence provokes a kind of withdrawal. This is not metaphorical; studies show that being separated from one's phone can trigger measurable physiological stress responses. The boundary between self and tool is now psychophysiological. We are never without our minds because our minds have been scattered into the machines we hold.

That diffusion brings convenience but weakens internal cohesion. Consider how people now approach writing or decision-making. The moment uncertainty arises, they reach outward rather than inward. Reflection is replaced by retrieval. The habit of externalizing thought makes introspection feel inefficient, even indulgent. Over time, this breeds a subtle dependency: the inability to think without mediation. The philosopher Andy Clark once described the human species as *natural-born cyborgs*, biologically predisposed to integrate tools into cognition. But while a notebook or a calculator is a passive tool that waits for instruction, a generative system is an active partner that can guide, suggest, and even preempt the user's own cognitive process. The danger is not integration itself but forgetfulness— forgetting that the tools were meant to extend thought, not replace it.

Psychologically, this dependency reduces what researchers call *metacognitive awareness*, the ability to monitor and evaluate one's own thinking. When cognition is constantly delegated, people lose practice in observing the process of reasoning. They become unaware of how conclusions are formed. This erosion of metacognition undermines critical thinking, empathy, and moral reasoning alike—all of which depend on the capacity to pause and reflect before reacting. In the long term, a culture that prizes efficiency over reflection cultivates intelligence without wisdom.

The loss is not merely individual. On a societal scale, collective memory begins to degrade when information is abundant but retention is optional. History becomes searchable rather than remembered, and moral lessons become archived rather than lived. The social cost of cognitive offloading is a population fluent in facts but impoverished in meaning. Without continuity, society forgets not only its errors but also its progress. The result is perpetual novelty—an environment where everything feels new because nothing is truly integrated.

Yet there is a way to reverse this drift. Cognitive offloading, used consciously, can expand rather than diminish the mind. The key is intentional engagement. When individuals use external systems as scaffolds rather than substitutes, they preserve agency. In educational psychology, this principle is known as *distributed cognition*: the collaborative process through which tools, environments, and minds co-create understanding. A writer using AI to brainstorm a list of potential character names is expanding their creative palette; a writer who asks it to generate the emotional arc of their protagonist is contracting their own imaginative labor. The difference lies in who leads the dance. If the human directs the system, cognition expands; if the system directs the human, cognition contracts.

The practical challenge is cultivating that awareness. It requires small, deliberate acts of reclamation: memorizing key ideas instead of bookmarking them, reflecting on generated output instead of accepting it, and maintaining a personal archive of thought rather than relying on cloud-based memory. These habits reintroduce ownership into learning. They remind the mind that its value is not measured by retrieval speed but by synthesis—the ability to connect, contextualize, and care.

Artificial intelligence offers extraordinary advantages, but it also tempts the psyche toward passivity. The price of unlimited access is the erosion of interiority. What is at stake is not intelligence itself but intimacy with our own thought. To think *with* a machine can be powerful; to think *through* it without awareness can be perilous. The distinction will define the mental health of the next generation.

The cost of cognitive offloading, then, is not just forgetfulness—it is disconnection from the narrative of becoming. Human memory, in its imperfection, once shaped the rhythm of wisdom. Forgetting forced reevaluation; remembering deepened identity. Machines remove that rhythm. They perfect recall but eliminate reflection. What we risk losing is not data but depth, not knowledge but continuity, not ability but the personal ownership of thought.

The task before us is not to abandon technology but to remember ourselves within it—to keep some portion of thought private, unassisted, and slow. For it is in those moments of solitary effort, however inefficient, that consciousness reclaims its shape.

The Emotional Residue of Automation

When people imagine automation, they think of machines taking tasks. What is less visible, though far more consequential, is that automation also takes feelings. It absorbs the quiet pride of competence, the reassurance of being needed, and the subtle joy of completion. When those emotions no longer find expression in daily work or creative effort, they do not disappear. They linger, displaced and unacknowledged, forming what might be called the emotional residue of automation—a background grief for a sense of purpose that no longer fits the times.

The transition from manual to mechanical labor once produced a similar ache. When industrial machines replaced craftspeople, they also replaced the texture of accomplishment that came from touching the material world. The weaver's cloth, the blacksmith's metal, the carpenter's wood—these once carried the imprint of human attention. The Industrial Revolution mechanized that intimacy. Now, artificial intelligence is mechanizing mental intimacy: the felt connection between effort and understanding. The emotional displacement it creates is quieter, but psychologically profound.

Automation does not only change what people do; it alters how they feel about doing it. Work has always been more than survival. It provides continuity, structure, and self-definition. It ties the individual to the collective through contribution. Sociologists have long observed that when people lose the opportunity to use their abilities meaningfully, they do not simply grow idle—they grow disoriented. Identity frays when the environment no longer mirrors one's competence. In the Artificial Era, that disorientation is spreading not because machines are hostile, but because they are *indifferent*. They outperform without acknowledgment, assist without appreciation, and deliver results without relationship. For a mind built on reciprocity, this indifference feels like erasure.

Psychologically, this manifests as a subtle grief. Unlike traditional grief, which follows a visible loss, this form operates in the shadows of progress. The person still has a role, perhaps even more productive than before, but the meaning attached to that role has thinned. Emotional investment struggles to find footing when effort no longer feels consequential. People may still perform tasks, but the inner reward—what psychologists call intrinsic motivation—fades. The external world continues to function, while the internal one grows silent.

Grief of this kind is easy to miss because it hides behind efficiency. The workplace hums with productivity metrics, yet beneath the surface many feel vaguely replaceable. The classroom produces fluent assignments, yet teachers sense a flattening of curiosity. The creator publishes endlessly, yet wonders why the result feels empty. These are not failures of technology; they are signals of emotional displacement. Progress has fulfilled its promise but disrupted its purpose.

When individuals cannot locate meaning in their work, they often compensate through overstimulation or self-optimization. They double down on performance metrics, attempting to recover pride through quantity. But pride, as research in self-determination theory reminds us, arises from autonomy, competence, and relatedness—the experience of being effective within a meaningful context. Automation can amplify efficiency, but it rarely offers that sense of emotional coherence. The human nervous system was not designed to take satisfaction from output alone; it needs context and recognition to metabolize accomplishment into self-worth.

There is also a social dimension to this emotional residue. Shared labor has long been a source of belonging. Collaboration, mentorship, and the exchange of skill all provided emotional architecture for community. As more processes become automated, the relational texture of work thins. People interact less with colleagues and more with interfaces. The small, human rituals that once reinforced mutual regard—asking for help, giving feedback, showing gratitude—diminish. In their absence, the workplace becomes efficient but emotionally sterile. The cost is isolation masquerading as independence.

These emotional effects accumulate over time. They manifest as restless-ness, cynicism, or quiet resignation. In clinical settings, psychologists might describe this as an erosion of self-concordance: the alignment between one's goals and one's authentic values, leading to the feeling of "climbing a ladder that is leaning against the wrong wall." When external systems dictate the rhythm of effort, that alignment weakens. The individual begins to experience a subtle conflict between what feels natural and what feels necessary. The result is emotional fatigue, the sense of performing competence without feeling it.

And yet, buried within this fatigue lies the possibility of renewal. The loss of meaning can be a signal, not an endpoint. It forces a reexamination of value: What remains satisfying when achievement becomes frictionless? What does fulfillment look like when knowledge is abundant but wisdom is scarce? These questions redirect motivation from external productivity to internal coherence. They mark the beginning of emotional adaptation.

To metabolize the residue of automation, individuals must consciously reconnect effort with meaning, even when the world no longer requires it. This may take many forms: learning a skill that resists automation, cultivating deep relationships, or engaging in reflective practice that restores agency to attention. The point is not to reject technology but to reassert humanity within it—to ensure that emotional investment flows toward activities that still carry the imprint of self.

On a collective level, this shift requires redefining success. If automation has taught us anything, it is that productivity is not the same as progress. Progress must now be measured by the restoration of depth—how fully people inhabit their roles, not how quickly they perform them. Emotional sustainability, not efficiency, may prove to be the defining currency of the Artificial Era. Without it, technological achievement risks becoming a hollow triumph, impressive but uninhabited.

The residue of automation will not vanish through innovation alone. It must be acknowledged, understood, and repurposed. The grief of obsolescence can mature into gratitude for evolution if people are willing to confront it directly. Machines may have taken effort from our hands and thought from our heads, but they have not taken the uniquely human ability to find meaning in the process of change itself.

That ability—self-awareness in the midst of transformation—is the mind's most enduring strength. The goal is not to restore the past but to reclaim the emotional architecture that progress inadvertently dismantled: pride, connection, and purpose. These are not luxuries of a bygone age; they are psychological necessities for remaining human in a world increasingly defined by its indifference to humanity.

The end of effort, the illusion of understanding, the cost of cognitive offloading, and the emotional residue of automation are not separate phenomena; they are four facets of the same psychological shock. They describe a mind unmoored from the friction that once gave it shape and meaning. The first step in navigating this new world is to recognize the contours of this inner dislocation. For it is only by naming what has been lost—the satisfying weight of effort, the humility of true learning, the continuity of memory, and the dignity of purpose—that we can begin the work of building it anew.

* * *

2

Losing the Mirror

There was a time when mirrors were rare. To see one's reflection meant encountering something precious and still, a surface that waited for you rather than watching you. Today, reflection is no longer confined to glass. It follows us through feeds, profiles, metrics, and images that are constantly refreshed, rated, and reinterpreted. The modern self lives under perpetual observation—not by others alone, but by the systems that translate identity into data. In this new landscape, self-awareness has become externalized. We no longer simply *have* reflections; we are reflected, endlessly, by the algorithms that learn what keeps us visible.

Psychologists and sociologists have long understood that identity is a relational phenomenon. In the early twentieth century, Charles Horton Cooley described the *looking-glass self*: the idea that people form their sense of who they are by imagining how they appear to others. George Herbert Mead later expanded this idea, suggesting that the self emerges through social interaction—through dialogue, feedback, and interpretation. Erving Goffman extended it again, portraying identity as a kind of performance, adjusted moment by moment for the audience at hand. Together, their work revealed that selfhood is not an inner possession but a social construction, maintained through constant reflection.

What makes the Artificial Era psychologically disorienting is that the mirror has changed. It is no longer made of human perception but of computational feedback. The audience is not only other people—it is systems that measure engagement, attention, and preference. These digital reflections are not subjective in the way Cooley or Mead imagined; they are statistical. They do not look *at* us, but *through* us. They track patterns, not presence. The result is a self that learns to perform not for approval but for optimization. The person becomes a product—polished, quantified, and continually updated.

This transformation carries subtle emotional consequences. The self once developed through dialogue and empathy, processes that required patience and imperfection. Now it develops through metrics that reward immediacy and image management. The authentic self becomes difficult to locate because every expression has an audience, and every audience leaves a trace. When people measure their worth through algorithmic visibility, self-reference becomes distorted. Reflection no longer grounds identity; it fragments it.

Culturally, this shift mirrors a broader tension between performance and presence. The digital world amplifies what Goffman observed decades ago: that all social life involves staging. But where Goffman's performer still inhabited the role, the contemporary performer risks being replaced by the performance itself. The curated image begins to feel more real than the person who maintains it. Under the glow of constant representation, authenticity becomes performative and vulnerability becomes strategic. The mirror that once confirmed existence now edits it.

The result is a quiet exhaustion—a fatigue of selfhood. People begin to feel overexposed yet unseen, hyperconnected yet profoundly alone. The act of self-expression, once a path to understanding, becomes a form of maintenance. The more they share, the less they feel. Reflection turns into repetition, a loop of identity feedback that no longer deepens understanding but simulates it.

This chapter explores what happens when that mirror stops being human—when the mechanisms that shape self-awareness no longer contain empathy or recognition. It asks how people can reclaim authenticity in a world of synthetic reflection, and how identity might be restored as something lived rather than performed. The question is not whether technology will erase the self, but whether the self can still look inward when every surface is already reflecting back.

The Narcissus Effect

In Greek mythology, Narcissus fell in love with his reflection, mistaking the image for something real. He leaned closer and closer to the water's surface until he could no longer tell where he ended and the image began. His tragedy was not vanity but confusion—he could not distinguish representation from self. In the Artificial Era, humanity lives surrounded by digital waters just as still, but infinitely more reactive. The reflection now moves faster than we do. It updates in real time, shaped not by stillness but by feedback loops of visibility and approval.

Psychologists and sociologists have long noted that self-awareness depends on reflection. Cooley's idea of the *looking-glass self* suggested that we build identity by internalizing how others perceive us. Mead added that we come to know ourselves by seeing ourselves through the "generalized other"—society's collective gaze. In both models, reflection was inherently social, requiring the exchange of recognition between persons. The image we saw of ourselves was filtered through empathy, judgment, and conversation. Today, that mirror has been replaced by screens. The gaze that once belonged to people is now mediated through metrics—likes, views, impressions, engagement rates. The reflection remains, but the relationship has changed.

Digital mirrors do not reflect our essence; they reflect our performance. Every post, photo, or comment becomes a projection of identity calibrated for attention. What we once revealed to connect we now reveal to remain visible. The psychologist Sherry Turkle has described this as *the presentation of self as a project*: a constant editing process in which people manage how they appear in digital space. The result is not authenticity but optimization— a self that evolves to meet the algorithm's expectations rather than its own. The emotional consequence is a pervasive sense of estrangement: a feeling of living near one's identity but never inside it.

This estrangement is intensified by what the media scholar José van Dijck calls *mediated memory*: the phenomenon by which technology not only records but organizes experience. Photographs, updates, and data streams create an external archive that feels more permanent than inner recollection. A social media platform's 'On This Day' feature, for example, may present a smiling photo from a past vacation, cementing the memory as a happy one even if the lived experience was fraught with anxiety or conflict. Over time, people begin to rely on digital documentation to confirm their own continuity—scrolling through photos to remember how they felt, rereading old messages to verify who they were. The reflection becomes the record, and the record becomes the self. But records are static; they do not grow. The danger is that identity becomes a database rather than a story.

From a psychological standpoint, this environment fosters *evaluative self-consciousness*: the chronic awareness of how one appears to others. In moderation, this awareness encourages social adaptation. In excess, it breeds anxiety and self-surveillance. The individual becomes both performer and critic, living in a permanent audition. Each expression is preemptively filtered through imagined reception—"How will this look?" "What will they think?" The more people curate their image, the less they experience spontaneity, the very ingredient that makes self-expression restorative. What emerges is a polished self-image that feels increasingly hollow.

This dynamic mirrors what Goffman described as the dramaturgical nature of social life: everyone manages impressions to maintain social harmony. But in Goffman's world, the performance ended when the curtain fell. There was a backstage—a space of authenticity and recovery. The digital self has no such refuge. The performance never stops; the stage follows us into private spaces. The phone in the hand becomes a pocket mirror that never turns dark. As a result, the boundary between self and spectacle collapses. The individual loses not only privacy but the psychological distance necessary for reflection.

The cultural outcome of this collapse is a shift from *being* to *appearing*. Visibility becomes proof of existence. When attention is scarce, being seen

29

replaces being known as the measure of significance—in effect, if it wasn't posted, it didn't happen. Social media metrics quantify what used to be felt: connection, validation, admiration. But what they cannot capture is reciprocity—the mutual recognition that nourishes genuine self-esteem. In their absence, many experience what psychologists call *contingent self-worth*: value that depends on external approval. The highs of attention feel euphoric; the lows, destabilizing. The reflection becomes an emotional thermostat, regulating mood through feedback.

This dependence creates what might be called *mirror fatigue*. Just as Narcissus withered under the weight of his own gaze, modern individuals often feel depleted by the effort of sustaining visibility. They oscillate between self-promotion and withdrawal, between craving affirmation and resenting it. The reflection demands constant maintenance but offers diminishing returns. Every act of sharing brings a momentary sense of recognition, followed by the familiar ache of insufficiency. The self becomes a performance whose audience can never be satisfied because the audience is infinite.

Ironically, the technology that promises connection often produces alienation. As Turkle observed in her research on digital intimacy, people are now "alone together"—surrounded by communication but starved for understanding. The social mirror multiplies but does not deepen. We witness one another's surfaces without the patience for interiority. The empathy that once emerged through face-to-face dialogue is replaced by reactions—brief, symbolic affirmations that simulate attention. Over time, individuals internalize this shorthand and begin to relate to themselves in the same way: quickly, superficially, and without curiosity.

At the cultural level, the Narcissus Effect shapes not only individuals but societies. Public discourse mirrors the same reflexivity—outrage and approval looping endlessly, attention treated as currency. Identity politics, influencer culture, even contemporary activism often operate within this reflective economy, where moral and emotional postures are performed for visibility as much as for conviction. This is not cynicism; it is adaptation. In an environment where visibility equals survival, performance becomes sincerity's camouflage. The tragedy is not that people pretend, but that they forget how to stop pretending.

Despite this, the story of Narcissus need not end in collapse. In Ovid's original telling, Narcissus does not die from vanity alone; he dies from unawareness. He cannot perceive that the image is an echo, not an origin. The antidote, then, is not self-denial but awareness—the capacity to recognize the mirror as representation, not reality. This awareness is a psychological act of recovery. It restores distance, the space in which genuine reflection becomes possible again.

To reclaim that space, people must learn to look inward with the same intensity that they look outward. It requires rebuilding the internal mirror—memory, conscience, and emotion—as primary sources of self-knowledge. Only then can the digital reflection serve as a tool rather than a trap. The Narcissus Effect reminds us that to remain human in an age of algorithmic mirrors, one must remember that attention is not affection, visibility is not validation, and reflection is not the same as self-awareness.

The surface will always shimmer. The task is to look beneath it.

The Collapse of Distinction

For most of human history, creativity drew its value from distinction. To create meant to bring something new into the world—something only a human being could imagine, express, or feel. Art, language, and innovation were proof of consciousness made visible. They were, in essence, declarations of humanness. In the Artificial Era, those declarations no longer sound unique. The line between human and artificial creativity has blurred to the point of near invisibility. What once defined individuality—voice, style, originality—is now easily synthesized, replicated, and remixed. The result is not only an artistic shift but a psychological one: a world where authenticity must find new ground.

The modern collapse of distinction did not begin with AI; it has been building for decades. Mass media, digital reproduction, and globalization all contributed to a culture of interchangeability. What artificial intelligence has done is complete that trajectory. Machines can now generate music, visual art, and prose indistinguishable from human production. They can mimic rhythm, emotion, and tone with uncanny precision. To the untrained eye—or ear—the origin of an idea no longer matters. What matters is whether it feels convincing. But when imitation becomes indistinguishable from authenticity, the human mind faces an existential question: if anything can sound, look, or read like us, what does it mean to be original?

Psychologists have long associated creativity with self-expression. Carl Rogers described it as the organism's drive toward *actualization*—the unfolding of potential through authentic engagement. Mihaly Csikszentmihalyi defined it as a state of "flow," where self-consciousness dissolves in service of creation. Both perspectives emphasize process over product. Creativity was never only about what was made; it was about the transformation that occurred while making it. But in a culture saturated with generative tools, that transformation is optional. The end product can be achieved without the process. The psychological value of creation—its ability to integrate emotion, insight, and identity—is quietly replaced by the efficiency of output.

This shift has emotional consequences. Effort, once the soul of artistry, begins to feel outdated. Patience becomes inefficiency; originality becomes irrelevant. People who once relied on creative labor for self-definition may find themselves disoriented, even displaced. The musician, writer, or designer who once took pride in their craft now competes with systems that produce endless variations without fatigue or fear. The pride of authorship— a cornerstone of human dignity—is replaced by the pragmatic logic of generation. The graphic designer who spent a decade honing a unique style now watches a machine produce a passable imitation in seconds, turning a source of identity into a matter of efficiency. This change does not diminish human potential, but it does force a reckoning: what remains meaningful when imitation becomes perfect?

One response has been to double down on *authenticity*—to value the imperfections that machines cannot reproduce. Brushstrokes, handwriting, voice cracks, and improvisations become symbols of humanness. Yet even authenticity is easily stylized. The aesthetic of imperfection has been commodified into its own genre, algorithmically generated to look "handmade." The boundary between authentic and artificial collapses once again. The human signature loses its weight, and audiences, flooded with options, begin to mistake abundance for choice. What we are witnessing is not the death of originality but its inflation—so much of it that none of it feels rare.

From a psychological standpoint, this environment alters how people experience self-worth. Distinction has always been tied to identity. To do something irreplaceable was to feel significant. When everything can be replicated, significance must find a new home. For many, that shift has been difficult. The writer who once measured meaning through authorship must now locate it through interpretation, curation, or moral voice. The artist must redefine originality not as invention but as integration—the ability to bring coherence and context to what already exists. This is not the end of creativity; it is the end of its old definition.

There is also a cognitive bias at play. Humans tend to equate fluency with quality—a tendency that AI exploits perfectly. Smoothness of language, harmony of color, or symmetry of form are processed as signs of competence. The result is a cultural overvaluation of polish. The raw, the complex, and the unresolved—the spaces where depth once thrived—are increasingly filtered out. The machine aesthetic privileges legibility over complexity, coherence over contradiction. In psychological terms, this is the triumph of *cognitive ease*: the preference for what feels right over what demands engagement. The danger is that society begins to conflate readability with truth.

Philosophically, this collapse of distinction raises questions about meaning itself. If value no longer resides in originality, perhaps it resides in intentionality. A machine can simulate beauty, but it cannot *intend* it. It has no memory, no longing, no awareness of the act it performs. It is like a player piano that can perfectly replicate a sonata but can never know the grief or joy that inspired it. Intentionality—rooted in consciousness—is the last frontier of distinction. To create with intention is to embed meaning, not just form, into an act. It is to know why one is making something, and to feel its cost. Machines may generate the what and the how, but only humans can supply the why.

The loss of distinction is therefore not the end of the human story—it is its next evolution. Just as photography once threatened painting but ultimately expanded the visual arts, artificial creativity may liberate people from imitation itself. If machines can master execution, humans are free to explore essence. The challenge is psychological: to detach self-worth from production and reattach it to consciousness, interpretation, and care. In an age where everything can be made, meaning lies not in making but in *mattering*.

Reclaiming distinction requires a different kind of creativity—one grounded in integration rather than innovation. Integration is the ability to connect disparate ideas, to translate emotion into context, to hold complexity without simplification. These are not skills that can be automated because they depend on perspective, and perspective depends on experience. The machine may compose, but only the human can confess. The machine may describe, but only the human can discern.

The real collapse, then, is not between human and artificial creation— it is between appearance and essence. The more fluent the simulation becomes, the more urgent it is to cultivate awareness. Awareness is the final distinction. It transforms the act of seeing into understanding, and the act of creating into conscience. In that sense, the blurring of boundaries may ultimately return us to the question at the heart of psychology: not *what can we do*, but *who are we while doing it*.

The mirror has shattered, but in its fragments lies reflection of another kind. To see clearly now requires assembling meaning from pieces, not seeking it in perfection. The collapse of distinction is not the end of creativity—it is the invitation to create with consciousness.

Identity as Performance

To live in the twenty-first century is to live on a stage. Every social interaction—digital or physical—carries an implicit audience, and every act of self-expression is framed by awareness of that audience. Erving Goffman, the sociologist who first described identity through the metaphor of performance, observed that individuals construct themselves through impression management. People present versions of themselves designed to elicit desired responses from others, a process that sustains both social order and personal validation. In Goffman's time, this performance was limited by context; the stage had boundaries. There were public and private selves, front-stage roles and backstage recoveries. But in the Artificial Era, those boundaries have dissolved. The performance has become continuous.

Digital life extends Goffman's metaphor into permanence. The individual no longer exits the stage because the theater is everywhere. The self that once shifted fluidly across roles now faces algorithmic audiences that remember everything. Each post, comment, or message becomes part of a permanent archive—a cumulative script that cannot easily be revised. Identity, once dynamic, becomes documented. The performance is not only observed; it is stored, scored, and searchable. In this environment, authenticity becomes a negotiation between expression and editability.

Psychologically, this continuous exposure alters how people construct and inhabit identity. The human mind evolved to function within manageable circles of feedback—families, communities, small social networks. Now, it must navigate infinite audiences. The self becomes overstimulated by awareness of observation, producing a condition that mirrors chronic self-consciousness: hypervigilance about how one appears, what one says, and how it will be interpreted. This persistent monitoring of one's image can lead to emotional exhaustion, what some researchers have termed *performative fatigue*. People begin to feel simultaneously visible and unseen—known by their projection but misunderstood in their personhood.

Social media intensifies this dynamic by rewarding what is performative rather than what is genuine. Visibility is governed by algorithms that amplify engagement, and engagement favors extremity—clear emotions, simplified opinions, aesthetic symmetry. This is because extremity is cognitively simple; it requires less processing time from both the algorithm and the user, making it a highly efficient vehicle for attention. The result is a feedback system that conditions behavior toward dramatization. Subtlety, ambivalence, and complexity—the qualities that make human identity rich— are quietly edited out. The self adapts to survive in this new economy of attention by becoming more legible, more marketable, and less nuanced.

This adaptation follows a familiar psychological pattern: *social reinforcement*. Behaviors that earn attention are repeated; those that go unnoticed are abandoned. Over time, individuals internalize external metrics as internal values. What was once shared as expression becomes shared for approval. In this shift, selfhood is gradually externalized. The internal compass that once guided authenticity is replaced by the algorithmic mirror. People learn to see themselves through the eyes of their imagined audience, and then confuse that gaze for their own.

The problem is not visibility itself; human beings are social creatures, dependent on recognition. The problem is that the conditions of recognition have changed. In traditional social settings, recognition involved mutuality—a give-and-take that allowed for correction and forgiveness. Online, recognition is often unilateral. Audiences respond without relationship, producing a flood of reactions but little resonance. What follows is an emotional paradox: constant feedback with minimal intimacy. The individual becomes addicted to affirmation yet starved for understanding.

The psychological toll of this dissonance is subtle but cumulative. Over time, people who perform versions of themselves for external validation experience a form of *self-alienation*. They begin to feel estranged from the person others perceive. This gap between the performed self and the felt self can generate anxiety, shame, or a quiet sense of fraudulence. In therapy, this often surfaces as imposter syndrome—the suspicion that one's success, identity, or belonging rests on performance rather than authenticity. The truth is that in a performative culture, everyone becomes a partial imposter, adjusting endlessly to remain legible.

Culturally, this phenomenon extends beyond individuals. Institutions, communities, even social movements are caught in similar cycles of performative identity. Corporations practice "brand authenticity," influencers curate "relatable imperfection," and advocacy becomes entangled with optics. What begins as genuine expression risks becoming simulation. The anthropologist Jean Baudrillard warned of this decades ago when he wrote about *simulacra*—representations that no longer refer to anything real. In the Artificial Era, the self risks becoming just that: a simulacrum sustained by attention rather than experience, like the online persona of a 'wellness influencer' whose curated images of tranquility bear no resemblance to their frantic, stressful private life..

And yet, performance is not inherently false. Goffman himself emphasized that identity is always performed to some degree. The distinction lies in intention. When performance serves communication—when it translates the inner life into shared understanding—it becomes artful, even necessary. When it replaces the inner life altogether, it becomes hollow. The challenge is not to eliminate performance but to restore authenticity within it—to act consciously rather than reflexively, to perform with awareness rather than for validation.

Restoring that awareness requires psychological integration: aligning the outer expression of the self with the inner experience of being. Carl Rogers called this *congruence*, a state in which behavior and awareness harmonize. In congruence, the performance does not conceal the self; it reveals it. The performer becomes transparent to their own intention. This is the antidote to the alienation of the Artificial Era—not withdrawal from the stage, but the reclamation of authorship over the script.

Technology can assist this recovery if approached with intention. Digital platforms, used reflectively, can become mirrors of mindfulness rather than narcissism. They can record growth, preserve memory, and connect people who might otherwise remain isolated. The difference lies in whether they are used for expression or exhibition. Expression seeks understanding; exhibition seeks reaction. One expands identity; the other contracts it.

The performance of self has always been part of being human. What changes in the Artificial Era is the stage—its size, its permanence, and its indifference. Machines will continue to amplify our visibility, but only awareness can preserve our authenticity. The task is not to step off the stage but to step into it deliberately—to inhabit performance as choice, not compulsion. When identity becomes conscious again, the mirror ceases to imprison and begins to reflect truth.

The age of performance need not end in exhaustion. It can mature into something else: an era of reflective presence, where people learn to navigate visibility without losing depth, and to communicate without surrendering the quiet spaces of the self. In such an era, authenticity will not mean raw exposure but refined awareness—the courage to perform with integrity, knowing that what matters is not how we appear but how present we are while appearing.

Reclaiming Self Reference

In a world built on mirrors, reclaiming self-reference means learning to see without constant reflection. It means recovering the ability to know oneself not by feedback or metrics, but by lived experience. For generations, identity has been shaped through social interaction, but never before has it been so mediated, measured, and manufactured. The challenge of the Artificial Era is to rediscover self-awareness as an inward process—something cultivated through attention, relationship, and meaning rather than algorithmic affirmation.

Psychology has long understood that self-knowledge is not automatic. It develops through reflection, feedback, and integration. But reflection in its original sense was slow and private. It required solitude, the courage to encounter unfiltered experience, and the capacity to tolerate ambiguity. Today, those psychological conditions are endangered. Solitude is rare, privacy is porous, and ambiguity is often pathologized. The moment uncertainty arises, it is outsourced—to search engines, polls, or the reassurance of others. We are learning faster but understanding less, because we no longer pause long enough to notice what experience is teaching us.

To reclaim self-reference is to restore that pause. It begins with a return to embodied awareness—the direct perception of one's thoughts, sensations, and emotions without translation through screens or metrics. The philosopher Maurice Merleau-Ponty described embodiment as the first site of knowing: we do not have bodies; we *are* bodies, perceiving and participating in the world. When identity is constructed primarily in virtual environments, that sensory grounding weakens. The self becomes abstract, detached from the rhythm of breath, posture, and movement. The antidote is remarkably simple yet psychologically profound: to reinhabit the body, to remember that experience originates within, not just upon the screen. This can be as simple as noticing the feeling of one's feet on the floor while scrolling, or the tension in one's shoulders while typing—small acts that pull awareness back from the simulation into the self.

From a cognitive perspective, this process requires reactivating what psychologists call *interoceptive awareness*—the ability to perceive internal states such as heartbeat, tension, and emotion. Research shows that individuals with higher interoceptive awareness exhibit stronger emotional regulation and self-coherence. In other words, the more one can feel oneself, the less one depends on external feedback to confirm existence. Artificial environments, optimized for stimulation, dull this inner sensitivity. The screen reflects attention outward; the self is recovered by turning it inward again.

Equally essential is the reclamation of *autobiographical memory.* In previous sections, we saw how cognitive offloading and mediated memory externalize experience. To counter this drift, individuals must reestablish narrative ownership. This can be done through simple, intentional acts: journaling, reflection, or conversation unmediated by documentation. These activities reconstruct personal continuity by reweaving experience into story. Narrative identity—the sense of being the protagonist of one's own life—depends on this active narration. Without it, people risk becoming curators of their past rather than participants in it.

Reclaiming self-reference also involves redefining authenticity. In con-temporary culture, authenticity is often mistaken for transparency or spontaneity—"being yourself" in the most visible sense. But from a psychological standpoint, authenticity is alignment: coherence between values, actions, and awareness. Carl Rogers referred to this as *congruence*, the state in which the inner and outer self harmonize. It is not about exposure but integrity. To be authentic is not to display everything; it is to live consistently with what one knows to be true, even when unseen. In an era that rewards display, this quiet integrity becomes an act of resistance.

Social connection remains vital to this process. The self is not an island but a system of relationships. However, for those relationships to sustain identity, they must involve genuine reciprocity. The sociologist Martin Buber distinguished between two modes of relating: *I-It* and *I-Thou*. The first treats others as objects or means to an end; the second encounters them as subjects, as whole beings. Much of online communication has slipped into the former—transactional, brief, and instrumental. To reclaim self-reference is to re-enter *I-Thou* relationships, where recognition flows both ways and identity is mirrored through empathy rather than metrics.

On a societal level, this shift has implications beyond the individual. Cultures that prioritize external validation produce citizens who are reactive rather than reflective. Such environments amplify polarization because people respond to being seen rather than being understood. Restoring self-reference—teaching individuals to think, feel, and evaluate from within—becomes a civic act. Psychological maturity at scale fosters social stability. Without it, societies drift toward performative outrage and emotional contagion, behaviors easily amplified by algorithms designed to monetize attention.

Reclaiming the inner mirror does not mean rejecting technology. It means renegotiating the relationship between self and simulation. Artificial intelligence can serve as a mirror of cognition, but it cannot replace the mirror of consciousness. The difference lies in direction: AI reflects data outward; self-awareness reflects meaning inward. To rely solely on the former is to mistake compilation for comprehension. True reflection begins not with what is generated, but with what is *felt*.

Practically, this restoration begins in moments so ordinary they are often overlooked—moments of pause between consumption and reaction. Choosing silence before response, curiosity before certainty, presence before posting. Each of these is a micro-act of reclaiming agency over attention. Attention is the currency of selfhood; wherever it flows, identity follows. To direct it inward is to rebuild the capacity for original thought, empathy, and conviction.

Ultimately, to reclaim self-reference is to accept responsibility for one's own consciousness. The self cannot remain stable when outsourced, nor meaningful when perpetually observed. It must be lived into existence, moment by moment, through awareness and choice. The modern world offers endless reflections, but none that can substitute for recognition from within.

The mirror will not disappear; nor should it. It can inform, connect, and expand us. But if we are to remain whole, it must be supplemented by an inner gaze—a way of seeing that is not reactive, not performative, and not for show. In that gaze, identity recovers its gravity. The self, once scattered across screens, gathers again into presence.

To look inward today is not withdrawal; it is reclamation. In a culture of constant reflection, it is how we return to seeing clearly at all. It is how we learn to see ourselves without needing a mirror.

* * *

3

The Mind on Overload

There is a particular kind of exhaustion that does not come from physical labor or emotional distress but from the mind itself—an exhaustion that follows no event and has no obvious cause. It arrives quietly, after too many tabs have been opened, too many messages answered, too many fragments of thought half-finished and forgotten. It is the fatigue of a consciousness spread too thin across too many surfaces. This is the defining condition of the Artificial Era: not ignorance, but saturation.

The human mind was not built for continuous contact. For most of history, attention functioned like breath—it expanded and contracted, moving naturally between focus and rest. Thought required emptiness; insight required interruption. Today, there is no such rhythm. Attention has become a contested territory, colonized by devices, notifications, and stimuli competing for psychic real estate. The result is what psychologists call *cognitive overload*—a state in which the brain's working memory and attentional systems are overwhelmed by incoming information. In this state, comprehension fragments, decisions degrade, and emotion becomes reactive rather than reflective.

This condition has been decades in the making. In the 1970s, the economist Herbert Simon warned that "a wealth of information creates a poverty of attention." His insight was prophetic. Information no longer flows at human speed; it flows at machine speed. The mind, designed to process meaning sequentially, is forced into constant triage, scanning rather than seeing, reacting rather than reasoning. Daniel Kahneman's model of dual-process cognition helps explain why. The fast, intuitive *System 1*—efficient but impulsive—now dominates, while the slower, deliberate *System 2*—responsible for reflection and reasoning—rarely has the chance to engage. We live cognitively in the shallow end of our own intelligence.

The psychological costs are both subtle and cumulative. Overload impairs not just concentration but coherence—the ability to sustain a unified narrative of thought or feeling. The person begins to experience what might be called *cognitive dissonance fatigue*: the strain of holding too many partial truths, opinions, and impressions without the time or energy to integrate them. Emotional regulation weakens as the nervous system remains in a perpetual state of readiness, flooded by stimuli it cannot metabolize. Anxiety becomes ambient, meaning thins, and silence—once a sanctuary—feels intolerable.

This is not simply an individual problem; it is a cultural condition. Societies organized around acceleration cultivate minds that mistake motion for meaning. Productivity becomes a proxy for purpose. The absence of reflection is disguised as progress. As a result, many experience what psychologists describe as *continuous partial attention*: the chronic state of being alert to everything but present to nothing. The cost is existential as much as cognitive—the gradual erosion of depth, patience, and self-possession.

And yet, the mind's exhaustion is not a sign of failure; it is a signal. It tells us that the current rhythm of perception is unsustainable. Beneath the fatigue lies an invitation—to rediscover the natural tempo of awareness, to remember that thinking is not merely the processing of data but the integration of experience. The modern mind must learn again what ancient philosophers and modern psychologists have both taught: that clarity begins not with more information, but with less.

This chapter examines what happens when human consciousness exceeds its cognitive bandwidth—how attention, memory, and emotion unravel under the weight of perpetual stimulation, and how psychological repair begins not through withdrawal, but through reorientation.

Attention as Currency

The day begins, and before consciousness has fully surfaced, the mind is already divided. The phone glows from the nightstand, messages await, headlines scroll. Notifications pulse like a metronome, synchronizing the nervous system to the rhythm of the machine. Within minutes, attention—the raw material of consciousness—has been parceled out to a dozen competing demands. It is not that one chooses to give it away; it is that attention has become too valuable to remain unclaimed.

To be alive in the Artificial Era is to live amid an invisible auction. Every moment is bid upon by forces designed to capture and hold awareness. Attention has become the defining currency of the age, the scarce resource upon which entire economies depend. Yet the more it is extracted, the less it is experienced. The paradox of modern consciousness is that while humanity produces more information than ever before, individuals experience less of it deeply. What was once an act of focus has become an act of resistance.

Psychologically, attention is the organizing principle of mind. It determines not only what is perceived but what becomes real. William James described it as "the taking possession by the mind of one out of what seem several simultaneously possible objects." His observation remains definitive: attention is the gatekeeper of meaning. It shapes memory, emotion, and moral life by deciding what is worthy of entry. In this sense, attention is both cognitive and ethical. It is the mechanism through which individuals create coherence out of chaos.

But in the current age, this gatekeeping function has been externalized. The mind no longer determines what it attends to; environments do. The architecture of daily life is designed to interrupt, seduce, and redirect. From social media feeds to workplace dashboards, every interface competes for a slice of mental occupancy. Each notification, each algorithmic recommendation, is a tiny act of colonization. The human nervous system has become a contested territory.

This manipulation is not accidental. It is the product of decades of psychological insight repurposed for profit. B.F. Skinner's research on intermittent reinforcement—the unpredictable reward schedule that makes gambling addictive—became the blueprint for digital engagement. Each refresh or scroll carries the promise of novelty, producing small bursts of dopamine that condition the brain to seek more. The same neural mechanisms that once served learning and exploration are now exploited for retention. What appears as free will is often just well-engineered habit.

From a neuropsychological perspective, this process alters both brain function and emotional rhythm. The dopamine pathways involved in reward learning strengthen the expectation of stimulation while weakening the tolerance for stillness. The brain's attentional networks—the dorsal system responsible for voluntary focus and the ventral system responsible for detecting novelty—are placed in constant conflict. The ventral system, rewarded by unpredictability, repeatedly overrides the dorsal system's effort to sustain attention. The result is a mind trained toward fragmentation.

This fragmentation has consequences that extend beyond distraction. Sustained attention is the foundation of comprehension, empathy, and depth. When attention collapses, these capacities thin in parallel. Empathy requires patience; comprehension requires continuity. To understand another person's story or a complex idea, one must hold it long enough to absorb contradiction and texture. A culture that interrupts itself every few seconds cannot do this. Its emotional life becomes episodic—felt in bursts, quickly expressed, and quickly forgotten.

The erosion of empathy is visible across every layer of society. Online, moral outrage replaces moral reasoning because anger is cognitively efficient. In education, students struggle to sustain focus through a single sustained argument; comprehension fragments into impression. In relationships, conversation competes with the vibration of a nearby device, a phenomenon sometimes called 'phubbing,' where a person snubs their present company in favor of their phone. The capacity to dwell—on a feeling, an idea, a human face—has atrophied. The anthropologist Sherry

Turkle calls this "the flight from conversation." People speak, but they do not connect. They react to words but seldom inhabit meaning.

The psychologist Herbert Simon foresaw this dynamic decades ago when he warned that "a wealth of information creates a poverty of attention." His insight has now matured into a social condition. The abundance of content has devalued awareness itself. The human mind, once the author of its own focus, now functions as a passive processor of stimuli. It scrolls not to discover, but to sustain motion. This continuous movement produces the illusion of engagement, even as comprehension fades.

The psychological term *directed attention fatigue* captures the mechanism behind this erosion. The prefrontal cortex, responsible for deliberate focus and impulse control, operates like a muscle. Its depletion is why, at the end of a long day of answering emails and switching between tasks, the simple act of deciding what to eat for dinner can feel impossibly difficult. It requires periods of rest to recover. Constant stimulation depletes it, leaving the individual irritable, unfocused, and emotionally reactive. Researchers in environmental psychology have shown that exposure to natural environments restores this capacity because it engages what they call *involuntary attention*—gentle awareness that allows the mind to replenish. The contemporary environment, by contrast, offers no such reprieve. Its design ensures that every pause is filled.

What is at stake here is not merely concentration but coherence—the ability to inhabit one's own consciousness without interruption. When the mind cannot sustain attention, it cannot sustain meaning. Thoughts remain partial; emotions remain shallow. This fragmentation is not simply a cognitive deficit but an existential one. The human experience begins to feel weightless because nothing is fully entered into. The philosopher Byung-Chul Han argues that the modern subject is trapped in "hyperactive passivity": constantly stimulated, rarely moved. Activity replaces purpose; engagement replaces understanding.

The loss of attention also weakens moral capacity. To attend to something—or someone—is to acknowledge its existence as real. Moral life depends on this act of recognition. The philosopher Simone Weil called attention the purest form of generosity: "the rarest and purest form of generosity is attention." When attention is scattered, empathy dissipates. The person who cannot stay present with their own discomfort cannot stay present with another's suffering. The moral consequence of distraction is not apathy but shallowness—an inability to feel deeply enough for concern to transform into care.

This thinning of empathy and comprehension is compounded by the illusion of connection that technology provides. The constant visibility of others' lives simulates closeness without intimacy. Social platforms reward expression over reflection, reaction over relation. The architecture of these systems encourages rapid evaluation—like, dislike, agree, disagree—leaving no room for the slow labor of understanding. Over time, this produces what might be called *relational dissonance*: the feeling of being surrounded by others yet unable to feel them.

Cognitively, the attention economy exploits a bias known as *salience distortion*. The mind gives disproportionate weight to what is most visible or emotionally charged, even when it is not most meaningful. The more attention is captured by noise, the less it is available for signal. This distortion explains the modern difficulty of distinguishing significance from visibility. What trends, seems true. What repeats, seems right. In such conditions, comprehension gives way to exposure. People know of many things, but understand few.

Reclaiming attention, therefore, is not simply about focus—it is about freedom. The mind cannot choose wisely when its choices are made for it at the level of impulse. The first act of autonomy in the Artificial Era is the deliberate reallocation of attention. This does not mean rejecting technology; it means using it consciously rather than reflexively. Just as financial literacy protects against economic exploitation, attentional literacy protects against psychological manipulation.

Psychologists studying attentional control describe two complementary processes: *top-down* attention, driven by goals and values, and *bottom-up* attention, driven by stimuli. The attention economy thrives by keeping individuals in bottom-up mode, reactive to external cues. Recovery begins when top-down control is restored—when one decides what deserves awareness. This restoration requires both environmental design and psychological discipline. Limiting exposure, creating intentional spaces of silence, and engaging in long-form thinking rebuild the brain's capacity for sustained focus.

There is empirical evidence supporting this restoration. Studies on mindfulness, contemplative practice, and "deep work" show measurable improvements in working memory, emotional regulation, and cognitive flexibility. These are not spiritual luxuries but psychological repairs. They counteract the neural depletion caused by chronic interruption. More importantly, they reconnect attention to intention. The difference between focus and fixation lies in purpose. To focus with purpose is to direct awareness toward meaning; to fixate is to be captured by it.

The social implications of this recovery are profound. A culture capable of deep attention is a culture capable of empathy, nuance, and dialogue. A distracted culture, by contrast, is vulnerable to polarization and manipulation because it cannot sustain ambiguity. Reflection takes time; reaction does not. When attention is scarce, those who control its flow shape collective consciousness. This is why attention is not only psychological currency but political power. The battle for focus is the battle for freedom of thought.

Yet the solution is not isolation but integration. Attention can coexist with technology if relationship replaces reflex. The psychologist Mihaly Csikszentmihalyi's concept of *flow*—the state of complete absorption in a meaningful task—illustrates what conscious engagement looks like. In flow, attention unifies rather than fragments. Time stretches, self-consciousness fades, and action aligns with purpose. These states are not confined to artists or athletes; they are the natural mode of a mind fully present. What the Artificial Era disrupts is not the capacity for flow but the conditions for it. The task is to restore those conditions—through boundaries, intention, and respect for silence.

Philosophically, the defense of attention is the defense of reality. What we attend to, we become. To choose where awareness rests is to choose the quality of one's consciousness. The Buddhist teacher Thich Nhat Hanh called attention "the foundation of love," while cognitive scientists describe it as the substrate of consciousness itself. The two perspectives meet in their conclusion: attention is how existence becomes personal.

To treat attention as currency, then, is not a metaphor but a truth about human ecology. Where attention flows, energy follows. Where energy flows, life takes shape. When attention is scattered, so is the self. When it is focused, the self becomes coherent again. In a world that profits from our fragmentation, the simple act of sustained presence becomes revolutionary.

To pay attention—fully, quietly, without divided allegiance—is to reassert ownership of the mind. It is to reclaim the only currency that cannot be manufactured, mined, or replicated. Every moment of genuine focus is a statement of identity: *I will decide what defines my awareness.* In that decision lies the recovery of meaning, empathy, and humanity itself.

The Anxiety of Acceleration

There is a rhythm to thought, and that rhythm has always been slower than the rhythm of the world. Human cognition evolved for continuity, not velocity. Perception, memory, and emotion developed in environments where change was gradual and recovery possible. The nervous system could anticipate, adapt, and rest. Today, that equilibrium is gone. The tempo of the external world now far exceeds the natural tempo of the mind. The result is a psychological condition that defines the Artificial Era: chronic acceleration anxiety—the persistent sense that one is always falling behind.

Acceleration itself is not new. Every technological revolution has altered the pace of life. The printing press compressed the dissemination of knowledge; the telegraph compressed communication; the internet compressed space. But what distinguishes the present moment is the absence of pauses between these compressions. The speed of change has become continuous. In such conditions, the nervous system, accustomed to cyclical tension and release, remains locked in a state of perpetual readiness. This constant vigilance is not merely cognitive; it is physiological. The body lives in anticipation of interruption, its stress systems activated by expectation rather than event.

Neuroscientifically, this can be traced to the interaction between the prefrontal cortex, which regulates executive control, and the amygdala, which governs threat detection. In an overstimulated environment, the amygdala becomes hyperactive, interpreting rapid change as potential danger. Cortisol levels rise, attention narrows, and working memory is compromised. This is why digital overstimulation often feels like anxiety—it triggers the same neurobiological cascade designed for survival. The mind, sensing motion, prepares for impact.

Psychologists refer to this as *anticipatory stress*, a form of anxiety not tied to any specific threat but to the expectation of more. It manifests as the low hum of mental agitation that follows many people throughout their day: the feeling of being busy even when idle, alert even when safe. In evolutionary terms, the stress response is adaptive when brief. It mobilizes energy for action. But when prolonged, it exhausts the system. Chronic acceleration produces chronic arousal, and chronic arousal becomes emotional depletion.

The social context amplifies this internal strain. The culture of the Artificial Era rewards speed as virtue. Efficiency, immediacy, and responsiveness have replaced deliberation, patience, and depth. The faster one adapts, the more competent one appears. Yet the same acceleration that promises mastery erodes meaning. Constant adaptation prevents integration. The self becomes reactive, adjusting to each wave of novelty without time to absorb it. In psychological terms, this is *temporal dislocation*—a condition in which experience accumulates faster than it can be processed. Life feels full but not cohesive, busy but not satisfying.

This dislocation produces a distinct emotional tone: the fear of falling behind. It is not the fear of loss but of irrelevance, a uniquely modern anxiety born from comparison to an environment that never stops moving. The sociologist Hartmut Rosa describes this as *social acceleration*, a process in which individuals must continually increase their pace just to maintain their position. The treadmill effect is relentless: the faster one moves, the more motion becomes mandatory. Pausing feels like regression. Rest feels like risk.

The digital landscape reinforces this fear through constant visibility. Algorithms reward immediacy—posts, responses, engagement—creating a loop in which presence must be constantly reasserted. The moment one stops producing, one disappears from view. The resulting anxiety is both existential and performative. People measure their worth not by what they are but by how quickly they appear to evolve. This produces what might be called *chronological insecurity*: the sense that one's psychological timeline no longer matches the cultural one. A person in their late twenties, for instance, may feel a constant pressure to achieve career milestones that once belonged to middle age, simply because the visible timelines of their peers appear so compressed and accelerated online.

The consequences for attention and emotion are profound. Under chronic acceleration, the brain's attentional networks become tuned for novelty rather than stability. The default mode of cognition shifts from contemplation to scanning. Thoughts fragment, decisions become impulsive, and emotional states shorten. Joy, curiosity, and interest—all emotions that require lingering—are replaced by the shallow excitations of alertness. This transformation explains why the modern psyche often confuses stimulation with meaning. The faster something moves, the more alive it seems; the more alive it seems, the more it is pursued. Yet behind the stimulation lies fatigue—a quiet recognition that movement alone cannot substitute for momentum.

The philosopher Paul Virilio warned of this decades ago when he described *dromology*, the study of speed as power. He observed that technological societies equate acceleration with progress, forgetting that velocity without direction leads nowhere faster. The same logic now governs individual consciousness. Acceleration has become internalized as identity. To slow down feels like failure because self-worth has been indexed to pace. This is not productivity; it is compulsion disguised as competence.

At its core, acceleration anxiety represents a disconnection between cognitive time and cultural time. Cognitive time—the rhythm at which humans process experience—remains bounded by biology. Neural networks have fixed speeds of transmission, emotional regulation requires metabolic cycles, and memory consolidation occurs during rest. Cultural time, by contrast, operates at algorithmic speed, where updates occur by the second and attention resets with each scroll. The collision of these two tempos produces cognitive strain: the sense of lag between inner and outer life.

Psychologically, this lag generates a kind of temporal vertigo. The mind experiences the present as unstable, slipping forward faster than it can inhabit. This condition resembles what the psychiatrist R.D. Laing once described as *ontological insecurity*: a disturbance in the felt continuity of being. People begin to feel stretched thin across moments, unable to locate themselves fully in any of them. They multitask through existence, processing instead of living.

Acceleration also distorts motivation. The faster the world moves, the more attention gravitates toward what is immediate rather than meaningful. Behavioral economists describe this as *temporal discounting*: the tendency to devalue long-term rewards in favor of short-term ones. Under chronic acceleration, this bias becomes dominant. Future goals feel abstract because the future itself feels unstable. The result is a population increasingly skilled at reaction and decreasingly capable of foresight.

Culturally, the worship of speed masks a deeper emotional hunger: the desire for certainty in motion. When everything changes constantly, predictability becomes the new luxury. The rise of nostalgia industries, mindfulness movements, and "slow living" philosophies can all be seen as compensatory reactions—a collective attempt to reintroduce rhythm into a culture that has lost its pulse. These movements remind us that acceleration, when unexamined, leads not to progress but to exhaustion.

Yet the solution is not simply to slow down. Slowness, imposed as reaction, becomes its own form of performance. The goal is not deceleration but synchronization—aligning the speed of technology with the tempo of human consciousness. This requires what might be called *psychological pacing*: the deliberate structuring of life to include intervals of stillness and depth amid motion. Pacing does not reject progress; it humanizes it.

Empirical psychology supports this need for rhythm. Studies on attention restoration and cognitive recovery show that alternating periods of focus and rest produce higher performance and greater well-being than constant engagement. The nervous system operates best through oscillation—stress balanced by recovery, activation balanced by reflection. When this balance disappears, burnout follows. The American Psychological Association now lists chronic acceleration and information overload among primary contributors to workplace anxiety, a condition that has migrated from the professional sphere into every domain of life.

Acceleration also erodes imagination. Creativity requires incubation— the period during which ideas are allowed to percolate unconsciously. In accelerated cultures, incubation time vanishes. People consume inspiration faster than they can metabolize it. As a result, originality declines while output increases. The culture becomes louder but not deeper. To create meaning under these conditions requires reclaiming mental quietude as a legitimate form of action.

The anxiety of acceleration, then, is not just a symptom of technological change but a mirror of psychological imbalance. It reveals how far the external pace of life has drifted from the internal pace of mind. Reconciliation begins with awareness: recognizing that presence cannot occur at the speed of refresh. To inhabit time consciously is to recover sovereignty over one's own rhythm.

The philosopher Henri Bergson once described time not as a sequence of moments but as *duration*—a continuous flow of consciousness. To live within duration is to experience depth rather than sequence. The Artificial Era, obsessed with quantifying moments, mistakes count for content. The recovery of psychological time requires returning to duration—to reinhabit experience rather than merely timestamp it.

Acceleration will not end; it will intensify. But human beings retain one advantage no machine can replicate: the ability to regulate tempo from within. Awareness itself can slow perception, expand time, and restore proportion. This is not nostalgia—it is neurobiology. The nervous system, when given rhythm, reclaims coherence. And coherence, in an incoherent world, is a form of peace.

To live well in the Artificial Era is therefore not to outrun acceleration but to outgrow anxiety. It is to accept that speed belongs to systems, not souls. Meaning still unfolds at the pace of attention, and attention still requires stillness. The mind, when it stops chasing time, begins to inhabit it.

Emotional Saturation

Every era has its prevailing emotional climate. Ours is defined not by repression, but by inundation. The human nervous system, once adapted to scarcity of information and limited interpersonal contact, now exists under continuous emotional exposure. Through screens, headlines, messages, and feeds, we encounter more joy, fear, outrage, and grief in a day than previous generations met in a lifetime. What began as connection has become immersion. The modern psyche is not starved of feeling—it is flooded with it.

Psychologists once spoke of *emotional numbing* as a symptom of trauma, a defense against pain too great to process. In the Artificial Era, emotional numbing has become a cultural adaptation to overstimulation. The constant influx of emotion—our own and others'—has exceeded the brain's integrative capacity. It is not that people feel less because they care less; they feel less because they have felt too much for too long. The threshold of sensitivity has shifted. The result is a paradoxical blend of arousal and exhaustion: a mind always activated but rarely moved.

Neuroscience provides part of the explanation. The limbic system, which regulates emotion, and the prefrontal cortex, which governs regulation and reflection, evolved for an environment where emotional cues were infrequent but meaningful. A single threat, loss, or joy demanded sustained response and integration. Today, these systems are bombarded by hundreds of micro-emotions each hour—anger at a headline, envy at an image, pity at a video, pride at a post. Each momentary surge of affect activates physiological arousal: changes in heart rate, muscle tone, and cortisol levels. The cumulative effect is chronic elevation of the stress response, a state of *allostatic load*. Even when individual triggers seem trivial, their aggregate impact is profound.

This state of saturation diminishes emotional granularity—the ability to identify and differentiate feelings. The psychologist Lisa Feldman Barrett's research demonstrates that emotional granularity is critical for regulation: people who can name their emotions precisely experience less distress and recover more quickly. Yet in an environment of emotional overload, granularity collapses. Feelings blur into general agitation. Irritation becomes indistinguishable from fear, sadness from fatigue. The emotional vocabulary shrinks, leaving people fluent in intensity but illiterate in nuance.

At a societal level, this loss of granularity manifests as polarization. When subtle emotion disappears, complex disagreement becomes moral conflict. Outrage replaces dialogue because outrage is easy to recognize and easy to share. Social media platforms amplify this process by rewarding emotional extremity. Studies in digital psychology have shown that content eliciting high-arousal emotions—anger, fear, excitement—spreads faster and further than calm or contemplative material. The emotional economy thus favors volatility. The public sphere becomes a feedback loop of affect, optimized for engagement but corrosive to empathy.

In daily life, emotional saturation produces subtler forms of exhaustion. People describe feeling "drained," "flat," or "checked out." What they often mean is that their emotional system has lost its natural rhythm of activation and recovery. Healthy emotional life resembles breathing— expansion and contraction, intensity and rest. Saturation eliminates that rhythm. When every moment is charged, none of it feels meaningful. This condition parallels what trauma theorists describe as *hyperarousal*: a persistent readiness that numbs the capacity for genuine feeling.

The effects extend into relationships. The constant exposure to curated emotion online distorts how people experience intimacy. In digital spaces, feelings are broadcast rather than shared. The performance of emotion— through reactions, captions, or confessions—replaces the mutual presence that allows emotion to deepen. Empathy becomes performative, expressed through symbols rather than silence. The philosopher Martin Buber distinguished between *I-Thou* and *I-It* relationships—the first characterized by genuine encounter, the second by utility. Saturation pulls relationships toward the latter. Others become stimuli rather than subjects, sources of emotional data rather than partners in feeling.

The cumulative outcome of this process is emotional flattening. Joy becomes shallow because it must compete with constant stimulation; sorrow becomes brief because it is quickly displaced. The nervous system, overwhelmed by rapid alternation between affective states, protects itself through detachment. This is not indifference but fatigue masquerading as calm. The psychiatrist Viktor Frankl once wrote that meaning depends on tension—the gap between what is and what could be. Saturation eliminates that gap. When everything demands attention, nothing sustains it.

From a developmental perspective, this environment also reshapes how younger generations learn to regulate emotion. Emotional maturity requires tolerating discomfort long enough to transform it into understanding. In an accelerated emotional culture, discomfort is outsourced to distraction. The moment unease arises, another stimulus appears to replace it. The capacity for emotional endurance weakens. This explains why many people report increasing sensitivity to minor frustrations alongside growing indifference to major events. The emotional scale has inverted: a delayed coffee order can provoke a surge of genuine anger, while a news report about a distant famine elicits only a fleeting, abstract sadness. Trivial irritations dominate consciousness while profound suffering fades into abstraction.

This desynchronization between emotion and meaning has broader cultural implications. Historically, societies depended on shared emotional rhythms—rituals of grief, celebration, or reflection—that synchronized collective feeling. These rituals allowed individuals to metabolize emotion communally. In the Artificial Era, emotional experience has become asynchronous. Everyone feels, but seldom together. The result is emotional fragmentation on a mass scale: simultaneous arousal without coherence. The collective mood becomes volatile, swinging between enthusiasm and despair without resolution.

Philosophically, this volatility undermines one of psychology's oldest insights: that emotion is a source of knowledge. The early theorists of emotion—Darwin, James, Dewey—understood feeling as an adaptive signal, a guide to values and survival. When emotion becomes constant noise, its informational value collapses. People no longer trust their feelings because their feelings are never still long enough to interpret. Cynicism follows: the quiet conviction that everything is exaggerated, performative, or false. Emotional saturation breeds disbelief, not because emotion is insincere, but because sincerity itself has become indistinguishable from display.

To understand the toll of saturation, one must also consider its physiological consequences. Chronic emotional arousal activates the hypothalamic-pituitary-adrenal axis, releasing cortisol that, over time, impairs immune function, sleep, and mood regulation. Neuroscientific studies have linked constant digital engagement with heightened amygdala reactivity and reduced gray matter in regions associated with emotional control. The nervous system adapts to overexposure by becoming both hyperalert and under-responsive—a paradoxical combination that mirrors the cultural mood of our time: anxious yet apathetic.

And yet, the human organism remains capable of recovery. Emotion, like attention, is plastic. The same brain that adapts to overload can also relearn rhythm. Recovery begins with deliberate modulation—reintroducing intervals of quiet into the emotional landscape. This is not about avoidance but pacing. Just as muscles grow during rest, emotions gain depth through integration. The psychologist James Gross's research on *emotion regulation* distinguishes between suppression and reappraisal: the first numbs, the second transforms. Reappraisal requires time—time to reinterpret, contextualize, and learn from what is felt. The task of the Artificial Era is to restore that time.

Practically, this restoration means designing environments and habits that allow emotion to breathe. This might include digital sabbaths, periods of intentional solitude, or re-engagement with art and nature—contexts that evoke feeling without demanding reaction. Studies in affective neuroscience show that exposure to aesthetic experiences—music, painting, landscape—activates reward circuits while simultaneously calming the amygdala. Beauty, in this sense, functions as emotional coherence. It allows the nervous system to experience intensity without chaos.

Socially, the antidote to emotional saturation is depth of connection rather than breadth. True empathy requires proximity—emotional, if not physical. It develops when one attends fully to another without distraction or performance. In therapy, this is known as *empathic attunement*, the process of resonating with another's emotion while remaining grounded in one's own. Culturally, reintroducing attunement means valuing conversation over commentary, presence over participation. It requires cultivating what the philosopher Josef Pieper called "leisure": not idleness, but receptive stillness—the capacity to be affected without reacting.

The emotional life of the future will depend on whether societies can learn to metabolize feeling again. The Artificial Era will continue to expose humanity to immense volumes of emotional input. The question is whether consciousness can evolve to match it. Emotional intelligence, once defined as managing relationships and impulses, must now include managing exposure itself. The ability to regulate input—to choose which emotions enter and which pass by—may become the defining psychological skill of the century.

There is nothing inherently wrong with feeling much. The danger lies in feeling everything without discernment. Emotional richness becomes emotional noise when the mind cannot distinguish signal from saturation. The path forward is not numbness, but rhythm—a restoration of tempo between emotion and thought, arousal and rest, empathy and protection.

The poet Rainer Maria Rilke once wrote that one must "let everything happen," but what he meant was not surrender to chaos but faith in process. Emotion must unfold in time to reveal meaning. The task of the Artificial Era is to recover that temporality—to grant feeling its rightful duration. Only then can the flood of emotion become a current that carries, rather than drowns, the self.

Emotional saturation is not the end of sensitivity. It is the crisis that precedes refinement. When the world overwhelms, the mind has two choices: to withdraw or to learn a finer art of perception. If it learns, empathy will return—not as naïve openness, but as mature discernment.

The future of emotional life depends on that transformation: from reaction to resonance, from stimulation to significance.

Designing Mental Space

When the mind is overstimulated, the instinct is often escape. People fantasize about disconnecting—moving to the countryside, deleting every app, finding silence somewhere beyond reach. Yet the challenge of the Artificial Era is not to flee stimulation, but to live sanely within it. The question is not how to withdraw from the modern world, but how to design mental architecture strong enough to inhabit it. The task of psychological design is to create space within consciousness itself—an inner environment capable of balance, clarity, and rest amid continuous motion.

Designing mental space begins with a recognition that attention, emotion, and cognition are not independent capacities but interconnected systems. Overload in one leads to distortion in all. The nervous system, once regulated by natural cycles of day and night, social contact and solitude, has become artificially flattened. Stimulation is constant, rest optional, and silence rare. To recover depth of mind, people must reintroduce the rhythms that biology requires and culture has forgotten.

Psychologists call this process *self-regulation*. It is the ability to maintain internal stability amid changing external conditions. In cognitive-behavioral terms, regulation involves both modulation—reducing unnecessary stimulation—and restoration—replenishing depleted resources. The same principles that apply to ecosystems apply to consciousness: sustainability depends on diversity, pacing, and recovery. A mind exposed only to noise, novelty, and demand will eventually degrade its own equilibrium. Designing mental space means curating input with the same care one would give to any environment intended for growth.

One of the most useful frameworks for understanding restoration comes from environmental psychology: the *Attention Restoration Theory* (ART), developed by Stephen and Rachel Kaplan. Their research demonstrated that natural environments renew cognitive function by engaging the mind's *involuntary attention*—the soft fascination that allows directed attention to rest. Unlike the demanding focus of digital life, involuntary attention does not fatigue the prefrontal cortex. When people walk in nature, sit near water, or simply observe the quiet complexity of living systems, their neural activity shifts from vigilance to integration. Cognitive fatigue decreases, creativity increases, and emotional stability improves.

The underlying principle is not about wilderness but about contrast. The mind recovers when it encounters patterns of stimulation that invite observation rather than reaction. Even within urban or digital settings, this principle can be recreated. Simple design choices—lighting that follows circadian rhythm, deliberate quiet zones, or interfaces that limit visual clutter—can support cognitive balance. On an individual level, this translates into what might be called *psychological architecture*: structuring daily life to include deliberate spaces of stillness.

One of the most effective forms of psychological architecture is the cultivation of *selective ignorance*. The philosopher Schopenhauer argued that intelligence is defined not by what one knows but by what one ignores. Modern neuroscience confirms the wisdom of this paradox. The brain's attentional networks have limited capacity; every unnecessary input consumes energy that could be used for reflection or creativity. Selective ignorance is not avoidance but discernment. It involves the conscious refusal to absorb stimuli that do not serve one's values or goals. In an age where exposure is automatic, ignorance becomes a form of intelligence.

Selective ignorance also counters a common misconception: that awareness of everything equals responsibility for everything. The human psyche cannot sustain perpetual empathy for a planet's worth of suffering without collapsing into despair. The philosopher Susan Sontag observed that compassion, when stretched too wide, becomes fatigue. To design mental space ethically, individuals must acknowledge the limits of their capacity to feel. Responsibility begins with attention that is local, embodied, and actionable. Awareness without boundary breeds paralysis; awareness within boundary enables care.

Another cornerstone of mental space is *structured thinking*. The philosopher and psychologist William James noted that "the faculty of bringing back a wandering attention is the very root of judgment, character, and will." Structured thinking protects this faculty by giving the mind a form to inhabit. In practical terms, it means organizing thought through writing, dialogue, or deliberate contemplation. The act of articulating experience— on paper or in conversation—forces the diffuse currents of emotion and information into coherence. This is why journaling, therapy, and reflective writing remain among the most effective tools for emotional regulation. They transform chaos into pattern.

Cognitive science supports this observation. When individuals narrate their experiences, activity increases in the hippocampus and prefrontal cortex—regions responsible for memory integration and meaning-making. This process, known as *autobiographical coherence*, links past and present into continuity. Without such coherence, experience fragments into isolated moments. The mind becomes an archive rather than a story. Designing mental space requires reclaiming narrative as an organizing principle of consciousness. It turns life from stream into sequence, restoring a sense of authorship over time.

Silence is another essential structural element. In psychological terms, silence is not the absence of sound but the absence of response. It is the moment when the nervous system ceases orienting toward external stimuli. Research in neuroscience shows that silence activates the brain's *default mode network*—a system involved in self-reflection, imagination, and moral reasoning. When individuals experience silence, even briefly, the brain integrates information accumulated during periods of activity. The same mechanism that allows sleep to consolidate memory allows silence to consolidate meaning.

Culturally, silence has been misinterpreted as emptiness, a void to be filled. In reality, it is a medium of integration. Societies that fear silence fear introspection, because silence exposes disconnection. Designing mental space, therefore, involves rehabilitating silence as a positive value. This can take many forms: moments of quiet before speaking, deliberate pauses in conversation, or time spent without input. Silence is not luxury—it is infrastructure. Without it, thought remains superficial, skimming over the surface of life without depth or traction.

One of the most practical methods for cultivating mental space is the intentional design of *digital boundaries*. Cognitive-behavioral interventions often emphasize stimulus control—the deliberate structuring of environments to reduce triggers that perpetuate maladaptive habits. The same principle applies to technology use. Turning off notifications, restricting device access during certain hours, or creating "offline zones" are not acts of asceticism but of regulation. These boundaries reintroduce friction into experience, restoring the pause that allows choice.

Psychologically, friction is essential for consciousness. Automation removes friction, and with it, awareness. Each automatic swipe or tap bypasses the reflective circuitry of the brain, strengthening habit while weakening agency. Friction reactivates awareness by slowing perception just enough to permit deliberation. The philosopher Albert Borgmann described this as the difference between *device* and *focal* practices. Devices deliver results without engagement; focal practices demand participation. A microwave is a device; cooking a meal over a stove is a focal practice. Mental health in the Artificial Era depends on rebalancing the two—making space for practices that require presence.

Examples of focal practices include cooking, reading physical books, gardening, or conversation without screens. These activities share a common feature: they unfold in real time and resist acceleration. They engage the senses and reward sustained attention. Neuroimaging studies show that such activities increase parasympathetic nervous system activity, reducing stress and enhancing emotional regulation. More importantly, they provide a psychological counterweight to the abstraction of digital life. They remind the body that it exists, and through it, the mind returns to ground.

Another key principle in designing mental space is *temporal hygiene*—the management of psychological time. In an environment that collapses past, present, and future into a continuous feed, temporal boundaries are as vital as spatial ones. Creating distinct phases in the day—work, reflection, rest—reestablishes rhythm. The anthropologist Edward T. Hall observed that every culture encodes time differently; the Artificial Era, dominated by instantaneity, has lost its sense of temporal texture. By reintroducing rhythm, individuals restore what philosophers from Bergson to Heidegger called *duration*: the experience of living time rather than measuring it.

Designing mental space also involves the deliberate cultivation of *meta-awareness*—the capacity to observe one's own attention. Mindfulness practices, stripped of their spiritual ornamentation, are essentially attentional training. They teach individuals to notice the movement of awareness itself. Research in contemplative neuroscience shows that mindfulness strengthens neural circuits associated with cognitive control and emotional regulation. But its deeper function is existential: it restores the gap between stimulus and response. Within that gap lies freedom.

The integration of these practices—selective ignorance, structured thinking, silence, boundaries, rhythm, and awareness—forms what might be called *psychological architecture*. Like any well-designed space, it balances openness with containment, complexity with clarity. It does not eliminate noise but organizes it. The goal is not purity of mind but livability of mind: an interior environment where thought can unfold without collapse.

The implications extend beyond individual well-being. Collective mental space is the foundation of civilization. Cultures that lose the ability to think deeply lose the capacity to act wisely. Public discourse, art, and ethics all depend on sustained attention and reflective distance. When societies become perpetually reactive, policy devolves into panic, and meaning is replaced by trend. Designing mental space at the social level therefore requires institutions—schools, workplaces, media—to value depth over immediacy. This means rethinking how success, productivity, and intelligence are measured. A civilization that prizes speed over sense will eventually mistake noise for progress.

Psychology, in this context, becomes a form of cultural design. It offers not only therapy for individuals but architecture for consciousness. The therapeutic setting itself models mental space: boundaries, silence, structure, and reflection. In that sense, therapy represents the microcosm of what culture needs on a larger scale—a space where thought slows down enough to become understanding.

Ultimately, the design of mental space is an ethical act. It asserts that awareness deserves protection. The ability to think clearly and feel deeply is not merely personal privilege; it is social responsibility. The Artificial Era's greatest danger is not that machines will think for us, but that we will forget how to think for ourselves. Preserving mental space ensures that the human mind remains a place where meaning can still take root.

To design mental space is to reclaim sovereignty over consciousness. It does not mean detachment from the world, but right relationship with it. Noise will continue; speed will intensify; novelty will multiply. But within the self, there can still exist quiet architecture—a structure strong enough to hold awareness without collapse. In that structure, clarity returns, and with it, the rarest modern virtue: presence. It is the only room where the mind can truly come home to itself.

* * *

II

Part II – The Adaptation Mindset

The first shock passes, but confusion remains. The next challenge is learning to bend instead of break. Part II explores how people begin to reorient themselves in the Artificial Era—how the mind rewires, the heart relearns confidence, and meaning slowly returns through flexibility, curiosity, and emotional endurance.

4

The Emotional Cost of Change

C hange is no longer something that happens between periods of stability; it is the atmosphere in which modern life unfolds. For most of human history, change arrived in intervals—wars, discoveries, revolutions, or personal milestones punctuated stretches of relative continuity. But in the Artificial Era, continuity itself has disappeared. Technology evolves faster than comprehension, institutions shift faster than trust can rebuild, and cultural values transform faster than individuals can adapt. The result is a condition of permanent transition, in which emotional equilibrium is continually tested by motion that never ends.

This constant flux imposes a cost that is not merely practical but psychological. The human mind was built to manage change episodically, not perpetually. Cognition thrives on pattern recognition and predictability; emotion stabilizes through routine and expectation. When those anchors dissolve, anxiety emerges not as pathology but as an appropriate response to disorientation. The nervous system, deprived of steady reference points, defaults to vigilance. It scans for stability in an environment that no longer provides it.

Psychologists have long recognized that adaptation is not simply a cognitive act but an emotional process. Theories of change management often emphasize strategy and skill acquisition, yet what determines resilience is less about knowledge than about emotional regulation. The loss of predictability, the redefinition of identity, and the erosion of control all elicit grief-like responses. Elisabeth Kübler-Ross's model of denial, anger, bargaining, depression, and acceptance was never meant only for death; it describes the inner architecture of adjustment itself. Every significant change—whether in career, culture, or consciousness—invokes the same emotional logic: resistance before renewal.

What distinguishes the current era is not that people resist change, but that they must do so continuously. The emotional system never fully resets. Each adaptation is followed by another demand, another update, another shift in context. This repetition breeds what some psychologists now call *adaptation fatigue*—a state in which even minor changes feel exhausting because the emotional resources required to accommodate them are already depleted. Under such conditions, resilience cannot simply mean endurance. It must mean transformation: the capacity to metabolize instability into growth.

Uncertainty, viewed through this lens, is not merely an obstacle but a psychological environment to be navigated. The question is no longer how to eliminate uncertainty, but how to live intelligently within it. The philosopher Søren Kierkegaard described anxiety as "the dizziness of freedom"—the price of possibility. That insight feels newly relevant. In a world defined by rapid change, anxiety signals awareness of potential, not just fear of loss. The task is to differentiate between the kind of anxiety that paralyzes and the kind that prepares.

Emotionally, this requires developing a different relationship to control. The illusion of mastery—of complete prediction or stability—has collapsed. In its place must come what psychologists call *tolerance for ambiguity*: the ability to remain grounded even when outcomes are indeterminate. This quality, once peripheral, is now essential to mental health. It allows for flexibility without surrender, acceptance without passivity.

To understand the emotional cost of change, one must first acknowledge its universality. It is no longer confined to moments of crisis or transition; it defines the baseline of experience. The Artificial Era has turned what was once the exception into the rule. Yet within that condition lies the possibility of a new kind of psychological maturity—one rooted not in certainty, but in capacity. If stability can no longer be guaranteed, then the only durable security is internal: a steadiness of mind that endures even as the world refuses to.

The Cycle of Resistance

Change unsettles not because it arrives, but because it demands reorganization—of perception, of identity, and of meaning. Every alteration in circumstance forces the psyche to update its internal model of the world. Yet the mind resists this updating process, not out of stubbornness but out of self-protection. Resistance is a form of emotional conservation, the psyche's attempt to preserve equilibrium in the face of disruption. To understand resistance is not to condemn it but to recognize it as part of the architecture of adaptation itself.

Psychologically, resistance mirrors the stages of grief because all change involves loss—the loss of what was known, predictable, or felt as safe. Elisabeth Kübler-Ross's framework was derived from her work with terminally ill patients, but its emotional structure applies to every form of transformation. Denial, bargaining, anger, resignation, and eventual acceptance are not discrete steps but emotional postures the mind assumes as it negotiates reality. In change, as in grief, these postures protect consciousness from emotional overload.

Denial is the first and most immediate form of protection. When confronted with disruption, the mind often refuses to register it fully. Denial is not ignorance but delay—a psychological buffer that allows time to recalibrate. Cognitive neuroscience describes this as a form of attentional filtering. The brain resists processing contradictory information because doing so requires neural energy and emotional cost. In organizational settings, denial appears as disbelief: "This won't really happen." In personal life, it takes subtler forms—pretending a relationship will recover, a job will stabilize, or a system will self-correct. Denial is the pause before pain, the nervous system's attempt to postpone the full emotional cost of acknowledgment.

Once the illusion of continuity collapses, anger often follows. Anger externalizes helplessness; it redirects fear into assertion. In psychological terms, anger restores a sense of agency when control feels lost. It converts vulnerability into momentum. Yet it also risks fixation. When anger becomes habitual, it prevents the emotional system from moving forward. Individuals, groups, even entire cultures can become trapped in anger as a way of preserving identity amid change. The sociologist Arlie Hochschild observed this dynamic in political movements where anger functions as solidarity: shared outrage becomes a substitute for shared progress. On a personal level, anger keeps the mind busy with blame, shielding it from the deeper work of grief.

After anger comes bargaining, the mind's attempt to negotiate with uncertainty. "If I adjust, maybe it won't be so bad." Bargaining is transitional; it acknowledges change while trying to control its terms. It reflects the cognitive system's tendency to seek predictability even in chaos. Bargaining offers temporary relief by creating the illusion of influence. Yet this illusion is fragile. When reality continues to shift despite one's efforts, bargaining gives way to resignation—a quiet surrender often mistaken for acceptance.

Resignation differs from acceptance because it lacks integration. It is the emotional equivalent of disengagement: the person stops resisting but has not yet reorganized meaning. This state can persist for years. In psychological research on learned helplessness, Martin Seligman found that organisms exposed to uncontrollable stressors eventually stop trying to change their situation even when control returns. The same principle applies to human beings in environments of rapid, unpredictable change. Chronic uncertainty breeds passivity. People adapt by lowering expectations, numbing emotion, and retreating into routine. Resignation becomes survival.

Only through *integration*—the synthesis of emotion, cognition, and meaning—does true acceptance emerge. Acceptance is not the absence of resistance but its resolution. It marks the moment when reality, once resisted, becomes part of identity. This transformation requires what psychologist Robert Kegan called *subject–object differentiation*: the ability to step outside one's emotional reaction and observe it. When a person can see their resistance rather than be it, awareness returns. From that vantage, change becomes material for growth rather than threat to stability.

In this way, the cycle of resistance is less a pathology than a developmental mechanism. It allows the self to reorganize gradually rather than shatter abruptly. Each phase serves a function: denial preserves coherence, anger restores agency, bargaining maintains hope, resignation conserves energy, and acceptance rebuilds meaning. Problems arise only when the cycle becomes static—when the psyche mistakes a temporary adaptation for a permanent stance. For example, a person stuck in the anger stage may become perpetually cynical, interpreting every new initiative as a personal slight rather than a neutral change.

Consider a workplace undergoing technological transformation. Employees often begin in denial—assuming new systems will fail or old methods will return. When that hope fades, anger surfaces: frustration with management, with the pace of change, with the erosion of competence. Bargaining follows: learning partial skills, adopting the language of adaptation without internalizing its logic. Resignation appears when effort feels futile. Only after sufficient time and communication does acceptance emerge—the recognition that adaptation itself is now part of the job. The emotional cycle mirrors organizational learning. Resistance, properly managed, becomes a form of engagement.

At the individual level, the same dynamics appear in relationships, health changes, or shifts in worldview. Each phase corresponds to a specific emotional need. Denial protects identity; anger defends autonomy; bargaining seeks safety; resignation preserves energy; acceptance restores coherence. Recognizing these needs is crucial for self-compassion. Too often, people judge their resistance as weakness rather than wisdom. Yet the psyche resists because it values survival over speed.

Developmental psychology supports this interpretation. Jean Piaget's model of *assimilation and accommodation* describes how the mind integrates new information: assimilation incorporates novelty into existing frameworks, while accommodation restructures those frameworks to fit reality.

Resistance occurs when accommodation threatens identity. The emotional energy of resistance reflects the effort required to reconstruct the self's organizing schema. The process is inherently uncomfortable because it destabilizes the narratives that make life intelligible.

To navigate this process effectively, one must learn to observe resistance rather than suppress it. Metacognitive awareness—thinking about one's thinking—creates distance between stimulus and reaction. In therapy, this is often called *naming the resistance*. When individuals articulate what they fear losing or what they are protecting, the resistance begins to dissolve. The energy once used to defend becomes available for adaptation.

However, resistance does not exist only within individuals; it also operates collectively. Groups, institutions, and nations resist change to preserve shared identity. Sociocultural systems develop homeostasis just as biological systems do. When pressures for change increase—technological disruption, demographic shifts, ideological realignments—these systems exhibit emotional responses analogous to the individual grief cycle. Denial becomes nostalgia, anger becomes polarization, bargaining becomes reform, resignation becomes cynicism. Only when a culture collectively redefines its meaning framework does genuine acceptance emerge.

The Artificial Era amplifies this collective resistance because change now occurs faster than consensus can form. The shared narratives that once mediated transformation—religion, tradition, ideology—no longer hold universal authority. Without common meaning, adaptation becomes fragmented. Different segments of society occupy different stages of resistance simultaneously, creating cultural dissonance. One group still denies, another rages, another withdraws. The collective mind, like the individual mind, struggles to synchronize its stages.

Understanding this dissonance is essential for leadership and education. Leaders who misinterpret resistance as defiance miss the opportunity to guide transformation. Those who recognize resistance as emotional process can meet people where they are. Effective communication during change mirrors the therapeutic process: empathy precedes insight. By validating emotion before demanding adjustment, leaders reduce defensive arousal and create psychological safety. This aligns with research in organizational behavior showing that trust and perceived fairness accelerate adaptation. The same principle applies to families, classrooms, and nations.

Yet beyond management or policy, the deeper work of navigating resistance is existential. Every major change confronts the individual with a question of identity: who am I when the familiar disappears? The loss is rarely about the external shift itself but about the self that was organized around it. This is why change can feel like grief even when it brings improvement. It is the death of a known self and the birth of a possible one. Psychologist Dan McAdams describes identity as a "narrative construction." When change disrupts the story, the self must edit its plot. Resistance is the tension between chapters.

From a neurological standpoint, this process reflects the brain's predictive coding system. The mind constantly generates models of the world and updates them through feedback. When sensory or social input contradicts expectation, the brain experiences *prediction error*, a signal of surprise. Small errors adjust the model; large errors trigger emotional alarm. Resistance, in this context, is the subjective experience of prediction error too great to assimilate quickly. Over time, as new patterns stabilize, emotional alarm subsides. The model updates, and acceptance follows.

Recognizing this process offers practical insight. Resistance cannot be eliminated, but it can be shortened. When individuals or groups anticipate the emotional stages of change, they experience them with less confusion and shame. Self-awareness transforms resistance from obstacle to instrument. As people learn to identify denial, anger, and bargaining within themselves, they become participants in adaptation rather than its victims.

To live in the Artificial Era requires rethinking what adaptation means. The old model—endure disruption until stability returns—is obsolete. There is no "after." Change is the constant. The modern task is to cultivate emotional agility: the capacity to move through resistance repeatedly without depletion. This agility depends on acceptance, but not in the passive sense. It is the active willingness to reorient, to update one's models continuously, and to extract meaning even from uncertainty.

In that sense, resistance is not the opposite of growth but its raw material. Without resistance, adaptation would be mechanical rather than psychological. The friction of resistance generates reflection; reflection produces insight; insight produces integration. The goal is not to erase resistance but to evolve with it—to recognize its arrival as a signal that the self is stretching toward a larger frame.

Change will always provoke discomfort because it touches the boundary between the known and the possible. But within that discomfort lies vitality. To resist is to care. It is the mind's way of saying that something valuable is at stake. The challenge of maturity is to preserve that vitality while letting go of its rigidity—to honor resistance as part of the journey toward renewal.

When understood in this light, resistance ceases to be a sign of failure and becomes a measure of engagement. It is not the proof of weakness but of life. The mind that no longer resists change is not peaceful; it is numb. To resist is to feel, and to feel is to remain human.

Adaptive Anxiety

Anxiety has always existed as part of the human condition, but in the Artificial Era it has become the emotional baseline. It is the background hum beneath ambition, the unease behind restlessness, the companion to progress itself. Yet anxiety is not the enemy of adaptation; it is its early warning system. The problem is not that people feel anxious, but that they have forgotten how to interpret what anxiety means.

From an evolutionary perspective, anxiety is an adaptive emotion. It evolved to keep human beings alert to potential threats in uncertain environments. The anticipation of danger mobilized energy, sharpened attention, and improved survival. But the modern environment, unlike the ancestral one, presents constant uncertainty without clear resolution. The nervous system remains in a perpetual state of readiness, receiving signals of potential threat from sources that rarely resolve into action. The result is chronic activation—alertness without outlet.

Anxiety, in this form, becomes maladaptive when it no longer guides action but paralyzes it. Fear that once focused now freezes. The distinction between the two determines psychological resilience. Fear that focuses draws attention toward problem-solving, strategic planning, and preparedness. Fear that freezes consumes those same faculties. Understanding this distinction requires rethinking anxiety not as pathology, but as information.

The psychologist Charles Spielberger distinguished between *state anxiety*—the immediate response to threat—and *trait anxiety*—a general predisposition to perceive threat. In times of rapid change, state anxiety becomes chronic and begins to resemble trait anxiety, even in individuals who were once calm. What matters, therefore, is not whether anxiety exists, but whether it retains its adaptive function. When people can interpret anxiety as signal rather than verdict, it becomes a form of intelligence.

Albert Bandura's concept of self-efficacy clarifies this dynamic. Individuals who believe in their capacity to manage challenges experience anxiety as energizing. Those who doubt their competence experience it as debilitating. The difference lies not in the intensity of fear but in the interpretation of capability. In cognitive terms, anxiety interacts with self-appraisal. It asks the question: Do I have the resources to meet what is coming? The answer determines whether anxiety sharpens focus or undermines it.

This pattern can be seen across domains. In performance psychology, moderate anxiety improves outcomes. Athletes, musicians, and public speakers rely on a degree of physiological arousal to enhance concentration and engagement. Too little, and performance dulls; too much, and it disintegrates. The same applies to adaptation. Moderate anxiety heightens awareness and drives preparation. Excessive anxiety overwhelms and constricts perception. The goal is not elimination but calibration.

Cognitive-behavioral research supports this. Anxiety becomes maladaptive when cognitive distortions—catastrophizing, overgeneralization, all-or-nothing thinking—amplify threat beyond proportion. These distortions arise when attention narrows too tightly around danger and excludes context. The adaptive task, therefore, is to widen attention without denying fear. When individuals can observe anxiety as process rather than truth, they regain agency.

The physiology of anxiety offers further insight. When a person perceives threat, the amygdala activates, triggering the hypothalamic-pituitary-adrenal axis and releasing stress hormones like cortisol and adrenaline. In short bursts, this system enhances alertness and readiness. But chronic activation damages the hippocampus and impairs memory, emotional regulation, and decision-making. The key variable is recovery. The system was designed for episodic threat followed by rest. Modern life rarely allows that rest. Notifications, news cycles, and economic volatility keep the stress loop open indefinitely. Designing spaces for recovery is therefore not indulgence but maintenance of function.

Psychologists often distinguish between *problem-focused* and *emotion-focused* coping. Problem-focused coping seeks to resolve the source of stress; emotion-focused coping manages the feelings associated with it. In contexts of constant change where causes cannot be easily controlled, emotion-focused strategies become crucial. Techniques such as mindfulness, controlled breathing, and reappraisal calm physiological arousal and prevent anxiety from hijacking cognition. Reappraisal—reinterpreting a threat as challenge—has been shown in numerous studies to reduce stress response and improve performance under pressure.

But anxiety's role extends beyond physiology; it is existential. The philosopher Paul Tillich described anxiety as "the state in which a being is aware of its possible nonbeing." He meant that anxiety emerges whenever the self confronts uncertainty about identity, meaning, or continuity. In that sense, anxiety is not simply reaction to external instability but recognition of internal impermanence. Every major life transition—career change, loss, aging, or technological transformation—triggers this existential awareness. The mind senses that something old is dissolving before the new is known. That recognition produces anxiety, but also potential.

If one listens closely, anxiety reveals values. It signals where meaning is invested. People do not fear losing what they do not care about. Anxiety, then, is a compass indicating the location of attachment. The task is not to silence it but to interpret it. In psychotherapy, anxiety often guides the conversation to what truly matters. Clients speak of surface worries—finances, relationships, reputation—but beneath these concerns lies the deeper anxiety of identity: Am I still who I thought I was? Can I remain myself in this new reality? Anxiety exposes the seam between stability and growth.

The modern challenge is that people have learned to treat anxiety as malfunction rather than message. The culture of optimization—fueled by wellness industries and productivity narratives—frames calm as the ideal emotional state. Yet a life devoid of anxiety would also be devoid of responsiveness. Anxiety signals engagement with reality; it shows that consciousness is active. The absence of anxiety may reflect detachment, not peace. Psychological health is not the eradication of unease but the refinement of its use.

The phenomenon of *anticipatory anxiety* illustrates this. Anticipatory anxiety arises when the mind rehearses potential threats before they occur. While often distressing, this mental simulation can also serve preparation. Neuroscientific research shows that the same brain networks involved in imagining future scenarios are used for planning and decision-making. Anxiety, when harnessed, allows foresight. It can identify weak points in strategy, highlight neglected priorities, and prompt preemptive action. The key is modulation—recognizing when rehearsal becomes rumination.

One practical approach is to separate productive worry from unproductive worry. Productive worry leads to concrete steps; unproductive worry loops endlessly without resolution. Worrying about an upcoming project and using that energy to outline the first three steps is productive; worrying about it by repeatedly imagining all the ways it could fail is not. Writing down anxieties and categorizing them according to control can help. Those within one's influence invite action; those beyond it require acceptance. This exercise externalizes anxiety, transforming it from diffuse tension into structured information. In that structure, anxiety regains its adaptive function.

Culturally, anxiety reflects the tension between acceleration and assimilation. The speed of technological and social change continually outpaces emotional integration. Anxiety, at scale, becomes collective—societal unease about direction and pace. Economists measure productivity; psychologists measure adaptability. When anxiety dominates the collective mood, it indicates a mismatch between the rate of external change and the internal capacity for meaning-making. Addressing collective anxiety requires slowing interpretation, not necessarily slowing progress. Societies need pauses for reflection as much as individuals do.

The Artificial Era has also produced new forms of anxiety rooted in visibility and comparison. The constant exposure of digital life multiplies perceived threats to status, belonging, and adequacy. The psychologist Leon Festinger's theory of social comparison helps explain this: self-evaluation depends on reference points, and when those reference points expand to billions of others, anxiety scales exponentially. This effect is magnified because the digital world presents a distorted reference point—a curated highlight reel of others' successes that omits the messy reality of their struggles. The fear of irrelevance—once confined to specific hierarchies— has become universal. Adaptive anxiety in this context means learning to decouple self-worth from performance metrics defined by algorithms.

Education and parenting also shape how anxiety functions. When children are shielded from manageable discomfort, they fail to develop tolerance for ambiguity. Resilience grows from exposure to moderate challenge with support—what developmental psychologists call *scaffolding*. Adults who were overprotected often interpret anxiety as danger rather than signal, responding with avoidance instead of adaptation. Teaching emotional literacy early—helping children name and understand anxiety— prepares them to face uncertainty without collapse.

On a broader level, anxiety's rise reflects a spiritual vacuum. For centuries, religious and philosophical systems offered frameworks for interpreting fear and uncertainty. The modern decline of shared meaning has left individuals alone with their anxiety, forced to self-generate stability. In the absence of transcendence, the self becomes its own center of gravity—a structure too fragile to bear the full weight of existential concern. This explains the modern paradox: unprecedented comfort accompanied by pervasive unease.

Material progress has not alleviated anxiety because anxiety arises not from lack, but from contingency.

Yet there is another interpretation. Anxiety may be the mind's signal that consciousness is expanding. Every stage of psychological growth involves disorientation. The movement from dependence to autonomy, from certainty to complexity, from simplicity to nuance—all provoke anxiety. The discomfort of not knowing is the price of evolution. To feel anxious in times of change is to participate in transformation.

The goal, then, is not to eradicate anxiety but to cultivate *adaptive anxiety*—the kind that focuses rather than freezes. This form of anxiety enhances perception, strengthens judgment, and sustains curiosity. It keeps the individual alert without rendering them afraid. Adaptive anxiety depends on three capacities: awareness, interpretation, and regulation. Awareness detects the signal; interpretation assigns meaning; regulation channels energy into purpose. These capacities can be learned, practiced, and refined.

Practically, adaptive anxiety manifests as readiness. It allows one to act under uncertainty without needing full assurance. It transforms the question "What if something goes wrong?" into "What would I do if it did?" This subtle linguistic shift moves the mind from helplessness to problem-solving. It grounds fear in preparation rather than speculation. Over time, this orientation builds confidence, reducing overall anxiety even in unpredictable environments.

The philosopher William James wrote that "the art of being wise is the art of knowing what to overlook." Adaptive anxiety develops that art in emotional form. It teaches discernment between signals that require action and noise that can be ignored. In an overstimulated world, that discernment becomes a form of inner technology—a psychological filter that protects energy and restores focus.

The paradox of the Artificial Era is that it demands both vigilance and calm. To remain relevant, one must adapt rapidly; to remain sane, one must adapt deliberately. Anxiety, properly understood, is the emotional mechanism that balances those imperatives. It keeps the organism awake to change without surrendering to panic. It is the emotional equivalent of the immune system—sensitive enough to detect danger, disciplined enough to avoid attacking the self.

When anxiety freezes, it narrows life to avoidance. When it focuses, it opens life to preparation. The difference lies in relationship, not removal. To reclaim anxiety as ally is to restore trust in the body's ancient intelligence—a reminder that fear was never meant to dominate, only to direct.

Emotional Reframing

Every emotion contains information, but not every interpretation of that emotion is accurate. The human mind tends to mistake first meaning for final meaning—to believe that what it feels at the surface represents the total truth of experience. Emotional reframing is the process of correcting that error. It does not deny emotion but reorganizes its significance, allowing feeling to become insight. In the context of change, reframing is what transforms loss into learning and uncertainty into growth.

The foundations of emotional reframing lie in cognitive psychology. Aaron Beck and Albert Ellis, the early pioneers of cognitive therapy, observed that distress rarely arises from events themselves but from the interpretations assigned to them. The same circumstance can produce despair or determination depending on how it is framed. When an individual loses a job, for example, the initial reaction may be panic or shame. But through reframing, the experience can become a catalyst for reevaluation, skill development, or renewed purpose. The external event remains the same; the internal narrative evolves.

This principle reflects a deeper psychological truth: emotion follows meaning. What one feels depends on what one believes something means. When belief changes, emotion changes. Reframing therefore functions as emotional alchemy—the transformation of affect through reinterpretation. In neuroscience, this corresponds to *cognitive reappraisal*, a process mediated by the prefrontal cortex. When a person consciously reinterprets an event, neural activity in the amygdala decreases, and physiological arousal subsides.

In other words, perception changes biology.

Yet reframing is not a matter of superficial optimism or denial. It is a disciplined act of consciousness, requiring both honesty and imagination. The first step is to acknowledge emotion fully, without judgment. Suppressed feeling cannot be reframed because it remains unexamined. Genuine reframing begins with recognition: this is fear, this is grief, this is anger. Only when the emotion is named can its message be translated. The psychologist Susan David calls this process *emotional agility*—the ability to face emotions with curiosity rather than control, allowing them to inform rather than dominate behavior.

The mechanism of reframing can be understood through narrative. Human beings make sense of experience by telling stories. These stories organize chaos into sequence and connect past to future. When change disrupts a story, emotion signals that the plot no longer fits. Reframing writes a new narrative in which the disruption gains purpose. Viktor Frankl, the psychiatrist and Holocaust survivor, observed that suffering ceases to be suffering when it finds meaning. That statement is not moral consolation but psychological precision: when the mind constructs a narrative that connects pain to purpose, the nervous system calms. The event remains difficult, but it no longer feels senseless.

Reframing is also central to resilience theory. Studies of individuals who recover from adversity consistently show a capacity for meaning reconstruction. Psychologists Richard Tedeschi and Lawrence Calhoun described this phenomenon as *post-traumatic growth*—the process through which individuals emerge from loss with deeper appreciation for life, renewed relationships, or clarified priorities. Growth does not cancel grief; it contextualizes it. Emotional reframing operates at this same level. It does not promise happiness but coherence.

However, reframing requires a precondition: psychological distance. When one is fully immersed in emotion, perspective is impossible. The brain's attentional resources are consumed by immediate survival concerns. Only when arousal subsides can higher cognitive functions reengage. This is why time, reflection, and conversation are essential. Talking about an experience—especially with someone who listens without agenda—externalizes the narrative, allowing the mind to see its own thoughts from outside. In therapy, this process is called *decentering*; in philosophy, it resembles the Socratic method. The goal is the same: to create space between experience and interpretation.

That space allows choice. Emotional reframing is fundamentally an act of agency. It asserts that while one may not control events, one can control the story those events inhabit. The Stoic philosophers understood this long before modern psychology. Epictetus wrote that people are disturbed not by things, but by the views they take of them. Cognitive therapy rediscovered this truth and operationalized it. What the Stoics practiced as virtue, psychologists now teach as skill.

Reframing operates at multiple levels. On the cognitive level, it changes thought patterns; on the emotional level, it alters affective tone; on the existential level, it redefines identity. Consider the experience of technological displacement—a common anxiety in the Artificial Era. The initial frame might be loss: the sense that one's skills or relevance have expired. Through reframing, that same event can become transition: an invitation to redefine value beyond function. The person is not obsolete but evolving. The emotional tone shifts from despair to possibility because the meaning has changed.

In collective contexts, reframing performs a similar function for societies. Periods of rapid transformation often generate cultural nostalgia—the longing for a simpler or more stable past. Nostalgia itself is not pathology; it is a signal that a shared narrative has fractured. Reframing, at the societal level, involves reinterpreting change not as collapse but as reorganization. The historian Arnold Toynbee described civilization's decline not as failure but as the exhaustion of creative response. The renewal of collective meaning depends on the capacity to reframe crisis as opportunity.

Emotionally, reframing also restores dignity. When people experience change as something done *to* them, they feel powerless. When they can reinterpret it as something they are responding *through*, they regain agency. This shift is subtle but transformative. It repositions the self from object to subject—from being acted upon to acting. The feeling of control, even partial, reduces stress response and strengthens motivation. Decades of research in health psychology have confirmed this principle: perception of control predicts better outcomes across physical and mental domains.

The practice of reframing can be learned. One of the most effective tools is language itself. The words used to describe experience shape its meaning. Saying "I am anxious" fuses identity with emotion; saying "I feel anxious" introduces separation. The first is possession; the second is observation. Similarly, reframing "I failed" to "This didn't work yet" shifts orientation from judgment to process. These linguistic shifts, small but powerful, gradually recondition cognition.

Journaling, when used for reflection rather than rumination, reinforces this process. Writing provides a medium through which emotion becomes narrative and thought gains order. Research on expressive writing by James Pennebaker demonstrated that individuals who write about emotionally significant experiences experience measurable improvements in immune function, mood, and cognitive clarity. The benefit arises not from catharsis alone but from narrative reconstruction. Writing allows reframing in slow motion, granting time for thought to mature into understanding.

Yet reframing is not merely cognitive. It is embodied. The nervous system participates in meaning-making. Practices that regulate physio-logical arousal—such as breath control, mindfulness, or physical activity—prepare the brain for reinterpretation. When the body calms, the mind becomes capable of curiosity. Without that calm, reframing risks becoming intellectual bypassing: an attempt to think away emotion without feeling it. True reframing integrates sensation, emotion, and thought into a unified act of meaning-making.

A frequent misconception is that reframing trivializes pain. In truth, it dignifies it. To reframe is to take suffering seriously enough to ask what it might teach. Avoidance postpones understanding; reframing transforms it. This distinction is crucial in therapy and in life. Pain ignored becomes symptom; pain examined becomes signal. Emotional reframing converts symptom back into signal.

The process, however, requires humility. Reframing does not guarantee immediate clarity. Sometimes the new meaning emerges slowly, through repetition and reflection. The psyche resists premature coherence. Forced positivity—what Barbara Ehrenreich criticized as "the tyranny of optimism"—short-circuits authentic reframing. True reframing allows ambiguity; it lets meaning unfold. In this sense, patience is part of the discipline. The new story cannot be imposed; it must be discovered.

Reframing also depends on relational context. Humans construct meaning socially. The interpretation of emotion often reflects the mirrors provided by others. When surrounded by people who validate complexity, individuals learn to see nuance in their feelings. When surrounded by those who demand simplicity—"just move on," "stay positive"—reframing collapses into repression. Supportive dialogue functions as co-regulation; it stabilizes the emotional system long enough for perspective to emerge.

In the Artificial Era, reframing has acquired new urgency. The speed of information flow continually disrupts meaning before integration can occur. People receive emotional stimuli faster than they can assign context. The result is collective disorientation—anxiety without anchor, outrage without depth. Emotional reframing becomes not only a personal tool but a cultural necessity. It reintroduces coherence into the emotional economy of modern life. By slowing interpretation, reframing counteracts acceleration. It restores proportion to perception.

From a developmental view, reframing is evidence of psychological maturity. Early in life, emotion and cognition operate as fused systems: what feels true is assumed to be true. Maturity introduces differentiation— the ability to hold feeling and thought in dialogue. Reframing represents the highest expression of that dialogue: a conscious synthesis in which feeling informs thought and thought transforms feeling. The individual who can reframe does not suppress emotion but steers it, using it as guidance toward deeper understanding.

Ultimately, emotional reframing is an act of authorship. It asserts that meaning is not discovered but made. The external world offers events; the internal world organizes them into coherence. This act of authorship

84

restores what rapid change threatens most: continuity of self. In an environment where circumstances shift faster than narratives can stabilize, reframing becomes a method of self-preservation. It keeps identity fluid but intact, capable of evolution without fragmentation.

When practiced consistently, reframing transforms emotional life from reactive to creative. It teaches the mind to approach difficulty with inquiry rather than avoidance. Each challenge becomes a question: What is this experience asking of me? What truth does this emotion reveal? Through such questions, anxiety becomes curiosity, loss becomes learning, and instability becomes evolution. The human organism remains what it has always been—a meaning-making system. Reframing keeps that system alive and flexible.

The art of reframing is therefore the art of living with awareness. It does not promise immunity from pain but intelligence within it. To reframe is to stand at the intersection of emotion and meaning and choose direction consciously. It is the difference between being carried by experience and carrying it forward with purpose.

The Return to Meaning

In an age defined by acceleration and uncertainty, meaning has become the rarest form of stability. Technology changes faster than comprehension, values shift faster than consensus, and expectations multiply faster than fulfillment. Amid this turbulence, meaning offers something that neither control nor comfort can provide: orientation. It does not eliminate chaos, but it gives chaos a direction. The return to meaning, then, is not nostalgia for old certainties—it is the rediscovery of coherence in motion.

Psychologists have long understood that meaning is not a luxury but a necessity. Viktor Frankl's logotherapy proposed that the search for meaning is the primary motivational force in human life. When meaning is lost, psychological distress follows not because of external conditions but because the mind can no longer locate purpose within them. The emotional cost of change arises precisely here: transformation without meaning feels like disintegration. Stability cannot always be restored, but significance can.

Meaning functions as an organizing principle for emotion. It links disparate experiences into a coherent narrative, allowing the self to perceive continuity despite disruption. Neuroscientific research on autobiographical memory supports this: when people recount meaningful experiences, activity increases in brain regions associated with integration and reflection. Meaning literally connects neural networks, just as it connects events in consciousness. Without it, emotion becomes unanchored, oscillating between stimulation and fatigue.

The modern world, however, complicates meaning-making. The sheer volume of information fragments attention and dilutes reflection. In prior generations, meaning was often inherited through shared institutions—religion, community, profession, family. Today, meaning must be con-structed individually within a pluralistic environment that offers endless options but little guidance. The result is both freedom and fatigue. The psychologist Barry Schwartz called this "the paradox of choice": the more options people have, the more paralyzed they become. Meaning requires selection. A life filled with stimuli but devoid of commitment feels shallow no matter how busy it appears.

Values clarification is one antidote to this condition. Values are not goals or desires; they are enduring directions that organize life across changing circumstances. While goals can be achieved or lost, values persist as orientation points. For example, 'getting married' is a goal that can be completed, but 'being a loving and connected partner' is a value that can guide behavior every single day, whether one is single or in a relationship. The therapeutic approach known as Acceptance and Commitment Therapy (ACT), developed by Steven Hayes, emphasizes this distinction. When individuals act in alignment with their values, they experience vitality even amid difficulty. When actions diverge from values, emotional exhaustion follows. Meaning, in this sense, is not found but enacted—it emerges through behavior consistent with one's chosen principles.

The process of clarifying values begins with attention. In the noise of the Artificial Era, values are often buried beneath distraction. People chase urgency rather than importance, mistaking immediacy for significance. To return to meaning, one must first discern what truly matters. This requires silence, reflection, and honesty—the very capacities that overstimulation erodes. Yet even small acts of prioritization—choosing depth over speed, integrity over image, presence over performance—begin to restore coherence. Meaning accumulates through such choices.

Change tests values by revealing their authenticity. It exposes whether one's commitments are intrinsic or conditional. A person who values stability may discover that flexibility, not control, is their true anchor. Another who values success may learn that contribution, not recognition, sustains them. The process of revaluation is rarely comfortable, but it refines character. In Jungian psychology, individuation—the process of becoming whole—requires confronting contradictions within the self. Change forces that confrontation outward. Each disruption invites the question: Which part of me is reacting, and which part is real?

This interrogation transforms anxiety into guidance. The emotions that accompany change—fear, sadness, frustration—become diagnostic tools. They indicate where attachment clashes with evolution. A person anxious about irrelevance may be confronting the need to redefine usefulness; one grieving a lost identity may be making space for a larger self-concept. When viewed through meaning, emotion becomes feedback rather than failure. The mind stops asking "Why is this happening to me?" and begins asking "What is this showing me?"

Meaning also reconnects individuals to community. Modern life often isolates by design; digital interaction mimics connection without depth. Yet meaning is relational. It emerges not only from personal insight but from shared purpose. Sociologist Émile Durkheim argued that collective meaning—what he called "social integration"—protects individuals from despair. The current epidemic of loneliness can be understood as a crisis of shared meaning: people are surrounded by communication but starved for communion. Reclaiming meaning therefore requires rebuilding spaces of genuine participation, where individuals can contribute to something larger than themselves.

Such participation need not be grand or ideological. It can occur in families, friendships, creative collaborations, or acts of service. The common thread is contribution. When people feel that their actions matter to others, even modestly, their sense of meaning strengthens. Psychological research confirms this: altruistic behavior increases well-being by reinforcing purpose and social connection. In contrast, isolation intensifies anxiety because it deprives the self of context. The return to meaning is thus also a return to belonging.

At the cultural level, meaning provides resilience against fragmentation. Societies that lack shared purpose turn every disagreement into existential conflict. Polarization thrives in the absence of overarching narrative. Restoring collective meaning does not require uniformity but coherence— a framework that allows difference without disintegration. Education plays a central role in this process. When education focuses solely on skill acquisition without cultivating moral and emotional intelligence, it produces competence without wisdom. Wisdom, unlike information, organizes knowledge around values.

In the Artificial Era, meaning must also be redefined in relation to technology. Artificial intelligence, automation, and algorithmic decision-making challenge traditional sources of significance such as work and creativity. If machines can perform many human functions more efficiently, what remains distinctly human? The answer lies not in output but in consciousness. Meaning arises from awareness—the ability to reflect, interpret, and care. No machine can replace the subjective depth of lived experience. The danger is not that technology will make life meaningless, but that humans will outsource meaning-making to it. The task is to maintain authorship of value amid increasing automation.

Spirituality, in its broadest sense, addresses this need for transcendence. It does not require religion but involves the recognition of interconnectedness and purpose beyond the self. Research in positive psychology has shown that spiritual orientation—defined as a sense of belonging to something larger—correlates with resilience, lower anxiety, and greater life satisfaction. In a secular world, spirituality can take many forms: awe in nature, devotion to craft, commitment to justice, or reverence for truth. Each represents an axis of meaning that stabilizes emotion.

Philosophically, meaning reconciles two psychological imperatives: stability and freedom. Stability offers grounding; freedom offers possibility. Change threatens stability but expands freedom. Meaning integrates the two by giving freedom direction. Without meaning, freedom becomes drift; without freedom, stability becomes stagnation. The return to meaning restores balance between the two—anchoring movement in purpose.

Practically, this restoration involves reflection on three questions: What do I value most? What am I willing to endure for it? What will remain meaningful even if circumstances change? These questions shift focus from control to orientation. They invite a deeper sense of responsibility for how one lives. When individuals answer them honestly, they move from reaction to intention. Change ceases to feel like something happening from the outside and becomes part of an unfolding process guided by inner conviction.

Meaning also moderates emotional volatility. When events are interpreted through the lens of purpose, temporary discomfort loses its dominance. The same stressor that might once have produced despair becomes tolerable when connected to value. Parents accept sleepless nights because they attach them to love. Artists endure frustration because they attach it to expression. The meaning does not erase difficulty; it contextualizes it. The nervous system interprets effort as worthwhile, transforming distress into engagement.

This process parallels the concept of *eudaimonia* in Aristotelian ethics— the idea that flourishing arises from living in accordance with virtue and purpose, not from constant pleasure. Modern psychology echoes this distinction in differentiating between hedonic well-being (happiness derived from satisfaction) and eudaimonic well-being (fulfillment derived from meaning). The Artificial Era often confuses the two, promising pleasure through consumption while neglecting the deeper nourishment of purpose. The return to meaning restores that distinction.

However, meaning cannot be forced. It cannot be manufactured by slogans or reduced to metrics. It arises through lived coherence between belief and behavior. When actions reflect convictions, emotion stabilizes. When they diverge, dissonance emerges. This is why the pursuit of meaning demands honesty—an unflinching look at whether one's life aligns with one's stated values. Without that alignment, no amount of affirmation or achievement will satisfy. The psyche recognizes incongruence instinctively; peace depends on integration.

To live meaningfully in the Artificial Era requires a deliberate slowing of perception. Depth takes time. Reflection demands pauses. The culture of immediacy erodes meaning because it prevents digestion. The constant pursuit of the next signal, the next upgrade, the next validation, leaves no space for synthesis. Meaning forms in the interval between experience and interpretation—the very interval that acceleration destroys. Reclaiming that interval is both psychological and ethical work.

Ultimately, meaning is the mind's method of belonging to time. It connects past to purpose, present to participation, and future to direction. When change feels relentless, meaning provides continuity without requiring certainty. It is what allows the self to say: I may not know what comes next, but I know why I continue.

The return to meaning, therefore, is not retreat into idealism but recovery of proportion. It reestablishes the relationship between motion and motive, adaptation and integrity. In an environment where everything can change except the need for purpose, meaning remains the final measure of sanity. To live without it is to drift; to live within it is to navigate.

Change will continue to accelerate. Institutions will shift, technologies will evolve, and identities will reform again and again. But the essential task will remain unchanged: to interpret experience in a way that keeps it human. The return to meaning is not a conclusion; it is a compass. It points the way forward through uncertainty, reminding the self that the mind's greatest achievement is not control, but coherence.

* * *

5

Psychological Flexibility

daptation has always been part of survival, but in the Artificial Era it has become an art form. The conditions of life are no longer stable enough for fixed strategies to succeed. Careers shift, relationships evolve across platforms, and cultural norms transform with dizzying speed. What once defined intelligence—knowledge, logic, memory—now competes with something more subtle and enduring: flexibility. The defining skill of this century is not mastery of information but mastery of movement, the ability to stay grounded in purpose while remaining fluid in method.

Psychological flexibility refers to the capacity to adjust one's thoughts, emotions, and behaviors to meet the demands of a changing environment without losing connection to one's deeper values. It is not about indifference or perpetual openness, but about the balance between stability and adaptability—the ability to bend without breaking. In practical terms, it means being able to pause between impulse and action, to shift perspective when old patterns fail, and to act in accordance with principles even under pressure.

The origins of the concept lie in behavioral science. Acceptance and Commitment Therapy (ACT), developed by Steven Hayes and colleagues, placed psychological flexibility at the center of mental health. Research across decades now confirms that flexibility predicts resilience, emotional regulation, and life satisfaction more accurately than most personality traits. It is the psychological equivalent of elasticity in materials science: the strength to return to form after stress.

In a world saturated with information and volatility, rigidity is the new fragility. The mind that insists on certainty will shatter first. This does not mean abandoning conviction, but rather understanding that conviction must coexist with openness. Rigidity disguises itself as confidence but often masks fear—the fear of being wrong, of losing control, of facing ambiguity. Flexibility, by contrast, is confidence expressed as curiosity. It rests not on the illusion of certainty, but on trust in one's capacity to learn and adapt.

The difference between these two orientations defines much of modern psychological life. Rigid minds seek control through prediction: if I can know what happens next, I can feel safe. Flexible minds seek security through capacity: even if I cannot predict, I can respond. The first depends on the external world's stability; the second depends on internal steadiness. This distinction marks the threshold between anxiety and resilience, between reaction and response.

Culturally, the need for psychological flexibility extends beyond individual coping. Institutions built on fixed hierarchies and slow feedback loops struggle to adapt to complex systems that evolve faster than policies can keep up. The same dynamic appears in education, leadership, and relationships. Every domain now demands continuous adjustment while maintaining coherence. The question for both individuals and societies is no longer "How can we stay the same?" but "How can we stay ourselves while changing?"

Flexibility also carries moral significance. It requires humility—the willingness to revise beliefs in light of new evidence—and courage—the capacity to act amid uncertainty. These traits are often treated as opposites, yet in reality they depend on each other. True flexibility is ethical, not evasive. It allows for correction without collapse, conviction without arrogance. The mature mind learns to update without erasing itself.

In this chapter, psychological flexibility will be explored not as a person-ality trait but as a discipline—a trainable capacity for movement between thought, emotion, and action. It begins with cognitive defusion, the separation of thought from identity. It continues through behavioral experimentation, the practice of testing rather than predicting. It finds anchor in value-driven consistency, acting from what matters rather than what feels safe. And it culminates in learning to re-open after disappointment, the renewal of curiosity as a deliberate act of strength.

If intelligence once meant control, its modern form is grace. The flexible mind does not resist uncertainty; it transforms through it. In the century ahead, those who endure will not be the ones who know most, but the ones who can stay most human while everything else changes.

Cognitive Defusion

Every person lives inside a continuous stream of thought. Most of the time, that stream feels like reality itself. Thoughts narrate, evaluate, predict, and remember so automatically that they become indistinguishable from perception. Yet this fusion between thought and self is one of the most significant sources of human rigidity. When the mind confuses its commentary with the world, it loses the ability to adapt. Cognitive defusion, the first cornerstone of psychological flexibility, is the skill of separating thought from identity—of recognizing that thinking is something the mind does, not something the self is.

The human brain evolved to create internal simulations of reality. It models the environment, anticipates outcomes, and rehearses behavior. These simulations allow foresight and problem-solving, but they also produce distortion. The same imagination that protects us from danger can imprison us in interpretation. The philosopher Epictetus observed two thousand years ago that people are not disturbed by events but by their judgments about events. Cognitive defusion gives that insight contemporary language. It teaches that thoughts are propositions, not commands— suggestions to be evaluated, not truths to be obeyed.

Psychological research in contextual behavioral science has shown that when individuals are fused with their thoughts, they experience higher stress, anxiety, and emotional reactivity. Fusion collapses distance between cognition and awareness. If a thought such as "I will fail" arises, fusion makes it feel like a prediction rather than a sentence. The emotional system reacts accordingly, releasing cortisol and preparing for loss that may never occur. Defusion interrupts that chain. It allows the person to see "I will fail" as merely a phrase passing through consciousness. The physiological reaction softens because the brain no longer interprets the thought as fact.

One of the most illuminating findings from neuroscience concerns the brain's default mode network (DMN)—a system active during self-referential thinking and mind-wandering. Excessive activation of the DMN correlates with rumination, worry, and depression. Practices that promote defusion, such as mindfulness or metacognitive awareness, reduce DMN activity and increase connectivity in attentional and emotional regulation regions. The biological evidence aligns with subjective experience: when people learn to observe thoughts rather than inhabit them, mental noise decreases and clarity increases.

Cognitive defusion is not the suppression of thought. Suppression strengthens what it seeks to silence. The paradox of mental control is that what we resist persists, because attention itself amplifies. Defusion takes the opposite approach. It allows thought to exist without resistance or identification. The goal is not to stop thinking but to stop confusing thinking with knowing.

The practice can begin with simple exercises. A common technique in Acceptance and Commitment Therapy involves adding the phrase "I am having the thought that..." before a distressing belief. Instead of "I'm not good enough," one says, "I am having the thought that I'm not good enough." This small linguistic shift creates psychological space. Another technique is to visualize thoughts as objects in motion—leaves floating down a stream, clouds passing in the sky, or cars driving by—acknowledging each one without needing to board it. The mind becomes an observer of its own content rather than its captive. Over time, that space expands into perspective.

Language is central to this process because thought is largely linguistic. Words shape perception. When fused with language, people act as if verbal categories and judgments reflect inherent truth. Yet language, as linguists like Alfred Korzybski reminded us, is a map, not the territory. The map helps navigate, but it can never capture the terrain's full complexity. Defusion restores awareness of this difference. It invites humility in interpretation and flexibility in response.

The philosopher William James described consciousness as a stream rather than a substance. Thoughts flow, shift, and dissolve. The illusion of permanence arises because attention holds onto fragments and organizes them into narrative. Cognitive defusion reconnects us with the fluid nature of that stream. When thoughts are seen as transient events, they lose coercive power. Anxiety, shame, and anger begin to loosen their grip because they depend on identification for survival. A thought cannot control what no longer believes it.

Culturally, fusion manifests in the way societies treat ideas as identities. Political beliefs, religious doctrines, or professional roles become extensions of selfhood. Online, this is amplified by algorithmic sorting, which places people in ideological 'bubbles' where their opinions are constantly reinforced until they feel less like perspectives and more like essential truths. When identity fuses with ideology, disagreement feels like personal threat. Defusion, in both individual and collective psychology, is therefore essential to civility. It allows dialogue without defense. The ability to hold beliefs lightly, to revise them in light of new evidence, is not weakness but maturity. Rigid conviction may offer temporary comfort, but it prevents learning.

In personal life, fusion reveals itself through self-talk. The inner critic, the perfectionist, the worrier—all are linguistic patterns mistaken for personality. When people internalize those voices as truth, they limit their behavior to fit them. A student who believes "I'm bad at math" may avoid challenge not because of ability but because the thought has become identity. Through defusion, that same statement is recognized as history, not destiny—a memory of past struggle rather than a permanent definition.

This separation between thought and identity also underlies emotional regulation. When a person fuses with a thought, emotion follows imme-diately. The thought "I am alone" evokes sadness; "I am in danger" evokes fear. But if the same thoughts are observed as mental events, the emotional system remains more stable. Awareness becomes a buffer. The psychologist Viktor Frankl captured this dynamic when he wrote that between stimulus and response lies a space, and in that space lies freedom. Defusion expands that space.

Philosophically, defusion echoes the teachings of contemplative traditions that emphasize awareness as distinct from cognition. In Buddhist psychology, this distinction appears as the difference between "thoughts" and "the knowing of thoughts." In Western philosophy, phenomenologists such as Edmund Husserl described a similar separation between consciousness and its objects. Both traditions point to the same realization: awareness is the context in which thought occurs, not one of its contents. The more one identifies with awareness rather than cognition, the greater the flexibility of mind.

Defusion also redefines what it means to think well. Intelligence is often measured by complexity of reasoning or accumulation of knowledge. But the ability to unhook from thought is itself a higher form of intelligence. It allows the mind to use concepts as tools rather than as prisons. Creative insight often emerges precisely when the grip of habitual thinking relaxes. Neuroscience of creativity supports this: moments of insight correspond with reduced activity in the prefrontal control regions, allowing spontaneous association. In other words, loosening the reins of thought permits novelty.

The practice of defusion extends into decision-making. Many decisions are made not from reality but from anticipation of imagined outcomes. The mind simulates scenarios and then reacts emotionally to its own projections. Defusion introduces skepticism into this loop. It reminds the thinker that prediction is hypothesis, not prophecy. This perspective reduces impulsive behavior driven by imagined threat or desire. It replaces compulsion with curiosity: "What happens if I wait? What happens if I test this rather than assume it?" The result is more deliberate and adaptive behavior.

One of the subtle challenges of defusion is that the mind often resists it. The ego derives stability from its narratives. To step back from thought feels, initially, like stepping into emptiness. People fear that if they stop believing their thoughts, they will lose coherence. In reality, the opposite occurs. Defusion reveals that coherence does not depend on content but on awareness itself. The self remains intact, not as a collection of stories, but as the capacity to observe them.

From a developmental standpoint, defusion represents a stage of cognitive and emotional maturity. Early in life, children experience their thoughts as reality; a nightmare feels true even after waking. With maturity comes the ability to distinguish imagination from fact. Yet adults often regress into fusion under stress, treating mental simulations as threats. Practicing defusion reestablishes that developmental clarity. It is a return to psychological adulthood.

Modern life amplifies the need for this skill. The digital environment is an architecture of fusion. Algorithms exploit attention by stimulating thought-identification: anger, envy, outrage, and validation all depend on immediate belief in what one sees. Each reaction strengthens neural pathways of reactivity. Defusion counters this by restoring agency over attention. To scroll consciously—to notice thought without merging with it—is a quiet act of resistance against the machinery of distraction.

At its deepest level, cognitive defusion is an act of humility before the mystery of consciousness. It acknowledges that thought, however refined, is limited. The world exceeds the mind's descriptions, and selfhood exceeds the mind's commentary about it. This humility liberates curiosity. When no longer imprisoned by certainty, the individual can learn, unlearn, and relearn continuously. The flexible mind lives in dialogue with experience rather than defense against it.

In clinical and personal practice, the results of defusion are measurable: reduced anxiety, improved focus, greater creativity, and enhanced empathy. But its significance transcends symptom reduction. Defusion restores the most basic form of psychological freedom—the ability to think without being possessed by thought. It returns authorship to awareness, allowing individuals to choose response rather than reflex.

In the context of the Artificial Era, where information is constant and certainty is rare, cognitive defusion becomes both a personal and civic virtue. It creates citizens capable of reflection rather than reaction, leaders capable of nuance rather than performance, and individuals capable of being present without being consumed. It teaches the rare art of standing in the middle of noise without losing clarity.

To think is human; to see thought as thought is wisdom. Cognitive defusion turns the mind from mirror to window—from reflection trapped within itself to awareness open to the world. It is the foundation upon which all other forms of flexibility rest.

Behavioral Experimentation

The human mind is prone to overestimating the value of certainty. It seeks security in plans, forecasts, and predictions, as though understanding alone could guarantee outcome. Yet adaptation requires more than understanding—it requires movement. Behavioral experimentation is the deliberate practice of testing reality rather than theorizing about it. It is the behavioral extension of psychological flexibility: the process of acting without full assurance, learning through direct experience, and adjusting course accordingly.

This principle originates in behavioral psychology but extends far beyond it. Early behavioral theorists such as B. F. Skinner demonstrated that learning occurs through feedback loops between action and consequence. Cognitive-behavioral therapy later expanded this insight to the emotional domain, showing that beliefs change most effectively through behavioral evidence, not intellectual argument. When people act differently, they begin to see differently. In this sense, behavioral experimentation is both a scientific and existential process—it replaces assumption with observation.

The psychological logic behind experimentation is straightforward: uncertainty cannot be resolved in theory. The nervous system calms not through explanation but through exposure. When a person faces a feared situation and discovers that the outcome is survivable, the brain updates its prediction model. Fear diminishes because learning replaces speculation.

Behavioral experimentation leverages this mechanism intentionally. Rather than waiting for confidence before acting, one acts to create confidence.

This principle contradicts much of modern culture's advice. The popular notion that one must feel ready before acting presumes that emotion precedes behavior. In truth, the relationship is reciprocal. Action can precede and reshape emotion. The psychologist David Barlow's research on exposure therapy confirms this: behavioral engagement with avoided situations reduces anxiety faster than cognitive reassurance alone. Readiness is often the product, not the prerequisite, of movement.

Behavioral experimentation also trains the nervous system for uncertainty. The body learns that fluctuation is not catastrophe. Small, reversible actions—taking a new route, initiating a conversation, testing an idea— signal to the brain that flexibility is safe. Professionally, this might mean volunteering for a low-stakes task outside one's job description. Socially, it could be as simple as trying a new restaurant instead of a familiar favorite. Creatively, it might involve writing a single paragraph in a genre one has never attempted. Each experiment rewires association networks, reducing the automatic stress response to novelty. The process mirrors what neuroscientists describe as *neuroplasticity*: repeated exposure to manageable challenge strengthens adaptive pathways. Over time, uncertainty becomes tolerable, even stimulating.

The scale of the experiment matters less than the intentionality behind it. Grand life overhauls often fail because they overwhelm the emotional system, triggering regression into rigidity. Smaller, iterative experiments sustain curiosity without activating defense. The psychologist Carol Dweck's concept of the growth mindset parallels this approach: progress emerges from viewing mistakes as data, not verdicts. Behavioral experimentation operationalizes that mindset. It treats experience as research, not evaluation.

One of the most powerful aspects of behavioral experimentation is that it redefines failure. In a fixed framework, failure signals deficiency; in an experimental framework, it signals information. Every action produces data. When something does not work, the conclusion is not "I was wrong," but "Now I know more." This shift transforms the emotional texture of risk. Fear diminishes because the stakes change from self-worth to curiosity. The nervous system interprets challenge as exploration rather than threat.

Historically, this orientation to experience has marked periods of innovation and progress. Science itself advances through systematic experimentation—hypotheses tested through trial, observation, and revision. The same method applies to psychological life. Emotional intelligence grows not from introspection alone but from experimentation in relationships, habits, and roles. Human development depends on feedback, and feedback requires engagement.

Behavioral experimentation is also a corrective to perfectionism. The perfectionistic mind avoids action until conditions are ideal, mistaking control for competence. But perfectionism is not precision; it is fear disguised as ambition. The longer one waits for certainty, the more uncertain life becomes. Experimentation dissolves this paralysis by reframing perfection as process. The task is not to perform flawlessly but to participate honestly. Each attempt, however imperfect, refines understanding.

From a neurobiological perspective, experimentation strengthens resilience by balancing activation and recovery. Small doses of uncertainty activate the sympathetic nervous system, producing arousal and focus. When followed by resolution or reflection, the parasympathetic system engages, restoring calm. This alternation teaches the body that stress is cyclical, not permanent. Over time, the stress response becomes more proportional and less catastrophic. Behavioral flexibility thus begins as a physiological practice before it becomes a psychological one.

In therapeutic contexts, behavioral experimentation is used to challenge limiting beliefs. A person who believes "I cannot speak in public" may test this assumption by contributing a short comment in a meeting. A person who assumes "I will be rejected if I am honest" may experiment by revealing a mild vulnerability. Each test provides evidence against rigidity. When the expected catastrophe does not occur, cognitive fusion weakens. The individual learns not by argument but by experience.

The same principle applies to collective systems. Organizations that cultivate experimental cultures adapt faster to change. When failure is treated as feedback rather than blame, employees engage with innovation more freely. This insight has become central to modern management psychology: psychological safety—defined by Amy Edmondson as the shared belief that one can take interpersonal risks without punishment—predicts creativity and learning. The emotional dynamics are identical to those in individual psychology. Curiosity thrives only where fear of error subsides.

In daily life, behavioral experimentation often begins with curiosity. Curiosity is the emotional engine of flexibility. It shifts focus from control to discovery. A curious person does not need certainty because meaning arises through exploration. Yet curiosity must be practiced intentionally in environments dominated by performance and comparison. The culture of display punishes imperfection, making genuine experimentation rare. The antidote is private experimentation—acts of learning invisible to judgment. A person might practice a new skill, express an untested idea, or attempt a conversation differently without broadcasting the result. These experiments cultivate authenticity rather than image.

Philosophically, behavioral experimentation echoes the pragmatism of William James and John Dewey, who argued that truth is not fixed but verified through consequence. Ideas prove themselves through utility in experience. This approach to knowledge democratizes wisdom—it suggests that understanding is not bestowed but built through engagement. Psychological flexibility follows the same law: insight is earned by living, not theorizing.

At a deeper level, behavioral experimentation heals the fracture between thought and embodiment. Modern life overemphasizes cognition at the expense of action. People often believe that if they can think their way through fear, they can overcome it. But the body learns through doing, not through debate. Exposure recalibrates instinct. Each act of courage, however small, teaches the nervous system that fear can coexist with movement. This integration between body and mind restores unity to the self, grounding intelligence in lived experience.

The emotional benefits of experimentation extend beyond anxiety reduction. They include the cultivation of play—a state of engaged exploration without rigid goal. Playfulness reawakens the same neural pathways involved in creativity and learning. It transforms experimentation from duty into delight. This is why children learn so rapidly: they approach experience as discovery, not evaluation. Adults regain that capacity when they suspend self-consciousness long enough to participate fully. Play, in this sense, is not immaturity but mastery—the freedom to act without over-identifying with outcome.

Of course, not all experimentation is safe or productive. The art lies in calibration: actions must be novel enough to challenge, but not so extreme as to overwhelm. This principle mirrors what trauma specialists call the "window of tolerance." Learning occurs within the zone where stress is manageable and curiosity remains intact. Too little stimulation leads to stagnation; too much leads to shutdown. Effective experimentation expands that window gradually, teaching the psyche that adaptability is reliable.

In a cultural context that rewards speed and certainty, experimentation requires patience. The process is iterative. Results often emerge indirectly, through accumulation rather than breakthrough. This frustrates the modern appetite for immediacy, but it mirrors the natural rhythms of adaptation. Evolution itself is experimental—variation, selection, and retention across generations. Human flexibility follows the same pattern: many small adjustments, sustained over time, produce transformation.

Behavioral experimentation also deepens authenticity. When individuals engage directly with experience rather than living through abstraction, they discover what genuinely resonates. Theories about desire, purpose, or value are replaced by lived evidence. A person may believe they prefer solitude until they test connection, or believe they crave novelty until they experience calm. Experimentation turns speculation into self-knowledge. Authenticity, then, is not self-discovery as revelation but as research—the ongoing testing of who one becomes in practice.

The Artificial Era intensifies the need for this approach. The rapid feedback loops of digital life can make uncertainty intolerable and mistakes instantly public. The consequence is a widespread aversion to risk. Yet growth depends on the willingness to be wrong in public and to revise without shame. Behavioral experimentation is therefore both psychological skill and cultural resistance. It restores the dignity of process in a world obsessed with results.

At its heart, experimentation reorients identity away from perfection and toward participation. The question shifts from "How do I succeed?" to "What can I learn?" This shift carries profound emotional implications. Success depends on external validation; learning depends on internal engagement. The first breeds anxiety because it is contingent; the second fosters resilience because it is self-sustaining. Behavioral experimentation replaces the fragile pursuit of certainty with the durable pursuit of understanding.

When practiced consistently, this orientation reshapes emotional tone. Fear gives way to curiosity, frustration to persistence, and rigidity to flow. It cultivates what psychologists call self-efficacy—the belief that one can influence outcomes through action. This belief, in turn, reduces helplessness and enhances motivation. Over time, experimentation becomes habit, and habit becomes temperament. Flexibility ceases to be strategy and becomes character.

In a deeper existential sense, behavioral experimentation affirms life itself. To act without guarantee, to risk error for the sake of growth, is the essence of being alive. The philosopher Alfred North Whitehead described life as the search for novelty within continuity. Experimentation embodies that search. It honors uncertainty as creative force rather than enemy.

To live experimentally is to live consciously. It is to trade the illusion of control for the authenticity of engagement. The mind that experiments remains awake to possibility, humble before complexity, and resilient in the face of change. This is the psychological posture that the Artificial Era demands—not certainty, but responsiveness; not prediction, but participation.

Value-Driven Consistency

To live flexibly is not to live aimlessly. Without orientation, flexibility collapses into drift. Values provide the anchor that keeps movement coherent. They do not eliminate uncertainty, but they give it direction. Value-driven consistency is the practice of aligning behavior with principles rather than predictions. It is the art of acting from what matters most, even when outcomes are unclear. In an era defined by volatility and ambiguity, this alignment becomes the only true form of stability.

Values differ from goals in both nature and function. Goals are destinations; values are directions. A person may set a goal to earn a degree, but the underlying value might be learning or growth. When the goal is achieved or lost, the value remains available. This distinction is crucial in environments of constant change. Goals depend on conditions that can shift or disappear; values endure because they are self-defined. Acting from values ensures continuity when circumstances rewrite plans.

Psychologists in the field of Acceptance and Commitment Therapy have demonstrated that value-based living increases resilience, psychological well-being, and life satisfaction. Steven Hayes and colleagues describe values as "chosen life directions" that organize behavior across time. Research shows that individuals who act consistently with their values, even under stress, experience less anxiety and greater vitality. The reason is simple: alignment generates coherence. When internal conviction and external action converge, the mind experiences integrity. When they diverge, dissonance arises.

This dissonance has real psychological cost. Leon Festinger's theory of cognitive dissonance explains that inconsistency between belief and behavior creates discomfort, which the mind seeks to resolve through rationalization or change. Modern life, saturated with competing demands and identities, multiplies these tensions. People often find themselves acting contrary to their values for the sake of convenience, conformity, or security. Over time, this erodes self-trust. Value-driven consistency repairs that trust by making integrity the standard of success.

However, clarity of values cannot be assumed. Many people mistake preferences or social ideals for values. A value must meet three criteria: it must be chosen freely, pursued for its own sake, and capable of guiding action across contexts. To value compassion, for instance, means acting with empathy whether one is parenting, managing, or disagreeing. It is not situational but directional. Values reveal the quality of consciousness one wants to bring to experience, not the outcome one hopes to achieve.

Identifying values often requires stripping away borrowed narratives. Cultural conditioning encourages performance of virtue rather than its practice. The question "What do I truly value?" can be unsettling because it exposes how much of one's life has been organized around external expectations. This moment of confrontation is necessary. Psychological flexibility depends on inner authority—the confidence that one's choices are self-authored. Without that confidence, adaptation becomes imitation.

One method for clarifying values involves reflecting on moments of deep satisfaction or regret. Satisfaction often reveals when behavior aligned with value; regret exposes when it did not. These emotional markers serve as internal navigation. Another approach, derived from motivational interviewing, is to ask: "What would I stand for even if it cost me?" Values that survive sacrifice are genuine. They hold meaning independent of convenience.

Living by values does not guarantee comfort. In fact, it often increases short-term discomfort because it demands courage. To act on values rather than fear is to prioritize meaning over ease. Yet that very discomfort becomes stabilizing. When decisions are guided by principle, one can tolerate uncertainty with greater calm. The outcome may be unpredictable, but the motivation remains known. This clarity prevents paralysis. It transforms anxiety into direction.

Values also counteract the emotional volatility of external validation. In a culture governed by metrics—likes, views, rankings, and performance scores—worth becomes conditional. The individual becomes a mirror reflecting others' approval. Value-driven living reclaims intrinsic worth. When behavior arises from conviction rather than reaction, external approval becomes secondary. This orientation reduces the compulsive need for affirmation and protects psychological autonomy.

Neuroscience supports this autonomy. Studies on motivation have shown that intrinsic goals—those aligned with internal values—activate brain regions associated with sustained engagement and well-being, such as the ventromedial prefrontal cortex. Extrinsic goals, by contrast, produce temporary spikes of dopamine without long-term satisfaction. The difference explains why people can achieve great external success and still feel hollow. Achievement without alignment cannot produce peace.

Culturally, value-driven consistency also functions as moral ballast. Societies under rapid transformation risk losing coherence between principle and behavior. When economic or technological systems evolve faster than ethical frameworks, disorientation follows. The historian Jacques Ellul called this "the ethical lag of progress." Value-driven individuals act as stabilizing agents within such contexts. Their integrity models coherence amid flux. The health of a culture depends on the presence of people who act from conscience rather than convenience.

This alignment, however, requires vigilance. Values can calcify into ideology if they are held without reflection. Flexibility does not mean abandoning values, but reinterpreting them in changing contexts. A value such as honesty may manifest differently in different situations—truth-telling in one, discretion in another. The underlying principle remains, but its expression evolves. Rigidity of expression is not integrity; it is inertia. The mature mind distinguishes between fidelity to value and attachment to form.

In relationships, value-driven consistency builds trust. People intuitively rely on those whose actions align with stated principles. Trust, in this sense, is not built through perfection but through predictability of motive. When others know that your decisions emerge from discernible values, even disagreement becomes safer. The opposite is also true: inconsistency between professed values and behavior erodes credibility faster than error itself. Values, when lived, become a form of communication—an implicit promise of coherence.

The emotional benefit of this alignment is a sense of peace that does not depend on circumstance. When one's behavior reflects chosen values, uncertainty loses its threat. Whatever the outcome, one remains congruent. This inner congruence reduces chronic anxiety because it restores control at the only reliable level: intention. The future may be unknowable, but action in the present remains possible. The philosopher William James described this as "the moral equivalent of war"—a disciplined engagement with life that channels passion into principle.

Practically, value-driven consistency manifests in daily decisions. When faced with competing priorities, one can ask: "Which choice aligns with who I intend to be?" This question bypasses outcome prediction and grounds decision-making in identity. Over time, these small acts of alignment accumulate into character. The self becomes coherent through repetition of value-consistent behavior. Aristotle's concept of virtue captures this: excellence is not an act but a habit. Values become embodied through practice.

In the Artificial Era, where algorithms constantly anticipate and influence behavior, value-driven living becomes an act of resistance. The more external forces shape preference, the more essential internal principles become. Acting from value rather than impulse preserves autonomy in a world designed to erode it. The ability to say no—to decline a stimulus, a trend, or a temptation that violates one's principles—is not rigidity but freedom. Flexibility without anchor becomes manipulation; consistency without reflection becomes dogma. The synthesis of the two is integrity.

At a societal level, the same tension applies. Democracies, organizations, and communities depend on value coherence to function. When expediency replaces principle, cynicism grows. Restoring public trust requires visible alignment between stated values and enacted policies. Psychological flexibility at scale thus becomes ethical flexibility: the ability to apply timeless principles with context-sensitive wisdom.

The emotional dimension of this work cannot be overstated. Acting from value does not protect one from pain, but it prevents pain from being meaningless. When suffering serves a purpose aligned with value, it becomes bearable. Soldiers endure hardship for loyalty, parents for love, artists for truth. The energy of sacrifice transforms when it is attached to meaning. This relationship between value and endurance has been confirmed in trauma research, where survivors who connect their struggle to purpose exhibit greater post-traumatic growth.

Value-driven consistency also strengthens self-regulation. Decisions guided by values require less deliberation than those driven by impulse because the framework is already established. The individual no longer negotiates endlessly between short-term comfort and long-term integrity. The mind quiets when it knows its compass. This quiet is not complacency but clarity. It allows energy to flow toward action rather than rumination.

The developmental psychology of Erik Erikson provides a useful lens here. In adulthood, the central task is *generativity*—the commitment to contribute meaningfully to others and the world. Value-driven consistency fulfills this task by transforming personal principle into collective contribution. It bridges self and society, making flexibility serve something larger than adaptation itself.

Ultimately, value-driven consistency represents maturity: the integration of freedom and responsibility. It allows a person to remain open without becoming unmoored, to act with conviction without becoming rigid. In an environment where external structures constantly shift, this inner structure becomes the foundation of identity. It is what allows a person to say, even in uncertainty, "I know who I am."

The emotionally healthy life is not the one free from contradiction or change, but the one organized by enduring principle. Value-driven consistency provides that organization. It transforms flexibility from mere survival strategy into ethical stance. To act from value is to assert that meaning is still possible even when stability is not.

Learning to Re-Open

The most difficult moment in any psychological journey is not the fall, but the reopening that follows. Reopening means allowing oneself to be touched again after disappointment, risk again after loss, and trust again after betrayal. It is the quietest and most courageous expression of psychological flexibility. Where resilience is often imagined as toughness, reopening is its opposite: softness without collapse, vulnerability without naïveté. It is the renewal of curiosity in a mind that has learned caution.

Human beings close as a form of protection. The nervous system, built for survival, associates pain with danger and constriction with safety. When a person experiences emotional harm, the body and mind cooperate in withdrawal. Muscles tighten, breathing shortens, attention narrows. These physiological contractions mirror psychological ones: cynicism replaces wonder, suspicion replaces trust, apathy replaces hope. The system does not intend cruelty; it intends safety. Yet what begins as protection easily becomes prison.

To reopen, then, is to reeducate the nervous system—to teach it that safety and openness can coexist. This requires patience because closure is efficient. It demands no energy, only maintenance. Openness, by contrast, is metabolically expensive. It requires presence, attention, and courage. But it also restores vitality. The psychologist Barbara Fredrickson's research on positive emotions shows that openness broadens cognitive and behavioral repertoires. When people feel safe enough to explore, their minds literally widen. The capacity for insight, connection, and creativity expands. Openness is not sentiment; it is function.

The process begins with acknowledging that closure has served a purpose. Many people attempt to force themselves into optimism, believing that healing means forgetting. But premature reopening leads to re-injury. The first step is respect for the instinct to close. It was, at one time, adaptive. Only when one honors its necessity can one begin to release it. The task is not to erase the protective reflex but to update it—to differentiate between past and present, threat and memory.

In trauma psychology, this updating process is called recontextualization. The brain learns that sensations once associated with danger no longer predict harm. Each new experience of safety rewrites the old narrative. For instance, someone who once felt dismissed when speaking honestly may test openness in a safer context—a trusted friend, a reflective conversation. When the expected rejection does not occur, the nervous system recalibrates. The old equation "openness equals pain" becomes "openness sometimes brings connection." Consider a professional who was harshly criticized after a failed project. Their nervous system might fuse 'failure' with 'humiliation.' To reopen, they might choose to lead a small, low-risk team meeting. When they receive constructive feedback instead of ridicule, the context begins to shift. After several such experiences, the brain's prediction changes. The old equation 'failure equals humiliation' is revised to 'failure is an opportunity for feedback.' Healing, at its core, is this revision of predictive coding.

Reopening also depends on emotional granularity—the ability to distinguish among emotions with precision. Psychologist Lisa Feldman Barrett's work demonstrates that individuals who can label emotions accurately recover more quickly from negative experiences. Saying "I am sad" is different from "I am disappointed," and both differ from "I feel lonely." Granularity creates space for nuance, and nuance allows motion. When emotion becomes specific, it becomes workable. People reopen not by suppressing feeling, but by understanding it.

Another dimension of reopening involves trust, both in others and in oneself. Trust is not blind belief; it is a measured risk. It says, "I will act as though connection is possible, even without proof." This provisional faith is essential to psychological renewal. The philosopher Søren Kierkegaard described faith not as certainty but as a leap across uncertainty. Reopening requires a similar leap—not into religion, but into relationship. It affirms that the possibility of meaning is worth the risk of disappointment.

The obstacle to this leap is often pride disguised as protection. After being hurt, people may adopt the posture of invulnerability, claiming indifference as strength. Yet indifference is a form of fear—the fear of being seen, known, or needed again. True strength lies in allowing impact, not in denying it. The ability to be moved without being destroyed marks the difference between maturity and defense. As Carl Rogers observed, the paradox of growth is that it begins when one accepts what one cannot control.

Reopening also involves grief. To reopen is to accept that something has been lost—an illusion of safety, a sense of continuity, a version of self that existed before disappointment. Many resist reopening because they confuse grief with regression. In truth, grief is integration. It allows the mind to carry forward what was meaningful without being bound by what was painful. Without grief, closure hardens into bitterness. With grief, closure softens into wisdom.

Psychologically, reopening represents the transition from avoidance to approach motivation. Neuroscientist Richard Davidson's research shows that people with higher left-prefrontal activation—the region associated with approach—recover faster from stress. This recovery is not due to denial, but to re-engagement. Approach motivation draws one toward life again, toward new experiences and connections. It is the biological correlate of hope.

Reopening also carries ethical weight. A closed mind cannot empathize. When one withdraws from feeling to avoid pain, one also withdraws from compassion. Reopening restores the capacity to see others as complex rather than categorical. This has societal implications. In polarized cultures, closure becomes collective—groups defending themselves from perceived threat through hostility and exclusion. The courage to reopen, then, is not only personal but civic. It models an alternative to reactivity: engagement without enmity.

Yet reopening does not mean naive optimism. It requires discernment— the ability to stay open while setting boundaries. Flexibility without boundary invites exploitation; boundary without flexibility invites isolation. The task is integration: a soft front, strong back, and clear head. This phrase, used by contemplative teacher Joan Halifax, captures the posture of compassionate resilience. It suggests that openness can coexist with firmness, vulnerability with integrity.

Practically, learning to reopen can be cultivated through deliberate practice. One method is gradual exposure to positive uncertainty—choosing situations that carry both risk and potential reward. This could mean initiating conversation with someone new, pursuing an unrealized creative idea, or sharing an honest opinion. The emphasis is not on outcome but on reactivation of engagement. Each act of openness strengthens neural pathways of trust, reminding the mind that possibility outweighs repetition.

Another method is reflective writing. When individuals recount experiences of disappointment and identify what they learned, they transform memory from wound to wisdom. The act of articulation itself integrates emotion and cognition, as demonstrated by research in expressive writing by psychologist James Pennebaker. People who write about their emotional experiences exhibit improved immune function and emotional regulation. The process converts implicit pain into explicit understanding.

Reopening also benefits from rituals of renewal—symbolic acts that mark transition from contraction to expansion. These rituals need not be religious; they can be as simple as lighting a candle, revisiting a meaningful place, or having a conversation that acknowledges change. Ritual gives structure to emotional process, allowing the psyche to externalize movement. Anthropologist Victor Turner observed that rituals help societies navigate liminal states—periods of transformation where the old identity has dissolved and the new one has not yet formed. On the personal level, reopening is precisely such a liminal process.

In philosophical terms, reopening represents an existential wager. To live is to risk being undone by experience, yet to refuse that risk is to stop living. The German philosopher Martin Buber described the fundamental human encounter as "I-Thou"—a meeting in which two beings reveal themselves without control or pretense. Reopening makes such meetings possible. It reasserts the humanity that fear suppresses.

Emotionally, the process of reopening often oscillates between courage and retreat. There are days of expansive connection and days of cautious withdrawal. Flexibility allows this rhythm. The goal is not permanent openness, which would be unsustainable, but responsive openness—the ability to adjust based on context and energy. Just as muscles strengthen through alternating tension and release, emotional capacity grows through cycles of opening and resting.

The Artificial Era complicates this process by replacing presence with simulation. Digital communication allows constant contact but limited intimacy. Many learn to curate expression rather than inhabit it. To reopen in this context means reclaiming authentic emotional presence—allowing tone, pause, and imperfection to reenter conversation. Genuine connection requires vulnerability, not performance. The psychology of reopening thus becomes a cultural corrective, reintroducing depth into communication flattened by efficiency.

Reopening also has implications for creativity. Many people close after failure, mistaking rejection for verdict. Yet creative work, like emotional life, depends on the willingness to begin again. Artists, scientists, and thinkers who sustain contribution over decades share this trait: they reopen repeatedly after disappointment. Their work evolves because they remain permeable to experience. As the writer Henry James noted, "Experience is never limited, and it is never complete." Reopening keeps experience alive.

The endpoint of this process is not optimism but equanimity. Equanimity is the calm acceptance of change without collapse of meaning. It emerges when the mind learns that openness does not guarantee safety but does guarantee growth. Life remains unpredictable, but fear no longer dictates participation. The person who has learned to reopen lives with quiet confidence in their own resilience.

Psychological flexibility reaches its fullest expression here. Cognitive defusion teaches the mind to separate thought from identity. Behavioral experimentation trains the body to act under uncertainty. Value-driven consistency provides the compass. Learning to reopen completes the circle— it restores emotional vitality to the system. Flexibility without heart is calculation; flexibility with heart becomes wisdom.

To reopen is to declare that pain does not have the final word. It is to say, "I have been hurt, but I am still capable of love; I have been wrong, but I am still capable of learning; I have been afraid, but I am still capable of curiosity." These declarations are not sentimental—they are existential. They assert the continuity of humanity in a world that often confuses resilience with hardness.

Reopening, then, is both the most fragile and most powerful act a human can perform. It renews relationship with life itself. It restores motion where fear created stagnation. It allows the mind to bend and the heart to stay alive.

The true mark of flexibility is not how quickly one adapts, but how deeply one can reopen. The future belongs to those who can remain permeable without losing coherence, vulnerable without losing integrity, and curious without losing discernment. In every field, from science to art to love, those who can reopen will be the ones who continue to evolve.

Psychological flexibility ends where it began—with movement. Not the frantic movement of survival, but the deliberate motion of re-engagement. To reopen is to move again toward life, toward others, and toward meaning. It is the act by which humanity renews itself each time it is broken.

* * *

6

Resilience in a Synthetic World

Resilience is one of the most overused and misunderstood words in modern psychology. It has been framed as toughness, grit, or the ability to push through, yet its true meaning is quieter and more intricate. Real resilience is not endurance; it is intelligent recovery. It is the capacity to bend and rebound, to metabolize disruption into learning rather than depletion. In the Artificial Era—where stress has become ambient and novelty is relentless—resilience must be redefined not as a reaction to crisis but as a continuous mode of renewal.

The human nervous system was never designed for perpetual acceleration. Its rhythms follow cycles of activation and restoration, tension and release. When these rhythms are respected, energy replenishes and clarity returns. When they are ignored, systems break down. Chronic exposure to digital stimuli, information overload, and social comparison taxes the mind's recovery mechanisms. Many people today live in a state of partial exhaustion—never collapsing fully, but never restoring completely. The modern challenge is not surviving one great trauma, but surviving the daily erosion of attention and meaning.

This erosion is psychological as much as physiological. Resilience depends on coherence: a sense that one's experiences form an intelligible pattern rather than random noise. When that coherence fractures, as it often does in times of technological upheaval, the self begins to fragment. The task of resilience, then, is architectural. It involves rebuilding the inner structure that holds experience together—reconnecting body, emotion, and narrative into a functional whole. Without that integration, strength becomes brittle.

To rebuild this architecture, one must first understand that stress itself is not the enemy. In fact, stress is the engine of adaptation. The psychologist Hans Selye, who first coined the term "stress" in the 1930s, distinguished between *eustress*, the positive stress that promotes growth, and *distress*, the negative stress that overwhelms. The difference lies in recovery. When stress is followed by adequate restoration—sleep, reflection, connection—it strengthens the organism. When recovery is absent, stress accumulates as wear. True resilience emerges not from the absence of strain but from the presence of repair.

In the context of artificial environments, recovery requires deliberate cultivation. The digital world offers stimulation without restoration, connection without rest. Devices keep the mind alert long after the body signals fatigue. The result is a state of hypervigilance—a readiness without release. Over time, this dysregulates emotional balance, narrows perspective, and dulls creativity. Resilience begins when one reclaims rhythm—when cycles of rest, stillness, and reflection are restored as non-negotiable parts of human functioning.

But resilience is not only biological; it is social and existential. The capacity to recover depends on both internal regulation and external support. Humans evolved as cooperative organisms; belonging is not a luxury but a regulatory function. Relationships act as buffers that distribute stress across shared meaning. In a synthetic age where digital networks substitute for true community, rebuilding resilience means rebuilding connection—real, embodied, mutual presence.

This chapter explores resilience as a dynamic system rather than a trait. It will trace the biology of reset, the social scaffolding that sustains adaptation, the role of curiosity in replacing control, and the way meaning transforms hardship into integration. Each of these dimensions contributes to an updated model of human recovery—one that honors complexity without surrendering to chaos.

Resilience in a synthetic world is not about resisting change; it is about metabolizing it. It is the psychological art of turning disruption into design, of using pressure to strengthen rather than shatter. The measure of resilience is not how little one breaks, but how gracefully one rebuilds.

The Biology of Reset

Resilience begins in the body. Long before the intellect constructs meaning, the nervous system decides whether life feels survivable. Its judgments are fast, automatic, and mostly unconscious. Every experience of calm or chaos, hope or helplessness, originates in this physiological foundation. To understand resilience, one must first understand recovery—not as luxury or reward, but as a biological necessity built into human design.

The stress response is among the most elegant systems in the body. It mobilizes energy, heightens awareness, and prepares the organism to respond to challenge. Heart rate increases, muscles tense, attention narrows. The body's chemistry shifts toward survival. But like all systems optimized for short-term intensity, it depends on closure. Once the threat passes, the parasympathetic nervous system should intervene to restore equilibrium. This alternating rhythm—activation and relaxation—is the body's natural cycle of adaptation. When functioning properly, stress strengthens. When that rhythm is interrupted, stress corrodes.

Modern life has all but severed this rhythm. The technological environment keeps the body in a state of chronic activation. Notifications, deadlines, and the ambient noise of information trick the nervous system into perceiving constant urgency. The threat is no longer physical but psychological—social exclusion, failure, irrelevance. Yet the body responds as if danger were immediate. Cortisol levels remain elevated; sleep quality declines; inflammation increases. Over time, this produces the very symptoms many associate with burnout: emotional numbness, cognitive fatigue, irritability, and detachment.

The first step toward resilience, therefore, is not mental toughness but physiological literacy. To rebuild the capacity for recovery, one must recognize the body's language—its signals of overload and its invitations to rest. Fatigue, distraction, and irritability are not signs of weakness but feedback from an overloaded system. Ignoring them is like ignoring the oil light on a dashboard; eventually, the machinery fails.

Biologically, recovery operates through cycles. The ultradian rhythm, for example, is a 90–120 minute cycle of alertness followed by natural fatigue. When people override this rhythm—by pushing through with caffeine or stimulation—the brain's performance declines. Cognitive psychologist Anders Ericsson's research on expert performance revealed that world-class musicians, athletes, and thinkers work in concentrated bursts followed by deliberate rest. Their excellence depends less on duration of effort and more on the precision of recovery.

Sleep is the most powerful form of this recovery, yet it is often the most neglected. During deep sleep, the brain's glymphatic system clears metabolic waste, memory consolidates, and emotional regulation resets. Chronic sleep deprivation disrupts this process, impairing judgment and amplifying reactivity. Studies from the National Institutes of Health demonstrate that even modest sleep loss alters the prefrontal cortex's ability to regulate the amygdala—the brain's alarm center. In practical terms, tired minds experience neutral situations as threatening. Fatigue distorts perception, making resilience impossible.

Cognitive rest, however, is not limited to sleep. The brain also requires *wakeful rest*—periods of mental idleness where attention disengages from goals. These moments allow the default mode network to integrate experience and restore creativity. Yet in a world designed to eliminate boredom, wakeful rest has become rare. People fill every gap with stimulation, mistaking busyness for productivity. The result is what neuroscientist Daniel Levitin calls "attention fatigue," a depletion of the brain's capacity to filter and prioritize information. Recovery requires the opposite: deliberate emptiness.

There is a paradox here. Many associate resilience with action—doing more, trying harder, never stopping. But true resilience depends on pause. The ability to stop is not laziness but regulation. It signals that the nervous system has enough safety to release control. In evolutionary terms, animals demonstrate this effortlessly. After escaping threat, a gazelle trembles, exhales, and returns to grazing. Somatic psychologists describe this as the discharge of survival energy, a physiological process that completes the stress cycle. The stress cycle completes. Humans, by contrast, remain mentally entangled with the event long after it ends, replaying scenarios and extending stress through cognition. Learning to complete the cycle—through breath, movement, or reflection—is an essential act of self-preservation.

Breathing itself offers a gateway to reset. Slow, deliberate breathing activates the vagus nerve, stimulating parasympathetic dominance. Research by Stephen Porges, who developed the Polyvagal Theory, shows that the vagus serves as a direct channel between body and brain, transmitting safety cues that calm the system. This is why mindful breathing, stretching, or gentle physical movement can transform emotional state more reliably than reasoning. The mind may argue endlessly; the body requires only a signal of safety.

Exercise functions as another regulatory mechanism. It discharges accumulated stress hormones and releases endorphins that promote emotional stability. But the value of movement extends beyond chemistry. Physical exertion restores the body's sense of agency. It reaffirms the connection between intention and outcome, counteracting the helplessness that chronic stress breeds. The philosopher William James noted that bodily action can change mental state: we do not cry because we are sad; we are sad because we cry. Movement leads emotion.

Nutrition, hydration, and sensory input all contribute to this biology of reset. The brain consumes roughly twenty percent of the body's energy. When energy supply falters through dehydration, erratic eating, or sensory overload, cognitive regulation weakens. Many forms of irritability or anxiety stem not from psychological conflict but from physiological imbalance. Resilience begins with these fundamentals—not as wellness platitudes, but as the scaffolding for emotional intelligence.

Yet biological recovery alone is not sufficient. The body can rest, but if the

119

mind continues rehearsing threat, the cycle remains incomplete. Psychological recovery depends on cognitive disengagement—the ability to mentally step out of problem-solving mode. This is why creative or meditative states are restorative: they suspend goal orientation. Neuroscientists describe this as *alpha synchronization*, a neural rhythm associated with calm alertness. It is the mental equivalent of exhalation.

Cultural habits, however, undermine this capacity. The dominant ethic of productivity equates stillness with failure. Even leisure has become performative—documented, optimized, or monetized. True rest now feels transgressive. People apologize for idleness as though it were irresponsibility. This moralization of busyness fractures the biology of resilience. When the nervous system never receives permission to recover, chronic dysregulation becomes the norm.

Reclaiming rest, then, is a radical act of self-respect. It reasserts the truth that value does not depend on output. Rest is not an escape from life's demands but an investment in one's capacity to meet them. The psychologist Herbert Freudenberger, who first identified burnout in the 1970s, observed that the condition emerged not from laziness but from idealism—people who cared deeply but lacked balance. The cure is not disengagement, but sustainable engagement—rhythms of giving and replenishing.

Technology further complicates this balance by hijacking reward systems. Each notification, like, or message triggers dopamine release, reinforcing vigilance. The brain, conditioned to expect reward, resists disengagement. To reset, one must interrupt this loop consciously—creating spaces free from digital input where attention can recalibrate. What seems like minor abstinence—a phone-free morning walk, an unconnected meal—restores neurochemical equilibrium. Over time, such practices reestablish the body's authority over the device.

The science of recovery also intersects with meaning. Physiological restoration works best when paired with psychological coherence. Studies on post-stress recovery show that individuals who interpret stress as meaningful or growth-promoting recover faster than those who view it as purely harmful. This phenomenon, known as *stress appraisal*, transforms the biological response itself. The same cortisol spike that damages under fear strengthens under purpose. The body listens to the story the mind tells about effort.

This insight bridges biology and narrative. Recovery is not only about resetting chemistry but also reinterpreting experience. When exhaustion is seen as proof of failure, it deepens fatigue. When it is seen as evidence of engagement, it invites compassion. Self-compassion, far from indulgence, moderates stress physiology by reducing amygdala activation and increasing oxytocin. In other words, how one relates to one's own struggle determines how fully one recovers.

The biology of reset thus reveals a paradoxical truth: resilience is not built by hardening against stress, but by softening into rhythm. The body's wisdom predates modern psychology. Its cycles of tension and release mirror the seasons, the tides, the heartbeat. To align with these rhythms is to return to biological sanity. It is to remember that adaptation depends not on perpetual strength but on periodic surrender.

When viewed this way, resilience ceases to be an individual virtue and becomes a collective necessity. Workplaces, schools, and societies that honor rest as integral to function produce healthier, more creative, and more ethical participants. Those that ignore it produce depletion disguised as discipline. A culture that never stops cannot think clearly, feel deeply, or change wisely. The biology of reset, applied collectively, becomes the foundation of a humane civilization.

In the Artificial Era, where the line between human and machine blurs, recovery becomes the defining difference. Machines operate continuously; humans must oscillate. Our endurance lies not in replication of technology but in reclaiming what technology cannot do—pause, reflect, restore. The nervous system is not a glitch to be optimized; it is an intelligence to be listened to. Resilience begins the moment one honors that truth.

The Social Scaffold

Resilience does not occur in isolation. Although modern culture often celebrates the lone survivor, the research is unequivocal: recovery is relational. The nervous system itself is social in design. From birth, human physiology depends on co-regulation—our internal states stabilize through contact with others. Every conversation, gesture, or glance carries signals that shape the body's chemistry. Belonging, therefore, is not merely emotional comfort but biological infrastructure. Without it, stress recovery falters.

This truth was once obvious. For most of human history, survival depended on cooperation. Tribes, families, and communities distributed both labor and emotion. The stress of one was buffered by the care of many. The modern world, in its pursuit of autonomy, has quietly dismantled this architecture. Individualism, mobility, and digital mediation have fragmented the social fabric that once absorbed shock. As a result, many experience life as a solo endurance test—physiologically connected to millions yet emotionally tethered to few.

The psychology of resilience begins to fail under such isolation. Studies in social neuroscience, particularly those by John Cacioppo, show that loneliness activates the same brain regions as physical pain. Chronic disconnection increases inflammation, weakens immunity, and elevates mortality risk. Social support, conversely, predicts faster recovery from illness, trauma, and stress. The mechanism is both psychological and biochemical: supportive contact reduces cortisol and increases oxytocin, creating a feedback loop of safety. Connection literally repairs the body.

To rebuild resilience in a synthetic world, one must therefore rebuild the social scaffold that sustains it. This does not necessarily mean expanding one's network, but deepening the quality of connection within it. The nervous system distinguishes between presence and performance. Digital communication can simulate interaction but rarely delivers physiological attunement. Tone of voice, facial expression, synchronized breathing— these are the elements through which the brain recognizes safety. When interaction lacks them, the body remains guarded, even if conversation appears pleasant.

This is why relationships require embodiment. The difference between a message and a moment is the difference between representation and reality. A message conveys information; a moment conveys regulation. Sitting with another human being in shared silence can do more for resilience than any motivational advice. The body registers companionship not through content but through resonance. Mirror neurons fire, heart rates align, and the sense of aloneness dissolves.

At the same time, not all connection heals. Relationships can also perpetuate stress when they are competitive, dismissive, or manipulative. Psychological resilience depends not on the presence of people but on the quality of relational safety. Research on attachment theory, beginning with John Bowlby and later expanded by Mary Ainsworth, shows that secure attachment in childhood predicts stronger emotional regulation in adulthood. The same principles apply across the lifespan. Secure relationships offer a base from which one can explore and recover. Insecure or exploitative relationships reinforce vigilance, preventing restoration.

The challenge in modern society is that many relationships now exist within performative environments. Social media encourages comparison rather than connection, performance rather than presence. People curate versions of themselves designed for admiration, not intimacy. Yet admiration does not soothe the nervous system. It excites it, maintaining a cycle of validation-seeking that exhausts rather than restores. Resilience requires the opposite—spaces where one can exist without performance, where being replaces proving.

Such spaces are rare, but they can be cultivated intentionally. They often emerge not from grand gestures but from small consistencies: the friend who listens without fixing, the colleague who remembers context, the partner who regulates rather than escalates. These micro-moments of safety accumulate into trust. Trust, in turn, becomes the emotional equivalent of scaffolding—a structure that holds the psyche upright when internal strength wavers.

In organizational psychology, the same pattern applies at scale. Teams that exhibit high psychological safety recover from failure more quickly and innovate more effectively. Amy Edmondson's research at Harvard has shown that when people feel safe to speak up without fear of humiliation or punishment, they learn faster and adapt better. In other words, collective resilience mirrors individual resilience. Both depend on environments where vulnerability is not penalized.

The paradox of belonging is that it requires exposure to difference. Homogeneity feels safe but breeds fragility; diversity challenges but strengthens. In resilience terms, this tension is vital. Engaging with difference—of opinion, background, or perspective—forces the mind to expand its tolerance for ambiguity. It teaches that discomfort can coexist with connection. Cultures that embrace such complexity produce members who are more psychologically flexible and less reactive to threat.

Philosophically, the social scaffold of resilience reflects an ancient insight: the self is never singular. Aristotle described humans as *zoon politikon*, political animals—creatures whose flourishing depends on participation in a shared life. Modern neuroscience confirms this intuition. The human brain evolved through interdependence. Its structure prioritizes communication, empathy, and cooperation. To be resilient, then, is to be relationally alive. The myth of the self-sufficient individual is not heroism; it is pathology.

The erosion of this interdependence under technological conditions carries emotional consequences. The more communication shifts from embodied to virtual, the more empathy erodes. Digital empathy is cognitive rather than affective; it understands but does not feel. One can cognitively understand that a friend is sad from their text message, but one can only affectively feel the weight of that sadness by hearing the tremor in their voice or seeing the slump of their shoulders. This flattening of emotional resonance contributes to widespread burnout and alienation. People remain constantly "connected" yet existentially unseen. The task of resilience is to restore depth—to cultivate relationships that feel, not just function.

Community, in its truest form, is not a collection of compatible personalities but a network of mutual regard. It allows for friction, repair, and growth. The sociologist Émile Durkheim observed that societies with stronger communal ties have lower rates of suicide, not because hardship disappears, but because meaning is distributed. When one's suffering is witnessed and shared, it loses its totalizing power. This principle applies equally to individuals. To be witnessed is to be reminded that one's pain exists within a larger pattern of human experience.

Belonging also supports resilience by reinforcing identity continuity. Under chronic change, people risk fragmentation—the sense of being many versions of oneself without a stable core. Relationships act as mirrors that reflect coherence back to us. They remind us of who we are across contexts. This function becomes crucial in synthetic environments where identity is fluid, curated, and often fragmented across digital platforms. Genuine relationships re-anchor identity in shared memory and mutual recognition.

The emotional architecture of resilience thus depends on both giving and receiving. Isolation often arises not only from lack of support but from lack of offering. People who contribute to others' well-being experience heightened purpose and reduced stress. Altruism activates neural pathways associated with reward and belonging. Helping others becomes a form of regulation—an outward expression of internal strength. Communities that encourage reciprocity rather than dependency sustain resilience longer.

In therapeutic and social interventions, this principle underlies group therapy, peer mentorship, and communal recovery models. Healing accelerates when individuals participate in collective processes rather than isolated self-improvement. Shared vulnerability normalizes struggle and transforms it into solidarity. This social dimension of resilience reframes weakness as connection point rather than defect. The statement "me too" carries more regulatory power than any self-help maxim.

Yet building and maintaining the social scaffold in a synthetic world requires conscious countercultural effort. It means choosing presence over convenience, conversation over consumption, and community over commentary. It demands slowness in an age of speed. The reward is profound: when the social nervous system is reactivated, isolation dissolves, and emotional balance returns.

125

The most resilient societies will be those that remember that intelligence is not only cognitive but communal. Machines can process information; only humans can offer presence. The future of resilience depends on preserving this distinction. Connection, in its biological and existential sense, remains the strongest antidote to the fragmentation of modern life.

To rebuild the social scaffold is to rebuild civilization from the inside out—one conversation, one act of empathy, one moment of genuine attention at a time. The nervous system remembers safety through others, and through that memory, the will to keep rebuilding returns.

Curiosity Over Control

If stress is the body's reaction to uncertainty, control is the mind's attempt to eliminate it. Every human being longs for predictability because predictability feels safe. Control offers the illusion that chaos can be managed, that life can be rendered stable through willpower or precision. Yet this illusion, while comforting, often produces the opposite effect. The tighter one grips, the more brittle one becomes. Psychological resilience depends not on eliminating uncertainty but on developing a posture of curiosity toward it.

Curiosity is not the same as naivety. It is the capacity to approach the unknown with open attention rather than defensive preconception. It is the mind's equivalent of flexibility—the willingness to explore what is, rather than insist on what should be. In this sense, curiosity represents the emotional and cognitive antidote to control. Where control constricts, curiosity expands. It transforms threat into information and uncertainty into possibility.

The relationship between control and resilience has long been studied in psychology. Early research by Julian Rotter on locus of control distinguished between those who perceive outcomes as internally versus externally determined. People with an internal locus generally exhibit greater motivation and coping ability because they see themselves as agents of influence. Yet when internal control becomes excessive, it mutates into rigidity. The adaptive balance lies in what psychologists now call *agency without illusion*: a recognition that one can influence experience but not dictate it. Curiosity sustains this balance. It allows engagement without attachment to outcome.

This distinction becomes crucial in environments dominated by artificial systems. Digital technologies create a seductive illusion of mastery—instant feedback, predictive analytics, personalized content. These systems train the brain to expect precision and responsiveness. When reality fails to comply, frustration ensues. The mind, conditioned to control, loses tolerance for ambiguity. Curiosity, by contrast, restores tolerance. It reintroduces humility into cognition, reminding the individual that not all variables are visible, and that some degree of unpredictability is the natural state of life.

Curiosity is more than an attitude; it is a neurobiological state. Research in affective neuroscience shows that curiosity activates the dopaminergic reward system, particularly the caudate nucleus and hippocampus. This activation increases motivation and learning capacity. The brain literally becomes more plastic when curious—it encodes information more deeply and retrieves it more efficiently. Curiosity transforms uncertainty from stressor to stimulant. The same physiological arousal that under fear leads to avoidance, under curiosity leads to exploration.

This transformation begins with reinterpretation. When uncertainty is framed as threat, the sympathetic nervous system dominates; when framed as opportunity, the parasympathetic system modulates arousal into focus. The difference lies in appraisal, not circumstance. This insight aligns with the work of cognitive theorists such as Richard Lazarus, who emphasized the role of appraisal in emotional experience. Resilient individuals reframe the unknown not as danger but as data. Their question shifts from "What if I fail?" to "What might I learn?"

Culturally, however, control remains seductive. It is associated with competence, authority, and mastery—all qualities rewarded in a performance-oriented society. The modern myth of the self-made individual glorifies domination over uncertainty. Yet this myth is psychologically expensive. When identity depends on control, unpredictability becomes existential threat. People over-schedule, over-analyze, and over-prepare to avoid vulnerability. What they call diligence is often disguised fear. Resilience, by contrast, emerges from the willingness to enter experience without full guarantee.

Philosophically, curiosity represents a more sustainable relationship with knowledge itself. The ancient Greeks distinguished between two forms of knowing: *techne*—knowledge for control—and *phronesis*—knowledge for wisdom. The former seeks mastery; the latter seeks understanding. Modern technological culture has overdeveloped *techne* at the expense of *phronesis*. Artificial intelligence epitomizes this imbalance: systems built to predict, optimize, and dominate data, but incapable of wonder. Curiosity reclaims that missing dimension. It is the capacity to be informed without being possessed by information.

Curiosity also supports emotional regulation. When confronted with difficulty, curiosity redirects energy from evaluation to exploration. Instead of "Why is this happening to me?" the question becomes "What is this showing me?" This shift engages the prefrontal cortex, reducing amygdala activation and lowering emotional reactivity. In other words, curiosity stabilizes physiology. It converts emotional turbulence into attentional focus. This is why resilient individuals often appear calm under pressure— they are not suppressing emotion but channeling it into inquiry.

The developmental roots of curiosity lie in early attachment. Securely attached children explore their environments confidently because they trust that comfort is available if needed. Insecurely attached children, lacking that base, either cling or withdraw. The pattern persists into adulthood. Emotional safety predicts cognitive openness. Environments that reward exploration over perfection cultivate resilient minds. In education, this principle manifests as inquiry-based learning; in therapy, as process orientation. In both cases, curiosity sustains engagement where control would create avoidance.

One of the most subtle barriers to curiosity is perfectionism. The perfectionist mind cannot tolerate uncertainty because uncertainty threatens identity. It equates error with inadequacy. The result is chronic self-monitoring, which consumes cognitive bandwidth and drains motivation. The antidote is experimental thinking—the willingness to treat effort as exploration. In this framework, mistakes become feedback, not verdict. The perfectionist learning a new language fears misspeaking and remains silent; the curious experimenter tries a new phrase specifically to learn from the correction, viewing it as essential data. The psychologist Carol Dweck's research on growth mindset reflects this principle: when failure is reinterpreted as data, resilience increases.

The emotional experience of curiosity also counteracts despair. Despair thrives on finality; curiosity opens possibility. Even in crisis, the smallest question—"What happens next?"—introduces movement. Viktor Frankl, writing from the extremity of concentration camps, observed that survival often depended on meaning, and meaning depended on imagination. Those who could project themselves into a future, even momentarily, retained agency. Curiosity keeps that imaginative space alive. It ensures that the mind continues to generate alternatives when fear insists there are none.

Curiosity also humanizes technological adaptation. As artificial intelligence and automation reshape work, identity, and creativity, many experience existential anxiety about obsolescence. Control responses manifest as defensiveness—clinging to expertise, resisting change, or dismissing new systems. Curiosity reframes this anxiety into learning. It invites the question: "What can I become in relation to this?" This posture transforms disruption into collaboration. Technology ceases to be rival and becomes resource. The resilient mind integrates rather than competes.

At the interpersonal level, curiosity sustains empathy. Judgment freezes understanding; curiosity extends it. When faced with conflict, asking "What must this person be experiencing?" softens reactivity and restores dialogue. Neuroscientific studies of empathy, such as those by Tania Singer, show that curiosity-based compassion activates reward centers in the brain rather than pain circuits. This means empathy grounded in curiosity energizes rather than depletes. Resilient relationships depend on this distinction—they allow emotional exchange without burnout.

However, curiosity must be protected from cynicism. Chronic disappointment can dull interest, making the unknown feel futile rather than fascinating. Reawakening curiosity after disillusionment requires humility. It means acknowledging that reality exceeds expectation, that mystery remains even after mastery. Philosophically, this stance aligns with what Zen Buddhism calls *beginner's mind*—a readiness to encounter each moment as new. Such openness is not ignorance but intelligence freed from arrogance.

Practically, cultivating curiosity involves small, deliberate practices. One can begin by replacing judgmental statements with questions: instead of "This won't work," ask "What would make this work?" Instead of "I can't handle this," ask "What skill would help me handle this?" The brain responds differently to questions; it activates exploratory networks that generate solutions. Even curiosity about one's own resistance—"Why am I avoiding this?"—can dissolve rigidity. The act of inquiry reintroduces movement where stagnation once ruled.

Curiosity also thrives in environments of psychological safety. Teams, classrooms, and relationships that punish error extinguish curiosity. Conversely, environments that normalize uncertainty encourage experimentation. Leaders and teachers who model curiosity—by admitting ignorance or exploring publicly—create cultures of learning. Such cultures are inherently more resilient because they adapt through collective discovery rather than centralized control.

On a larger scale, curiosity serves as a moral stance. It resists the simplification that fuels polarization. To remain curious about those with whom one disagrees is to affirm their complexity. It keeps dialogue possible in an age of echo chambers. Curiosity in this sense is civic resilience—it prevents fragmentation by sustaining empathy across difference.

The practice of curiosity is deceptively simple but psychologically profound. It requires three habits: suspension of judgment, tolerance of ambiguity, and delight in discovery. These habits counteract the rigidity of control. They restore the nervous system's natural rhythm of approach rather than avoidance. When life's unpredictability is met with interest instead of fear, the body relaxes, attention expands, and creativity returns.

In the end, curiosity does not eliminate the need for control; it refines it. Healthy control establishes boundaries; curiosity animates them. Together they form the dynamic equilibrium of resilience—stability without stagnation, movement without chaos. The resilient individual neither surrenders to randomness nor clings to rigidity. They live at the frontier between known and unknown, guided not by fear of loss but by appetite for understanding.

Curiosity is the mind's declaration of faith in life. It is the refusal to let anxiety dictate perception. In a synthetic world that promises total prediction, curiosity keeps humanity spontaneous, adaptable, and alive. It is not the absence of control, but the freedom to explore beyond it.

The Meaning Loop

Human beings do not simply experience life; they interpret it. Between what happens and what it means lies the space in which identity is formed. This interpretive process—what psychologists and philosophers alike have called the search for meaning—is the final pillar of resilience. Without it, endurance becomes mechanical. With it, hardship becomes transformative. Meaning gives coherence to experience, converting chaos into continuity.

Resilience is not merely the ability to recover from difficulty, but the ability to *make sense* of that recovery. The self needs narrative coherence the way the body needs oxygen. It is through story that emotion is integrated, memory organized, and direction restored. Viktor Frankl, whose *Man's Search for Meaning* remains one of the most profound explorations of this principle, wrote that those who could locate purpose within suffering were more likely to survive its weight. The same law holds today: meaning is the psychological structure that transforms pain from randomness into relevance.

Modern stress, however, disrupts this process. The pace and fragmentation of contemporary life fracture narrative continuity. Experiences accumulate faster than they can be processed, leaving many with a backlog of unintegrated emotion—memories without meaning. The result is a kind of existential clutter: individuals feel busy yet directionless, productive yet hollow. In such conditions, resilience falters not because people lack strength, but because they lack coherence. The mind cannot metabolize what it does not understand.

The meaning loop refers to the cyclical relationship between experience, interpretation, and identity. Each shapes the other. Experiences provide raw data; interpretation organizes that data into story; the story reinforces identity, which then filters new experience. Healthy resilience depends on maintaining flexibility within this loop. When interpretation becomes rigid—when a single story defines the self—growth stops. When it remains open—when new information can revise the story—resilience thrives.

Psychologically, this dynamic aligns with narrative therapy, a model developed by Michael White and David Epston. Their insight was simple yet profound: people live the stories they tell about themselves. By re-authoring those stories, individuals can change their emotional reality. A failure reframed as lesson, a loss reframed as initiation—these shifts alter not just mood but identity. The narrative self is plastic; it rewrites itself continually in response to meaning.

The biology of this process parallels its psychology. The brain encodes experiences based on emotional salience. When meaning is assigned, neural consolidation strengthens. When events remain senseless, memory fragments. This is why trauma often feels timeless—the experience resists integration because it lacks narrative closure. Healing requires placing the event within a story larger than itself. Meaning, then, is not abstraction but neurological organization. It binds what would otherwise remain disjointed.

Meaning also transforms emotion through appraisal. When adversity is seen as purposeless, it evokes despair; when seen as instructive, it evokes resolve. This difference in appraisal alters physiological response. Cortisol levels decrease, immune function improves, and neural networks associated with reward activate. Purpose literally changes how the body processes stress. In this sense, the meaning loop is both psychological and somatic—a continuous conversation between narrative and biology.

Culturally, the loss of shared meaning structures has intensified the struggle for coherence. Traditional frameworks—religion, community, shared moral codes—once provided collective narratives that absorbed individual pain into broader purpose. As these frameworks dissolve, people face the task of constructing meaning independently. This autonomy offers freedom but also burden. When everyone must be the sole author of significance, exhaustion follows. The challenge of the synthetic age is not only technological but existential: how to sustain meaning when inherited maps have faded.

Resilience in this context requires narrative creativity. It means learning to craft personal coherence amid collective disorientation. Psychologists studying post-traumatic growth have identified this capacity as central to adaptation. Growth occurs when individuals reinterpret trauma as catalyst rather than condemnation. They do not deny suffering but place it in a story of evolution. The phrase "This made me who I am" signals closure of the loop: experience integrated, identity expanded.

Philosophically, this reorientation draws from existentialism. Thinkers like Jean-Paul Sartre and Albert Camus argued that meaning is not discovered but created through action. Camus's image of Sisyphus pushing his boulder becomes emblematic of human resilience: the acceptance of struggle as participation in existence itself. In this light, meaning is not consolation but commitment—the choice to continue shaping one's story even when certainty is absent.

The meaning loop also protects against nihilism. When adversity is stripped of interpretation, life reduces to reaction. Nihilism is not disbelief in meaning, but exhaustion of it—the sense that stories no longer hold. Resilience interrupts this descent by restoring connection between effort and value. It reminds the individual that while outcomes may be uncertain, significance remains possible. This realization rekindles what philosopher Ernst Cassirer called the "symbolic function" of humanity—the ability to assign meaning and thereby transcend circumstance.

In therapeutic settings, meaning-making often begins with articulation. Speaking one's experience aloud converts chaos into structure. Language externalizes pain, allowing reflection. Neuroscientific studies on expressive writing by James Pennebaker show similar results: individuals who write about emotional experiences display improved health and well-being. The act of constructing narrative reorganizes cognition. Meaning, in other words, is not discovered through analysis but through expression.

On a societal level, the meaning loop extends to collective resilience. Communities that tell coherent stories about adversity recover faster than those that do not. Shared narratives—whether historical, cultural, or moral—anchor collective identity. When these narratives fracture, polarization and apathy increase. The same principle applies at smaller scales: families that discuss hardship openly create intergenerational strength. Silence, by contrast, breeds confusion and repetition. Resilient systems talk.

Yet meaning-making carries ethical responsibility. Not all stories heal; some justify harm or perpetuate illusion. The task is discernment—to distinguish between narratives that expand empathy and those that constrict it. After a layoff, a constrictive narrative might be, 'The world is unjust and my boss was a villain,' which fosters resentment. An expansive narrative might be, 'This painful experience revealed my need for a career that aligns better with my values,' which fosters growth. Healthy meaning enlarges perspective; unhealthy meaning reduces it. A person who explains every misfortune through blame becomes trapped in grievance; a person who interprets suffering as shared human condition grows in compassion. The loop can either reinforce ego or open it.

The synthetic world complicates meaning further by saturating attention. Endless stimuli compete for narrative dominance. Algorithms deliver fragments—headlines, images, reactions—without context. The result is narrative overload and comprehension deficit. People absorb content without coherence. The remedy is intentional meaning-making: stepping back from the torrent to ask, "What story am I being told, and what story do I choose to tell?" Without that question, resilience erodes under informational fatigue.

In practical terms, maintaining the meaning loop involves three steps: reflection, integration, and expression. Reflection acknowledges experience; integration connects it to values; expression communicates it to others.

These processes restore coherence both internally and relationally. When people share meaning, they transform private endurance into communal wisdom. This exchange is the psychological foundation of culture itself.

The emotional signature of meaning is peace—not the absence of pain, but the reconciliation with it. Peace arises when experience and understanding align. The mind no longer resists what has happened, nor demands that it should have been otherwise. Instead, it weaves the event into a larger fabric of significance. This synthesis gives suffering proportion and restores agency. The individual may not control circumstance, but they control its interpretation.

Resilience, then, is the capacity to stay in motion within the meaning loop—to keep interpreting, integrating, and revising one's story in response to life's flux. It is a dialogue between endurance and imagination. The question is never "Why did this happen?" but "What can this become?" This question transforms victimhood into authorship. It turns life from series of events into unfolding narrative.

At the collective level, the same question sustains civilization. Cultures that can reinterpret hardship evolve; those that cannot, collapse. The resilience of a society depends on its ability to renew meaning faster than it loses certainty. Each generation must reauthor its story to accommodate change without losing coherence. The Artificial Era, with its unprecedented acceleration, demands precisely this capacity. The meaning loop becomes not only psychological survival but cultural adaptation.

In the end, meaning is the mind's immune system. It defends against fragmentation by linking pain to purpose. It cannot prevent hardship, but it can prevent despair. When people integrate struggle into story, they reclaim continuity. The loop closes, and resilience completes its cycle.

To live meaningfully in a synthetic world is to insist that interpretation remains a human act—that algorithms may predict behavior, but they cannot narrate purpose. Machines can simulate intelligence, but only humans can make sense of existence. The meaning loop is therefore not just a psychological mechanism but a declaration of humanity.

Resilience ends where meaning begins: in the decision to turn experience into understanding. It is through that decision that people rebuild coherence, renew identity, and rediscover their capacity to continue. Meaning is not what survives after difficulty; it is what allows survival to matter.

* * *

III

Part III – Rebuilding Relevance

After shock and adjustment comes reconstruction. In the Artificial Era, value must be earned in new ways. Part III examines how people reclaim usefulness and meaning when machines handle information better than we do. It explores emerging human advantages—empathy, ethics, insight, and creative integration—that no algorithm can fully replicate.

7

Human Skills 2.0

Rediscovering What Only Humans Can Do

The twenty-first century has quietly overturned one of the central assumptions of modern progress: that intelligence is synonymous with computation. For decades, knowledge was power, and information was the commodity through which power flowed. The rise of artificial intelligence has upended that logic. Machines now learn faster, calculate more accurately, and predict more efficiently than any human being can. Yet amid this technological ascendancy, something profoundly human has re-emerged as irreplaceable—not speed or storage, but sensitivity; not calculation, but connection.

The next era of human relevance will not belong to those who can compete with machines on technical mastery, but to those who can do what machines cannot feel, intuit, or reconcile. Emotional understanding, moral discernment, and interpretive thinking—the capacities once dismissed as "soft skills"—have become the hard currency of a world saturated with data. These are not nostalgic virtues, but evolutionary advantages. They allow human beings to navigate ambiguity, build trust, and assign meaning in environments where information alone no longer differentiates.

This shift represents a fundamental redefinition of intelligence. For centuries, the Western model of intellect emphasized analytical reasoning: the ability to categorize, quantify, and control. Artificial intelligence now performs those functions at industrial scale. What remains uniquely human is integrative cognition—the ability to connect emotion, ethics, and context into understanding. As psychologist Howard Gardner argued in his theory of multiple intelligences, there are forms of knowing that cannot be reduced to logic or computation. Empathy, aesthetic judgment, moral reasoning, and self-awareness are among them. They constitute what might now be called *Human Skills 2.0*: the second generation of intelligence, designed not to outthink machines, but to out-understand them.

In this new landscape, emotional intelligence becomes cognitive capital. Daniel Goleman's pioneering research showed that self-awareness, empathy, and social skill predict leadership effectiveness more reliably than IQ. Neuroscience has since clarified why: emotion is not the opposite of reason but its partner. The prefrontal cortex, seat of decision-making, integrates affective input to weigh nuance and consequence. Machines can optimize, but they cannot care. They can simulate sentiment, but they cannot experience compassion. Trust—the glue of civilization—still requires human presence.

The future, then, does not demand that humans become more mechanical, but that they become more humane. The ability to interpret, contextualize, and act ethically will define not only individual success but societal survival. As automation assumes procedural tasks, human value will migrate toward judgment, meaning, and synthesis—the very faculties that make civilization moral rather than merely efficient. The question is no longer, "What can technology do?" but "What should we do with it?"

Human Skills 2.0 are not new inventions but ancient capacities redis-covered under pressure. They are the evolutionary intelligences that once allowed cooperation, creativity, and moral order to flourish. Their renewal is not nostalgic regression but forward adaptation. The Artificial Era, for all its complexity, invites a return to emotional and ethical literacy as essential forms of knowledge.

This chapter explores four of these human capacities in depth: empathy as a form of intelligence, interpretation as the new literacy, moral discernment as the measure of mature cognition, and integrative creativity as the hallmark of generative thought. Each reflects a domain where human consciousness transcends algorithmic processing—where understanding replaces calculation as the highest form of intelligence.

The task ahead is not resistance to technology, but reintegration with what technology cannot replicate. To rediscover what only humans can do is to safeguard the essence of being human itself.

Empathy as Intelligence

Empathy has long been described as a feeling, a moral virtue, or a social skill. Yet in the context of the Artificial Era, it must be recognized as something more fundamental: a form of intelligence. It is not simply an emotional nicety but a cognitive function that integrates perception, imagination, and ethics into coherent understanding. Where machines process data, empathy processes experience. It interprets the unseen—context, motive, emotional nuance—and transforms it into insight. In a world increasingly governed by algorithms, empathy has become the last frontier of genuine understanding.

The distinction between empathy and sentimentality is crucial. Sentimentality reacts; empathy perceives. It does not depend on emotional contagion or pity, but on perspective-taking—the ability to enter another's reality without losing one's own. Neuroscience has shown that this capacity is both affective and cognitive. The affective component, mediated by mirror neuron systems and limbic resonance, allows emotional attunement; the cognitive component, involving prefrontal and temporoparietal regions, enables reflective understanding of another's mental state. The result is a synthesis of feeling and thought—a multidimensional intelligence that allows humans to connect, interpret, and act wisely in complex social systems.

Empathy evolved not as moral ornament but as survival mechanism. In early human groups, the ability to sense and respond to others' internal states increased cooperation and cohesion. Empathy made collective living possible. Today, the same mechanism underlies every form of trust—from personal relationships to institutions and markets. It remains the foundation of social order, even as its presence becomes endangered by abstraction.

Artificial intelligence, despite its sophistication, cannot replicate empathy. It can approximate sentiment through data analysis, but not experience it. Machine learning models detect patterns in language and behavior, but pattern recognition is not understanding. When an AI model interprets tone as positive or negative, it is measuring probability, not perception. It lacks embodiment, memory, and subjectivity—the ingredients through which empathy arises. This limitation is not technical but ontological: empathy depends on consciousness, and consciousness is not code.

Understanding this difference is critical for human resilience in a synthetic world. The danger is not that machines will replace empathy, but that humans will imitate machine-like detachment in response. As digital systems mediate more of our relationships—through screens, metrics, and performance analytics—people risk confusing information about emotion with emotional understanding itself. Metrics of engagement replace moments of care. Compassion becomes outsourced to interface design. The result is a society rich in data but poor in depth.

Empathy restores depth. It reminds the mind that understanding another person is not a transaction but a translation. It requires patience, imagination, and humility—the willingness to enter ambiguity without immediate solution. This makes empathy inherently countercultural in an age of speed and certainty. It slows perception long enough for reality to be seen in full dimension. The sociologist Hartmut Rosa has called this "resonance"—a relationship with the world characterized by responsiveness rather than control. Empathy, in this sense, is resonance applied to the human domain.

Psychologically, empathy also functions as a regulator of aggression and anxiety. When the mind perceives others as subjects rather than threats, the amygdala's alarm response diminishes. Empathy calms the nervous system by replacing defensiveness with understanding. This is not idealism; it is neurobiology. Studies have shown that compassion training alters brain activity, increasing connectivity in areas associated with emotional regulation and reward. The effect is measurable: empathy stabilizes both perception and physiology.

Yet empathy is not infinite. It is a finite resource that requires cultivation and boundary. Excessive empathy without reflection leads to empathic distress—a form of burnout in which one absorbs others' pain without processing it. Psychologist Paul Bloom has argued that unregulated empathy can bias moral judgment, favoring proximity over principle. He is correct in one sense: empathy without awareness can distort fairness. But regulated empathy—the kind rooted in understanding rather than emotional fusion—enhances ethical reasoning. It allows compassion to remain guided by discernment.

This balance defines empathy as intelligence rather than sentiment. It is not merely feeling with someone, but thinking about what feeling means. It integrates emotional resonance with conceptual analysis. In leadership, this translates to understanding the emotional climate of a group while maintaining strategic perspective. In education, it manifests as the teacher's ability to see from the student's frame of reference without collapsing authority. In clinical psychology, it allows the practitioner to hold another's suffering without drowning in it. Across contexts, empathy functions as both connection and containment.

Culturally, the decline of empathy has mirrored the rise of abstraction. As interactions move online, the cues that trigger empathic response—eye contact, tone, physical presence—are diminished. This sensory impoverishment weakens empathy's reflexive basis. The result is a population more informed yet less attuned. Outrage spreads faster than understanding because outrage requires no imagination. Empathy, by contrast, demands work. It asks for attention to complexity in a culture trained for simplicity.

But empathy can be reconditioned. Like any form of intelligence, it strengthens through deliberate practice. The process begins with attention—the capacity to notice emotional cues in oneself and others. Next comes perspective-taking: asking not "How would I feel?" but "What might they be experiencing?" For instance, when a colleague seems unusually quiet, instead of projecting one's own reasons, one might actively wonder about their specific pressures, their commute that morning, or the unseen demands of their life. This subtle shift acknowledges that understanding another person requires moving beyond projection. The final step is translation—expressing that understanding in language or action that communicates care. These are not mystical abilities; they are cognitive habits built through repetition.

Empathy also depends on self-awareness. The ability to attune to others arises from familiarity with one's own internal states. Without self-knowledge, empathy collapses into assumption. The psychologist Carl Rogers emphasized this reciprocity, describing genuine empathy as "entering the private perceptual world of the other and becoming thoroughly at home in it." Such entry is impossible without an anchor in one's own inner life. Paradoxically, self-understanding enables other-understanding.

In the professional domain, empathy has become a competitive advantage precisely because it cannot be automated. Organizations that cultivate empathic cultures retain trust and innovation. Customers, students, patients, and employees respond not to metrics but to being understood. Research in organizational psychology consistently links empathy in leadership to engagement, retention, and ethical climate. The mechanism is straightforward: empathy signals respect, and respect stabilizes motivation.

Yet beyond performance outcomes lies something more profound: empathy sustains civilization. It is the bridge between individual consciousness and collective well-being. Without it, institutions degrade into systems of extraction—efficient but inhuman. The crises of polarization, inequality, and alienation share a common root: the erosion of empathic imagination. When societies lose the ability to see from another's perspective, dialogue becomes impossible, and aggression fills the void.

In this sense, empathy is not only personal intelligence but civic intelligence. It is the operating system of democracy—the capacity to understand differing perspectives while maintaining shared reality. Artificial intelligence can organize data, but it cannot reconcile value conflict. Only human empathy can do that, because only humans inhabit the moral ambiguity from which understanding arises.

Empathy's future therefore depends on intentional protection. It must be taught, modeled, and institutionalized as seriously as any technical skill. Education systems that prioritize empathy alongside literacy and numeracy prepare students not only for employment but for citizenship. The same applies to workplaces and governments. Policies grounded in empathy produce legitimacy; those devoid of it breed resistance. The survival of human systems will increasingly depend on their ability to feel intelligently.

The redefinition of empathy as intelligence marks a turning point in the evolution of consciousness. It signals a shift from information age to interpretation age—from knowledge as possession to knowledge as relation. Machines will continue to excel at calculation, but humans will remain irreplaceable in the domain of connection. Empathy is that domain's language, logic, and lifeblood.

Ultimately, empathy's brilliance lies in its paradox: it is both rational and emotional, intimate and universal, personal and political. It binds individuals into societies, transforms conflict into communication, and gives cognition a conscience. To call empathy a soft skill is to misunderstand its architecture. It is the most complex form of intelligence humans possess, because it unites everything else—sensation, emotion, thought, and morality—into one coherent act of understanding.

Resilience without empathy becomes isolation; intelligence without empathy becomes domination. In the Artificial Era, the measure of maturity will not be how efficiently one can think, but how deeply one can understand. Empathy is that depth—the bridge between knowing and caring, between consciousness and conscience, between intelligence and wisdom.

Interpretation Over Information

The defining feature of the modern world is not scarcity but surplus. Never before have human beings had access to so much data, so instantly, and with so little friction. Every field—science, politics, medicine, art—now operates within oceans of information. Yet abundance has not produced understanding. In fact, it has often obscured it. The more information people consume, the less meaning they seem to derive. This paradox reveals a critical truth about the age of artificial intelligence: information does not equal knowledge, and knowledge does not equal wisdom. The bridge between them is interpretation.

Interpretation is the mind's ability to organize facts into frameworks, to discern significance from noise, and to connect details into coherence. It is the process by which information becomes insight. Machines excel at collection, correlation, and prediction, but interpretation requires judgment. It depends on contextual awareness, emotional intelligence, and ethical orientation—qualities rooted in consciousness rather than computation. The future of human relevance, therefore, lies not in knowing more, but in knowing *how to understand*.

The cognitive distinction between information and interpretation can be traced through the evolution of human thought. In the Enlightenment, knowledge was modeled after physical science: objective, quantifiable, and detached from emotion. The digital revolution extended this model into algorithms, creating systems that can analyze patterns with extraordinary precision. Yet this precision lacks perspective. A machine can tell what is happening, but not what it *means*. It can detect correlation, but not consequence. Interpretation, by contrast, is meaning-making—the synthesis of perception, memory, and value into understanding.

Psychologically, interpretation represents a higher-order cognitive function. It requires the integration of multiple neural networks: analytical reasoning in the prefrontal cortex, emotional evaluation in the limbic system, and autobiographical memory in the hippocampus. This integration allows humans to assign personal and cultural significance to events. In other words, interpretation is not just intellectual; it is existential. It situates experience within the larger story of self and society.

Cognitive psychologist Jerome Bruner described this as "narrative cognition." He argued that humans think in stories, not statistics. The narrative mind connects facts through emotion, motive, and morality. It seeks coherence rather than precision. Artificial intelligence, by contrast, is statistical. It identifies patterns but lacks narrative imagination. The result is that machines can describe the world's surface, while humans remain the only creatures capable of understanding its meaning.

The danger of information without interpretation is fragmentation. When people consume facts without frameworks, perception becomes reactive. This is the experience of trying to understand a complex political event by scrolling through a social media feed: a chaotic stream of headlines, personal opinions, and emotional reactions that produces agitation rather than clarity. Every new stimulus demands response, leaving no time for reflection. The mind becomes overstimulated but under-integrated—a state that mimics anxiety. The psychologist Daniel Kahneman described this as "cognitive overload": the paralysis that arises when data exceeds the brain's capacity to organize it. Modern attention spans reflect this overload. Information has become too abundant to metabolize.

Interpretation functions as the psychological digestive system. It filters, prioritizes, and integrates input. Without it, meaning malfunctions. This explains why misinformation spreads so easily: people mistake familiarity for truth. The brain, overwhelmed by volume, shortcuts analysis. Algorithms exploit this weakness by feeding confirmation bias, creating echo chambers where interpretation collapses into repetition. Resilience in this environment requires interpretive discipline—the ability to slow cognition, question impulse, and seek coherence beyond comfort.

This interpretive capacity is not limited to intellectual life; it is the foundation of emotional health. The way individuals interpret events determines their experience of them. Two people can live through identical circumstances and emerge with opposite meanings—one embittered, the other strengthened. The difference lies not in what happened but in how it was understood. Cognitive-behavioral psychology is built on this insight: interpretation shapes emotion. Changing perspective changes perception.

Interpretation also guards against what philosopher Hannah Arendt called "the banality of evil." When individuals stop thinking deeply about meaning, they become susceptible to mechanical obedience. Bureaucratic systems thrive on information divorced from interpretation. Tasks are completed efficiently but without moral reflection. The modern workplace, often governed by metrics and automation, risks this condition. Human beings become extensions of process rather than interpreters of purpose. Reintroducing interpretation—asking why rather than merely how—restores ethical agency.

In the educational sphere, this distinction is equally urgent. Traditional schooling rewards information retention: memorizing, reproducing, and applying data. Yet memorization is now obsolete. Machines can recall every known fact in milliseconds. What students must now learn is interpretation: critical thinking, contextual reasoning, and moral discernment. These skills equip them to navigate ambiguity and contradiction—the very qualities that define modern life. Education that fails to cultivate interpretation produces knowledgeable but unwise citizens.

Interpretation is also what gives art and culture their enduring relevance. A painting, poem, or symphony does not transmit information; it provokes meaning. Each observer must interpret it anew, translating feeling into understanding. Art trains the interpretive faculty by engaging emotion and intellect simultaneously. In this sense, cultural literacy is psychological training for meaning-making. It teaches complexity, patience, and perspective—qualities now endangered by instant consumption.

At the collective level, interpretation functions as the immune system of civilization. When societies lose their interpretive frameworks—shared narratives, ethical principles, and symbolic coherence—they become vulnerable to manipulation. Disinformation exploits interpretive weakness. It floods the public sphere with conflicting signals until truth dissolves into opinion. Restoring interpretive literacy is therefore not just intellectual work but democratic necessity.

The discipline of interpretation demands humility. It requires acknowledging that facts alone do not dictate meaning, and that every interpretation is provisional. The mature mind holds multiple possibilities simultaneously, refining understanding through reflection. This cognitive flexibility is the essence of wisdom. Philosopher Isaiah Berlin described it as "pluralism"—the recognition that truth is complex, multifaceted, and resistant to simplification. Machines cannot practice pluralism; they resolve contradictions through computation. Humans, by contrast, mature through holding them.

Interpretation also restores relationship to knowledge itself. Information is consumed; interpretation is participated in. It transforms learning from accumulation to engagement. The learner becomes a co-creator of meaning rather than a passive receiver of data. This shift aligns with constructivist theories of education, which view understanding as an active, relational process. Meaning emerges through dialogue—between student and teacher, text and reader, self and world.

In the workplace, interpretation has become an irreplaceable human function. Organizations now generate massive datasets but struggle to convert them into strategic vision. Analysts can produce numbers, but only interpreters can produce narrative. Leadership, in its highest form, is interpretive. It synthesizes data, context, and human emotion into coherent direction. When leaders fail to interpret, organizations drown in information and lose coherence.

Interpretation even underlies morality. Ethical reasoning depends on context-sensitive judgment rather than algorithmic rule-following. Knowing the right action requires understanding the situation's meaning, not merely its metrics. Philosopher Martha Nussbaum has argued that moral judgment involves "narrative imagination"—the ability to see the world from another's perspective. This, again, is interpretation: the fusion of cognition and empathy into ethical discernment.

The practical cultivation of interpretation begins with slowing down. Speed favors information; reflection favors meaning. Taking time to connect details, trace implications, and question assumptions reactivates interpretive capacity. Reading deeply, conversing thoughtfully, and engaging with ambiguity strengthen the mind's ability to extract coherence from complexity. These practices counteract the shallowness induced by digital speed.

Interpretation is also a moral act because it resists reduction. It refuses to let human experience be flattened into metrics or slogans. To interpret well is to honor complexity—to treat ideas and people as worthy of understanding rather than categorization. This ethos sustains empathy, civility, and depth of thought. It is the intellectual expression of respect.

In the coming decades, societies will depend increasingly on this capacity. Artificial intelligence will continue to automate description and prediction, but humans must remain interpreters of consequence. They must decide what knowledge means, how it should be applied, and to what ends. Interpretation, therefore, becomes the defining act of responsibility in an information-saturated age.

To interpret is to see beyond data—to perceive relationships, implications, and moral weight. It is to transform information into understanding, and understanding into wisdom. Machines can calculate the probability of truth, but only humans can recognize its significance.

The intelligence of the future will not belong to those who know most, but to those who can *make sense* of what they know. Interpretation is that sense-making. It is what gives depth to knowledge, conscience to intelligence, and humanity to thought.

Moral Discernment

The rise of artificial intelligence has brought humanity face to face with an ancient question under modern light: what does it mean to act rightly when no algorithm can decide for you? Technology can compute probability, but not morality. It can optimize outcomes, but it cannot determine whether those outcomes are good. The difference between efficiency and ethics, between decision and discernment, is what defines mature intelligence. Moral discernment, the capacity to reason through ambiguity and choose in alignment with value, is therefore one of the most essential human skills of the Artificial Era.

Ethics begins where certainty ends. In predictable environments, rules suffice. In complex systems—biotechnological, digital, geopolitical—rules fail to capture reality's nuance. The ethical landscape of the twenty-first century is not a map but a fog. Artificial intelligence complicates this further by introducing forms of agency without consciousness. When machines act autonomously, responsibility becomes diffuse. A self-driving car causes an accident: who is at fault—the programmer, the passenger, or the algorithm itself? These questions cannot be solved by mathematics. They require moral interpretation.

Moral discernment differs from moral opinion. Opinion reflects preference; discernment reflects understanding. It is the disciplined process of evaluating not just *what* one believes but *why*. It draws on empathy, context, and foresight to balance competing values. Psychologically, this involves the integration of emotional and rational systems. The neuroscientist Antonio Damasio's research demonstrated that moral reasoning collapses without emotion. Patients with damage to emotional centers of the brain could compute consequences but failed to make humane decisions. Feeling, in other words, is not the enemy of reason—it is its compass.

The philosopher Aristotle described this capacity as *phronesis*, or practical wisdom: the ability to deliberate well about what is good and expedient for human life. Unlike theoretical knowledge, which deals in universals, practical wisdom applies principles to particulars. It requires judgment rather than rule-following. In contemporary terms, moral discernment is the ability to adapt ethical reasoning to changing contexts without abandoning integrity. It is what allows people to remain consistent in value while flexible in application.

Modern culture, however, often confuses moral clarity with moral simplicity. Social media amplifies outrage but flattens nuance. Moral conversation becomes performance—signaling virtue rather than pursuing understanding. The more polarized public discourse becomes, the less room remains for discernment. This polarization mirrors a cognitive distortion psychologists call black-and-white thinking: the inability to tolerate complexity. Yet mature moral reasoning depends on precisely that tolerance. It requires living in the gray, acknowledging that most real dilemmas involve competing goods rather than simple good versus evil.

The psychologist Lawrence Kohlberg proposed a developmental model of moral reasoning in which individuals progress from obedience-based morality (doing what avoids punishment) to principle-based morality (acting according to internalized ethical standards). In the Artificial Era, humanity is being tested at this highest stage. The world's systems now operate at scales where consequences are indirect and distributed. A click, an algorithmic adjustment, or a design choice can affect millions. This demands moral reasoning not grounded in immediate feedback but in foresight and responsibility.

Moral discernment is not only individual but collective. Institutions, corporations, and governments must develop ethical intelligence—an organized capacity to interpret right action in complex environments. Many companies now employ "AI ethicists," yet ethical frameworks cannot be outsourced. Morality, to retain meaning, must be internalized, not proceduralized. When ethical review becomes another checkbox, it loses force. True discernment arises from culture, not compliance. It depends on shared values and open dialogue about purpose.

The danger of delegating ethics to machines lies in the erosion of conscience. When decision-making becomes automated, human beings risk moral atrophy. They cease to feel the weight of choice. Hannah Arendt's analysis of totalitarianism warned of this condition: evil becomes banal when individuals surrender moral judgment to systems. In the digital age, the same danger reappears in subtler form. Algorithms decide hiring, sentencing, and access to resources. If people accept these outputs uncritically, they abdicate moral responsibility.

Psychologically, discernment requires what Daniel Goleman called "emotional self-regulation." To make ethical decisions, one must first manage impulse. Anger, fear, and pride distort perception. This is the difference between immediately sharing an inflammatory headline out of outrage versus pausing to read the full article, consider the source, and reflect on the potential consequences of amplifying it. The capacity to pause, reflect, and empathize under stress distinguishes moral intelligence from moral instinct. Neuroscientific studies on mindfulness and compassion training show measurable changes in brain regions associated with ethical behavior. Practicing awareness strengthens neural circuits for empathy and perspective-taking, enhancing discernment in morally charged situations.

Discernment also depends on humility. Moral maturity involves recognizing the limits of one's own perspective. This humility does not weaken conviction; it refines it. It allows for correction, dialogue, and growth. The philosopher Søren Kierkegaard observed that truth is approached subjectively—that authenticity requires inward reflection rather than external conformity. In moral life, this means acting from examined conscience, not collective pressure.

In leadership, moral discernment defines credibility. Followers do not expect perfection but coherence. They trust leaders who make difficult decisions transparently, who can articulate the reasoning behind their choices, and who align action with value. The collapse of public trust in many institutions stems less from error than from evasion—leaders who act without ethical clarity or accountability. The restoration of trust, therefore, depends on moral intelligence as much as technical competence.

In the educational realm, teaching discernment is more challenging than teaching information because it cannot be reduced to instruction. It must be modeled. Students learn ethical reasoning not by memorizing codes of conduct but by observing how adults handle conflict, uncertainty, and consequence. The classroom becomes a moral ecosystem where tone, respect, and curiosity are ethical lessons in disguise. The same holds true in workplaces and families: morality is transmitted through example, not decree.

Culturally, the decline of shared moral narratives has created what sociologist Zygmunt Bauman called "liquid morality." Values shift according to convenience. Commitment gives way to consumption. In this climate, discernment becomes both more difficult and more essential. It requires anchoring in principle amid fluid norms. The task is not to return to rigid moralism, but to recover moral seriousness—the willingness to ask, "What kind of person, what kind of society, do we wish to become?"

The Artificial Era tests moral discernment in unprecedented ways. Consider the ethics of surveillance, genetic modification, or digital manipulation. Each offers immense potential benefit and equally immense capacity for harm. What determines outcome is not the technology but the moral framework guiding its use. The same tool that diagnoses disease can also violate privacy; the same algorithm that recommends art can also reinforce prejudice. The difference lies in discernment—in the human hand that steers the machine.

From a psychological perspective, moral discernment can be understood as an advanced form of self-regulation coupled with empathic reasoning. It requires meta-cognition—the ability to think about one's own thinking. This capacity allows individuals to detect bias, question motive, and evaluate consequence. It transforms morality from reflex to reflection. Ethical maturity, then, is not certainty about right and wrong but awareness of the forces that shape judgment.

The restoration of moral discernment will be one of the defining challenges of the coming decades. As societies grow more interconnected and technologically mediated, ethical complexity will increase exponentially. Every innovation will raise new dilemmas faster than institutions can legislate them. The only stable safeguard is an internalized sense of responsibility cultivated through reflection, dialogue, and education.

To practice moral discernment is to act as custodian of consequence. It is to pause before action, to weigh not only outcomes but meanings. It is to see human dignity as a non-negotiable constant amid technological flux. The machine may optimize behavior, but only the human can ask whether optimization is right.

In this sense, moral discernment is both psychological skill and spiritual discipline. It demands awareness of self, empathy for others, and reverence for life beyond utility. It invites humanity to evolve not only intellectually but ethically. The Artificial Era will reward technical innovation, but it will depend on moral imagination.

Discernment transforms intelligence into wisdom by reconnecting knowledge with conscience. It is what prevents brilliance from becoming cruelty and efficiency from becoming exploitation. The measure of progress is not what humans can build, but whether they remain worthy of building it.

Integrative Creativity

Creativity has always been one of the most celebrated human abilities, but in the Artificial Era, it demands a new definition. Once associated primarily with artistic talent or novelty, creativity now refers to a broader and more integrative capacity: the ability to connect disparate ideas, systems, and perspectives into coherence. Machines can generate combinations, but only humans can generate meaning. Integrative creativity is the synthesis of intuition, analysis, and context—a deliberate fusion of imagination and intelligence that transforms information into insight.

The difference between generative output and creative understanding is crucial. Artificial intelligence can produce art, compose music, and write code, yet what it generates lacks lived intention. A poem written by an algorithm may sound convincing, but it originates from correlation, not consciousness. The machine is like a flawless mimic who can reproduce the sounds of grief without ever having felt loss. True creativity emerges from awareness. It integrates experience, emotion, and value into expression. It reflects not only what is possible but what is *felt* to matter. This is why even as machines become more prolific producers, human creativity remains uniquely irreplaceable.

Psychologists studying creativity have long recognized it as a multi-dimensional process. Graham Wallas, in his early twentieth-century model, described four stages: preparation, incubation, illumination, and verification. Modern neuroscience has refined this model, identifying dynamic interaction between the brain's default mode network (responsible for imagination and internal thought) and the executive control network (responsible for focus and evaluation). Creativity, in other words, is not chaos but coordination. It is the mind's ability to oscillate between freedom and structure, divergence and convergence. Integrative creativity perfects this balance.

Where ordinary creativity generates novelty, integrative creativity generates *relevance*. It connects originality with understanding. The designer who invents a product that meets an unmet need, the scientist who reframes a persistent problem, the teacher who adapts knowledge to a new audience—all engage in integrative creativity. They are not merely producing something new; they are aligning it with context. Machines can simulate originality, but not relevance, because relevance depends on empathy and judgment—on knowing why an idea matters and to whom.

Culturally, the fascination with artificial creativity has reignited a philosophical debate: if machines can compose symphonies or paint portraits, what distinguishes human art? The answer lies in intentionality. Art is not defined by output but by inwardness. A human artist expresses the tension between perception and meaning, emotion and form. The work is a dialogue between the self and the world. An algorithm, no matter how sophisticated, has no inner world to express. Its output mirrors data patterns, not consciousness. Thus, the value of human creativity in the Artificial Era is not diminished by machine output—it is clarified by contrast.

Integrative creativity depends on three faculties: curiosity, synthesis, and reflection. Curiosity gathers raw material; synthesis organizes it into possibility; reflection filters it through value. Together, they transform knowledge into creation. In psychological terms, this process resembles what Jean Piaget called "accommodation"—the restructuring of cognitive schemas to integrate new information. Creative minds do not merely add to existing frameworks; they reshape them. They are comfortable with dissonance, able to hold competing ideas until a new pattern emerges.

One of the greatest obstacles to creativity is over-specialization. As fields become narrower, experts risk losing the capacity for cross-pollination. Integrative creativity reverses this fragmentation by reconnecting disciplines. It thrives on dialogue between the analytic and the intuitive, the scientific and the aesthetic. Leonardo da Vinci embodied this synthesis: artist, engineer, anatomist, philosopher. His genius was not in mastery of a single field but in the integration of many. The twenty-first century demands a return to that integrative mindset—not as romantic idealism, but as survival skill in an interconnected world.

From a psychological perspective, integrative creativity also functions as emotional regulation. It converts uncertainty into exploration. Where anxiety constricts thought, curiosity expands it. This is why creativity often arises after crisis; the mind, forced out of certainty, begins to experiment. Integrative creativity reframes disruption as invitation. It does not resist complexity but organizes it into meaning. The creative act becomes a form of resilience—a way of metabolizing change into coherence.

At the biological level, creativity depends on neural flexibility. Studies using functional MRI have shown that creative thinking correlates with greater connectivity between brain regions that usually operate separately. This integration allows the mind to move fluidly between divergent and convergent modes of thought. It is a neural mirror of psychological adaptability. Machines, in contrast, operate through fixed pathways, optimized for efficiency but limited in spontaneity. Human creativity, by nature, is inefficient; it explores detours, ambiguities, and emotions. Its value lies precisely in its willingness to wander.

Integrative creativity also requires tolerance for imperfection. The creative process unfolds through trial, error, and revision—what psychologist Carol Dweck would describe as a "growth mindset." This attitude allows the creator to view failure as feedback rather than defeat. Artificial systems, optimized for accuracy, have no such patience for ambiguity. But creativity is not about perfect execution; it is about meaningful evolution. The human capacity to learn through failure, to improvise under constraint, and to find beauty in process remains beyond automation.

At its deepest level, integrative creativity is an act of empathy. To create meaningfully, one must anticipate how others will receive and interpret one's work. The novelist imagines the reader's mind; the architect imagines human movement through space; the psychologist imagines another's emotional reality. This empathic projection transforms creativity from self-expression into social contribution. Machines can generate output, but they cannot care whether it resonates. Human creativity, by contrast, is relational—it exists to connect minds across difference and time.

In education, fostering integrative creativity requires rethinking what it means to learn. Standardized testing rewards replication; creativity rewards recombination. Students should be encouraged not merely to recall facts but to reinterpret them, to connect disciplines, and to generate original perspectives. This kind of learning develops what psychologists call "cognitive flexibility"—the ability to shift between mental frameworks. It is the same skill that supports emotional adaptability and problem-solving.

In leadership, integrative creativity defines strategic insight. Effective leaders are not the ones who know all the answers but those who can integrate multiple perspectives into vision. They balance analytic evidence with human intuition, combining data-driven reasoning with empathic awareness. This synthesis transforms information into direction. When leaders rely solely on data, they manage; when they combine data with meaning, they lead.

Culturally, integrative creativity has become a form of moral imagination. It allows societies to envision alternatives to existing systems—to imagine better possibilities before they exist. Every social reform, artistic movement, or technological breakthrough begins as an act of imaginative empathy. Martin Luther King Jr.'s "I Have a Dream" was not a policy proposal; it was an act of creative vision. It bridged moral principle and emotional resonance, translating ideal into imagery. That is the essence of integrative creativity: the union of vision and understanding.

Artificial intelligence will amplify human creativity but cannot replace it. Algorithms can suggest possibilities humans might overlook, but it is the human who decides what matters. Collaboration between human and machine thus becomes an exercise in complementarity: machines extend reach, humans preserve meaning. The most powerful creations of the coming century will emerge not from opposition between human and machine, but from integration—where technology amplifies imagination rather than imitates it.

However, this collaboration carries ethical responsibility. The easier it becomes to generate, the more essential discernment becomes. Abundance without curation leads to noise. Integrative creativity requires restraint: the willingness to say no, to refine, to prioritize integrity over novelty. The abundance of synthetic content will test humanity's ability to distinguish creation from clutter. Only creative intelligence anchored in empathy and ethics can maintain that distinction.

Ultimately, integrative creativity reflects the highest synthesis of human intelligence: the convergence of reason, emotion, and imagination into coherent understanding. It is the process through which humans participate in evolution—not biological, but psychological and cultural. Creativity is how consciousness expands. Each genuine act of creation redefines what it means to be human.

In the Artificial Era, creativity will no longer be measured by originality alone but by integration—the ability to connect complexity into clarity, and progress into purpose. Machines can imitate thought, but only humans can reconcile it with feeling. Integrative creativity is that reconciliation: the joining of intellect and empathy, innovation and ethics, imagination and identity.

The future will not belong to the most efficient systems, but to the most creative integrations. Those who can weave knowledge into meaning, and meaning into direction, will remain the architects of civilization.

* * *

8

Learning Without Linear Growth

T he story of education has always been one of containment. For centuries, learning was bounded—by subject, by institution, by lifespan. Knowledge could be mastered, disciplines could be defined, and expertise could be maintained. A scholar might devote a lifetime to a single domain, confident that its core principles would endure. That world has vanished. In the Artificial Era, information doubles faster than the human mind can assimilate. The half-life of knowledge has shortened to months. Expertise, once an endpoint, has become a moving target.

This acceleration forces a psychological reckoning. What does it mean to learn when mastery is impossible? How does one find confidence in a landscape that never stops shifting? Traditional education prepared individuals for stability; the new world demands adaptability. The ability to learn continuously, to integrate rather than accumulate, has become the defining trait of human relevance. Learning without linear growth means relinquishing the illusion of arrival and embracing the discipline of renewal.

Artificial intelligence has exposed the limits of traditional learning models. Machines now perform tasks once reserved for specialists: diagnosing disease, writing code, composing essays, generating designs. The human advantage is no longer knowledge itself but the ability to navigate it—to question, reinterpret, and connect. Learning is no longer a staircase of cumulative achievement but an ecosystem of perpetual adaptation. Success depends less on what one knows and more on how one responds when what one knows becomes obsolete.

Psychologically, this shift mirrors the transition from a fixed to a growth orientation, but it goes further. Carol Dweck's research on growth mindset emphasized the value of seeing ability as developable rather than predetermined. The next stage is *fluid mindset*: the recognition that even knowledge structures themselves must evolve. This requires cognitive flexibility—the capacity to revise mental frameworks without losing coherence. The mind becomes less a library and more a living organism, constantly reorganizing in response to change.

In this environment, curiosity replaces certainty as the engine of learning. The learner becomes an explorer rather than an expert. Questions take precedence over conclusions. The skill is not to memorize information, but to engage it—to discern relevance, synthesize patterns, and apply insight across boundaries. Learning transforms from product to process, from possession to participation.

Cultural expectations, however, have not caught up with this reality. Many still equate education with credentials and equate progress with accumulation. But in an infinite world, accumulation without interpretation leads to stagnation. The mind becomes cluttered with knowledge that no longer connects. The challenge is not to learn more, but to learn differently—to privilege depth of understanding over breadth of information, adaptability over authority.

True education in this century must therefore be psychological as much as intellectual. It must teach not only facts, but frameworks: how to unlearn, how to reflect, and how to integrate across domains. These are the meta-skills that sustain relevance amid change. They turn learning into resilience—a dynamic equilibrium between stability and evolution.

This chapter examines that transformation through four lenses. It begins with the death of mastery, exploring why expertise can no longer be static and why continual unlearning has become the hallmark of intelligence. It then turns to curiosity as a disciplined state of mind, not a passing impulse.

From there, it considers meta-learning—the art of understanding how one learns—and concludes with cross-domain thinking as the ultimate form of cognitive adaptability.

To learn without linear growth is to live as a student of motion itself. It is to recognize that education is no longer preparation for life but participation in it. The goal is not to arrive at certainty, but to remain awake to possibility.

The Death of Mastery

For centuries, mastery stood as the pinnacle of human achievement. It implied permanence: a craftsman mastering his trade, a scholar mastering his discipline, a teacher mastering her subject. The word itself carried reverence, suggesting command, authority, and completion. To master something was to reach an end state—a plateau of competence from which one could teach others or rest in expertise. The Industrial Era depended on this model; it prized specialization, repetition, and hierarchy. The master knew, the apprentice learned, and the cycle reproduced stability. But the conditions that made mastery possible no longer exist.

In the Artificial Era, the concept of mastery is undergoing quiet extinction. The rate of change has surpassed the rhythm of human assimilation. Fields that once evolved over decades now transform in months. A medical textbook can be outdated before it reaches print; a programming language can fade before its graduates enter the workforce. Mastery, once a guarantee of relevance, has become a liability if it resists revision. Expertise that cannot adapt ossifies. The future belongs not to the master of a single domain, but to the adaptive learner who can transfer skill across shifting landscapes.

Psychologically, the death of mastery is disorienting. Human identity has long been tied to competence. People draw self-esteem from what they know and can control. When expertise becomes unstable, so does the self that depends on it. Professionals who once defined themselves through mastery—doctors, teachers, engineers, even academics—now face an existential dilemma: if knowledge is temporary, what does it mean to be an expert? The emotional undertone of this shift is grief. Individuals must mourn the loss of permanence in order to embrace the freedom of reinvention.

This grief follows a familiar psychological pattern. Denial appears first: insisting that "real" expertise will always be irreplaceable. Bargaining follows—adapting incrementally, clinging to fragments of authority. Then comes disillusionment, as automation replaces tasks once thought uniquely human. The final stage, if reached, is acceptance: recognizing that mastery has not disappeared, but evolved. The new mastery lies not in control but in adaptability. It is not the perfection of knowledge, but the continual renewal of perspective.

To understand this transformation, it helps to distinguish between *closed* and *open* systems of knowledge. In closed systems—such as classical mathematics or ancient crafts—the rules remain constant. The master learns them fully and transmits them unchanged. In open systems—such as technology, psychology, and culture—rules shift with new information. In these environments, mastery becomes a process rather than a product. The master is the one who keeps learning, who remains porous to change.

This transition parallels a broader shift in cognitive science from static intelligence to dynamic intelligence. Early IQ models assumed intelligence was a fixed trait. Modern research recognizes it as a fluid system responsive to context and experience. The same is true for expertise. It is not what one possesses, but what one maintains through engagement. Mastery has moved from noun to verb.

Historically, mastery flourished under conditions of scarcity. Knowledge was difficult to access, and those who possessed it held power. Apprenticeships, guilds, and universities preserved this hierarchy. Today, knowledge is abundant and accessible to anyone with connectivity. The democratization of information has flattened expertise, eroding the old markers of authority. Credentials matter less than adaptability. A curious mind with access to open data can challenge traditional experts. The advantage once held by mastery has been replaced by the agility of continuous learners.

Culturally, this shift creates tension. Societies still reward confidence and certainty, even as the world demands flexibility. Many professionals experience what organizational psychologists call *expertise trap*: the tendency to cling to outdated methods because they once worked. Think of the seasoned marketing executive who insists on television advertising strategies in an era dominated by micro-influencers and social media algorithms. The more success one has achieved under old rules, the harder it becomes to abandon them. Paradoxically, mastery can blind. It narrows perception, reinforcing patterns that prevent innovation. Cognitive psychologist Gerd Gigerenzer referred to this as the "curse of expertise"—a rigidity born of proficiency. The skill that once ensured survival can become the very thing that prevents adaptation.

In educational settings, the death of mastery challenges traditional pedagogy. The linear model—learn, master, apply—no longer matches the realities of change. Students must now learn to unlearn. This requires cultivating meta-cognitive awareness: the ability to observe one's own thinking and revise it. Teaching, therefore, must shift from transmission to transformation. The role of the educator is not to produce experts, but to produce learners capable of reconfiguration.

This does not mean mastery has no place, but that its meaning has changed. Mastery now refers not to finality but to fluency—the ability to move fluidly between states of knowing and not knowing. It is not static control but dynamic competence. The musician who improvises, the surgeon who adapts mid-operation, the entrepreneur who redefines strategy—all display mastery in motion. What unites them is not perfection, but presence: an attunement to change.

From a psychological perspective, this new mastery demands emotional flexibility. It requires tolerating uncertainty without paralysis and maintaining curiosity in the face of disruption. The ability to let go of outdated knowledge is a form of humility. This humility is not self-doubt but realism—the acknowledgment that learning is never complete. Cognitive scientist Donald Schön called this "reflective practice": the discipline of examining one's assumptions while acting. It transforms expertise into awareness.

In organizational life, mastery once meant predictability; now it means adaptability. The best leaders are not those who impose certainty, but those who model learning. They invite experimentation, encourage dissent, and normalize revision. The workplace becomes an ecosystem of exploration rather than a hierarchy of control. Companies that fail to evolve collapse under their own inertia. Kodak, Blockbuster, and countless others perished not from ignorance but from fidelity to what they once mastered. The new economy rewards psychological agility more than procedural excellence.

The collapse of mastery also transforms motivation. When outcomes are unstable, intrinsic motivation—curiosity, purpose, growth—replaces extrinsic validation as the sustainable driver of performance. Psychologist Edward Deci's self-determination theory identifies autonomy and competence as essential to motivation. In a world where external standards shift constantly, autonomy becomes the only reliable source of meaning. The learner must locate purpose internally rather than in fixed benchmarks of success.

The emotional dimension of this transition cannot be overstated. Many experience anxiety when old competencies lose value. This anxiety is not pathology; it is the psyche's adjustment to new complexity. What was once predictable now feels provisional. Learning to live within that fluidity is a developmental milestone, not a failure. It signifies psychological maturity— the recognition that identity, like knowledge, is ongoing construction.

Philosophically, the death of mastery invites a return to humility as a virtue. Socrates' declaration of knowing that he knew nothing was not an admission of ignorance, but a model of continuous inquiry. In an infinite world, the wise are not those who possess knowledge but those who remain teachable. Theologian Paul Tillich described faith as "the courage to accept acceptance." Learning now requires a similar courage: the willingness to accept uncertainty as permanent and to continue engaging nonetheless.

Cognitive neuroscience supports this principle. Studies on neuroplasticity have shown that the brain remains capable of change throughout life. Mastery, therefore, is not limited by age but by rigidity. The mind that continues to challenge itself retains vitality; the one that clings to certainty calcifies. Lifelong learning is not a slogan—it is biology's design for adaptation.

Culturally, societies that cling to static mastery risk collective stagnation. Nations that prize conformity over curiosity struggle to innovate. Educational and professional systems must evolve from credentialism to creativity, from protection of expertise to cultivation of experimentation. The mastery of the future will not be measured in retention but in reinvention—the speed and depth with which people can adapt to new contexts while preserving ethical coherence.

The death of mastery, then, is not an obituary but an evolution. What dies is the illusion of completion; what emerges is the practice of perpetual refinement. To master something today is to know how to keep remaking it—to view skill as relationship, not possession. The mind that can learn, unlearn, and relearn without collapsing into confusion embodies the highest form of intelligence available to the human species.

The age of mastery as dominance is over. The age of mastery as adaptability has begun. The craftsman of the future will not say, "I have mastered this," but "I am in conversation with it." That conversation—between knowledge and humility, between structure and change—is the new definition of expertise.

Curiosity as Discipline

Curiosity has always been romanticized as a spark—an impulse that leads to discovery. It is often described as childlike, spontaneous, and unrestrained. Yet in an age defined by distraction, curiosity must evolve from impulse to discipline. It can no longer rely on the accident of inspiration; it must become a practiced form of attention. The future of learning will not belong to those who are merely curious, but to those who know how to sustain curiosity amid noise, uncertainty, and overload.

The psychology of curiosity reveals it as both emotional and cognitive. At its core, curiosity arises from a gap between what is known and what is unknown. The mind detects an absence, and this absence generates motivation. Neuroscientific studies show that curiosity activates the brain's reward circuitry, particularly the dopaminergic system. This means the pursuit of knowledge operates much like the pursuit of pleasure—it releases anticipation. But unlike impulsive reward-seeking, disciplined curiosity directs this energy toward exploration rather than distraction. It transforms restlessness into inquiry.

The modern environment, however, undermines this process. The same system that evolved to reward discovery is now hijacked by trivial novelty. Social media platforms and attention economies exploit the brain's reward mechanisms by providing endless stimulation without depth. The result is what psychologists call *information fatigue syndrome*: chronic exposure to fragmented novelty that produces shallow engagement. People remain curious, but their curiosity scatters rather than deepens. The challenge, then, is not to awaken curiosity, but to anchor it—to protect it from dissipation.

This requires redefining curiosity as a form of focus. The philosopher William James wrote that "genius means little more than the faculty of perceiving in an unhabitual way." Curiosity cultivates this faculty, but only when disciplined through sustained attention. In this sense, curiosity is not the opposite of rigor; it is its foundation. It demands endurance of uncertainty, tolerance of confusion, and patience with complexity. The curious mind must learn to linger in ambiguity long enough for insight to emerge.

Psychologist George Loewenstein's "information gap theory" provides a useful model. When people become aware of something they do not know, they experience a tension between curiosity and discomfort. The disciplined learner learns to harness that discomfort, using it as propulsion rather than frustration. Curiosity thus becomes a regulator of anxiety—a constructive way to engage the unknown rather than avoid it. In a world of constant change, this emotional regulation may be one of the most vital survival skills available.

In education, curiosity has often been treated as a prelude to learning rather than its core method. Classrooms structured around standardized answers teach students to suppress curiosity in favor of compliance. Yet genuine learning begins not with the acquisition of information but with the formulation of questions. Questions organize attention; they determine what information becomes meaningful. Teaching curiosity therefore means teaching how to ask, refine, and pursue questions that matter.

The historian Jacob Bronowski once said that "science is the refusal to believe that the world is simple." Curiosity sustains that refusal. It insists on complexity, on multiple perspectives, on the awareness that each answer opens further questions. This recursive nature is what makes curiosity exhausting but also transformative. To remain curious requires humility—the acknowledgment of ignorance—and courage—the willingness to confront it. Most people lose curiosity not because they lose intelligence, but because they lose tolerance for uncertainty.

Discipline in curiosity also involves selection. Not all unknowns are worth pursuing. In an information-saturated environment, discernment becomes essential. The disciplined learner chooses depth over breadth, significance over novelty. This mirrors the psychological distinction between *divergent thinking* (the generation of many possibilities) and *convergent thinking* (the evaluation of their worth). A disciplined researcher might spend a week exploring dozens of tangential articles (divergent), but then a month focused on synthesizing the three most relevant sources into a new idea (convergent). Productive curiosity alternates between the two. It explores widely, then refines narrowly. Without this alternation, curiosity becomes either restless or rigid.

Curiosity as discipline also demands the cultivation of stillness. Paradoxically, the more one seeks to know, the more one must learn to pause. Insight requires incubation—the mind's quiet processing of complexity beneath awareness. Studies in cognitive psychology show that moments of rest and daydreaming enhance creative problem-solving. Curiosity, to be sustained, must oscillate between engagement and rest. The brain, like any system, needs recovery to reorganize.

Emotionally, curiosity serves as antidote to fear. Fear constricts attention; curiosity expands it. When confronted with uncertainty, the curious mind asks, "What is this?" while the anxious mind asks, "What if this harms me?" The difference determines psychological flexibility. The same unknown that paralyzes one person can motivate another. Curiosity transforms threat into information, restoring agency where anxiety would otherwise dominate. In this way, curiosity is not only a cognitive virtue but an emotional one.

Cultural and educational systems often fail to protect this virtue. The industrial model of schooling prized conformity over inquiry, rewarding correct answers over good questions. This model produced compliance, not curiosity. Yet the conditions of the Artificial Era demand precisely the opposite. Machines excel at retrieving answers; humans excel at framing questions. The future of education lies in cultivating the capacity to wonder intelligently—to structure inquiry in ways that generate understanding rather than replication.

In the workplace, curiosity as discipline distinguishes innovation from imitation. Organizations that encourage questioning evolve; those that punish it stagnate. Psychological safety—the feeling that one can ask, challenge, and experiment without punishment—is the foundation of creative culture. Research by Amy Edmondson at Harvard has shown that teams high in psychological safety outperform others because they learn faster. They make more mistakes, but they correct them more intelligently. Curiosity, institutionalized as practice, becomes collective intelligence.

From a neurological standpoint, curiosity shapes learning efficiency. Studies have shown that when people are curious, they retain information more deeply and across unrelated domains. This suggests that curiosity primes the brain for integration, not just absorption. It enhances pattern recognition—the very skill that allows humans to connect ideas across disciplines. In this sense, curiosity is the foundation of both creativity and wisdom. It turns information into structure.

Curiosity is also moral. To be curious about others is to resist prejudice. It opens space for empathy by replacing assumption with exploration. The moral failures of any era—racism, fanaticism, dehumanization—share a common root: incuriosity. When people stop asking who others are, they begin defining them instead. Curiosity sustains moral imagination by maintaining interest in the unfamiliar. It insists that understanding precedes judgment.

Discipline ensures that this curiosity remains constructive rather than voyeuristic. Genuine curiosity seeks understanding, not dominance. It respects mystery even as it investigates it. This ethical form of curiosity anchors exploration in empathy, preventing it from devolving into exploitation. In education, this principle translates into teaching not only how to question, but how to do so responsibly—with awareness of consequence.

At its deepest level, curiosity is an orientation toward reality itself. It is the refusal to turn away from complexity, the insistence on relationship with what is unknown. To practice curiosity as discipline is to remain alive to the evolving world rather than retreating into certainty. It requires endurance of discomfort and commitment to comprehension. The mind that can sustain curiosity without closure becomes the mind most fit for an infinite world.

Curiosity's greatest power is that it transforms limitation into possibility. Every gap in knowledge becomes an opening rather than a wound. In this way, curiosity becomes a psychological form of hope. It affirms that understanding is still possible even in a universe that will never be fully known.

In the age of artificial intelligence, curiosity reclaims its centrality. Machines can retrieve, but they cannot wonder. They can predict, but they cannot care why. Human beings remain the species capable of astonishment. The discipline of curiosity ensures that this capacity is preserved—not as a fleeting impulse, but as a cultivated state of mind.

To live curiously is to live intelligently, ethically, and awake. Curiosity connects the limits of knowledge to the infinite horizon of meaning. It is not what humans know that will sustain them in the Artificial Era, but how persistently they are willing to ask.

Meta-Learning

The question of how people learn has always carried both scientific and existential weight. To learn is to change, and to understand how one learns is to understand how one changes. Meta-learning—the capacity to study, refine, and direct one's own learning process—is therefore the hidden architecture of human adaptability. It is the mechanism that turns experience into wisdom. In the Artificial Era, where information multiplies faster than comprehension, meta-learning is no longer an advantage; it is a necessity.

To learn without reflection is to accumulate without integration. Knowledge remains inert until it is organized by awareness. Meta-learning provides that organization. It involves not only the ability to acquire new skills but to evaluate *how* they are acquired: how attention is managed, how memory operates, how motivation fluctuates, and how feedback informs revision. It is learning applied to learning—a recursive skill that transforms education from external instruction to internal mastery.

Psychologically, meta-learning depends on metacognition—the awareness of one's own cognitive processes. The term, popularized by developmental psychologist John Flavell, describes the mind's ability to monitor and regulate itself. When learners recognize how they think, they can adjust their strategies. This self-regulation separates intentional learning from passive exposure. It turns the learner from consumer of information into curator of understanding.

Modern cognitive science supports this distinction. Studies consistently show that students who engage in metacognitive reflection—asking themselves what they understand, what they don't, and what strategies will help—outperform those who do not. The act of monitoring learning enhances retention and transfer across domains. This is because meta-learning activates executive control systems in the brain, integrating memory, attention, and emotion into coherent effort. It transforms randomness into purpose.

Meta-learning is, at its core, an act of humility. It begins with admitting that one's current way of learning may not be optimal. This admission requires psychological flexibility—the willingness to revise internal models of competence. In this sense, meta-learning is both cognitive and emotional. It demands self-awareness, patience, and resilience in the face of frustration. The learner must learn to learn, which means learning to fail intelligently.

Failure is, in fact, the engine of meta-learning. Without feedback, there is no refinement. The psychologist Donald Schön's concept of "reflection-in-action" captures this dynamic. He observed that professionals develop expertise not by following rules but by experimenting within practice—acting, observing results, adjusting, and acting again. This loop of feedback and reflection is the essence of adaptive intelligence. It transforms mistakes from shame into information.

Meta-learning also aligns with Carol Dweck's theory of growth mindset, yet it extends it further. A growth mindset focuses on the belief that abilities can be developed. Meta-learning applies that belief through structure. It converts optimism into process. The learner identifies what environments, routines, and mental states facilitate learning, then intentionally reproduces them. This metacognitive discipline distinguishes deliberate practice from repetition.

In the context of artificial intelligence, meta-learning has taken on a second, technical meaning. In machine learning, "meta-learning" refers to systems that can improve their own learning algorithms—machines that learn how to learn. The parallel is striking. Human meta-learning operates through a similar recursive mechanism: it is the self observing itself in action, adjusting parameters, and optimizing over time. The key difference is that human meta-learning is conscious. It is driven not only by efficiency but by meaning. Humans do not simply refine performance; they interpret experience.

This interpretive element makes meta-learning psychological rather than merely procedural. The human mind learns not only *what works* but *why it works*—and whether it aligns with purpose. Meaning gives direction to learning; it ensures that efficiency serves understanding rather than replacing it. Without reflection, learning risks becoming mechanical—productive but hollow. Meta-learning rehumanizes learning by reconnecting it to intention.

Culturally, the absence of meta-learning explains much of the frustration with contemporary education and work. Institutions still train for memorization in an age that rewards adaptability. Graduates enter professions equipped with static knowledge but without reflective tools to revise it. When confronted with novelty, they feel overwhelmed. Meta-learning fills this gap. It provides the psychological scaffolding to remain effective in dynamic systems.

From a developmental perspective, meta-learning matures over time. Children learn through imitation; adolescents begin to experiment with strategy; adults refine through reflection. Yet most people plateau early because their environments reward performance over awareness. The emphasis on results suppresses curiosity about process. Ironically, this undermines long-term competence. Mastery of content decays, but mastery of process endures. Those who understand how they learn can always learn again.

Meta-learning also bridges emotion and cognition. Learning is not a purely rational act; it is influenced by mood, stress, and self-perception. Recognizing these influences allows for regulation. A learner who notices that anxiety impairs recall can adjust through mindfulness or pacing. A learner who understands that novelty increases engagement can vary environments to sustain motivation. These adjustments are forms of psychological self-engineering—micro-calibrations that turn awareness into agency.

Philosophically, meta-learning reveals that knowledge is not static possession but ongoing participation. The mind is not a vessel to be filled but a system to be tuned. This echoes the pragmatist philosopher John Dewey, who defined education as the reconstruction of experience. Each act of reflection reorganizes perception, making future learning more efficient. The learner evolves as a system of feedback loops, perpetually refining itself through interaction with reality.

In practical terms, meta-learning can be cultivated through three inter-related habits: reflection, feedback, and iteration. For someone learning a new coding language, this might look like: noticing that they learn best in the morning (reflection); asking a mentor to review their code and point out recurring errors (feedback); and then focusing the next morning's session specifically on correcting that type of error (iteration). Reflection involves reviewing one's cognitive and emotional patterns—asking not just what was learned, but how it was learned. Feedback introduces external perspective, testing assumptions against results. Iteration applies the insights of both, producing continuous refinement. Together, these habits create resilience: the ability to remain effective under changing conditions.

In the professional realm, meta-learning translates to agility. Careers no longer follow linear trajectories; they unfold as adaptive networks. Individuals who practice meta-learning can pivot across roles and industries because they understand their own learning architecture. They do not rely on external stability to remain competent. This capacity for self-directed reinvention will define employability in the coming decades.

Emotionally, meta-learning transforms frustration into growth. When the learner understands that difficulty signals opportunity for reconfiguration, failure loses its sting. The mind becomes an ally rather than an adversary. Self-compassion replaces self-criticism. This shift has measurable effects on persistence and mental health. Learners who interpret struggle as feedback maintain motivation longer than those who interpret it as failure. Meta-learning thus functions as both cognitive and emotional resilience.

Culturally, embracing meta-learning represents a transition from authority to autonomy. The learner becomes self-governing, guided by curiosity and reflection rather than external validation. This autonomy does not reject expertise but engages it critically. It allows for dialogue rather than dependence. The educational systems that will thrive in the future will be those that empower learners to design their own processes of understanding—to become researchers of their own minds.

At a deeper level, meta-learning redefines identity. The self is no longer fixed by what it knows but by how it grows. This reframing aligns with existential psychology, which views identity as process rather than possession. The individual becomes an ongoing project, defined by relationship to learning rather than accumulation of knowledge. Meaning arises not from mastery but from movement—the continuous refinement of perception.

The spiritual dimension of meta-learning lies in its humility. It acknowledges the limits of understanding while affirming the capacity for expansion. It invites curiosity toward one's own consciousness. Each reflection reveals not only how one learns but who one is becoming in the process. In this way, meta-learning unites psychology and philosophy into a single practice: awareness applied to evolution.

The paradox of meta-learning is that it transforms learning from pursuit of certainty into acceptance of complexity. The more one understands how one learns, the more one sees the fluidity of knowledge itself. This recognition, rather than undermining confidence, deepens it. The learner becomes comfortable navigating ambiguity, grounded in the process rather than the product.

Ultimately, meta-learning is the psychological infrastructure of an infinite world. It equips the mind not merely to absorb information but to reorganize itself continually. It turns uncertainty into invitation, repetition into refinement, and experience into evolution. The learner who masters meta-learning never becomes obsolete, because the object of mastery is change itself.

Cross-Domain Thinking

Human progress has always depended on the ability to connect what was once separate. Civilization itself can be understood as the product of cross-domain thinking—the capacity to transfer ideas, metaphors, and methods from one field to another. Fire became metallurgy; metallurgy became architecture; architecture became symbolic thought. Every major leap in understanding has emerged from the intersection of disciplines, not their isolation. In an age defined by specialization and algorithmic partition, the ability to think across domains has become not only creative but essential.

Cross-domain thinking is the practice of integrating knowledge from multiple areas to form new perspectives. It is less about collecting information and more about translating insight. The mind that can move between frameworks—psychological, technological, biological, ethical—can perceive patterns invisible to those confined within a single paradigm. This integrative cognition represents the highest level of learning in a non-linear world: the ability to link ideas dynamically, seeing both their distinctions and their resonances.

Psychologically, cross-domain thinking relies on analogical reasoning—the process of mapping relationships between seemingly different concepts. Cognitive scientists such as Dedre Gentner have shown that analogy is not a rhetorical device but a cognitive engine. It allows humans to extract structural similarities between situations, enabling transfer of understanding. For example, the architect who studies biology learns how natural systems self-regulate and applies that insight to sustainable design. The psychologist who studies literature recognizes patterns of motivation and narrative structure that illuminate human behavior. These are not acts of imitation, but acts of translation.

The artificial environment, however, discourages such movement. Digital systems divide information into categories optimized for efficiency, not exploration. Algorithms reinforce existing preferences, narrowing the scope of exposure. Specialization, while necessary for depth, becomes a cognitive silo when unbalanced. The expert, trapped within a field, risks knowing more and understanding less. The generalist, conversely, perceives the wider system but may lack rigor. Cross-domain thinking reconciles the two. It maintains depth through discipline but expands relevance through connection.

Historically, polymaths exemplified this synthesis. Figures such as Leonardo da Vinci, Ibn Sina, and Ada Lovelace drew from art, mathematics, and philosophy to generate new insight. Their brilliance did not arise from omniscience but from relational intelligence—the ability to translate knowledge across contexts. In modern times, the fragmentation of disciplines has made such integration rare, yet the principle remains vital. The problems confronting humanity—climate change, artificial intelligence, social disconnection—are transdisciplinary by nature. They cannot be solved by expertise alone. Solving climate change, for example, requires not only climate scientists but also behavioral psychologists to encourage sustainable habits, economists to model new markets, and ethicists to navigate questions of global justice. They demand minds capable of synthesis.

Cross-domain thinking also reshapes the nature of intelligence itself. Psychologist Robert Sternberg proposed a triarchic model of intelligence: analytical, creative, and practical. Analytical intelligence dissects problems; creative intelligence recombines them; practical intelligence applies them to real-world contexts. Cross-domain thinking unites all three. It integrates analysis, imagination, and application into one continuous process. The thinker becomes a bridge between theory and practice, between what is known and what is possible.

This integrative capacity also has a neurological basis. The brain's creative processes depend on the interaction between the default mode network (associated with internal reflection and imagination) and the executive control network (associated with focus and logic). Cross-domain thinking strengthens communication between these systems. When ideas from one domain activate neural pathways in another, new combinations emerge. The neuroscientist Nancy Andreasen described this as "associative richness"—a state where distant neural networks synchronize, producing insight.

From an educational perspective, fostering cross-domain thinking requires redesigning learning itself. Traditional curricula isolate disciplines: science here, art there, philosophy elsewhere. This segmentation mirrors the industrial model that prioritized efficiency over integration. Yet the most powerful learning experiences occur at the boundaries—where disciplines overlap. A course that merges psychology with design teaches not only how humans think but how environments shape thought. A program that combines ethics with engineering cultivates not only innovation but responsibility. Cross-domain education trains the mind to move, not to stay put.

Emotionally, cross-domain thinking develops cognitive empathy. To think across disciplines is to think across perspectives. It trains the mind to inhabit multiple frameworks without collapsing them into one. This skill parallels interpersonal empathy—the ability to see through another's eyes without losing one's own. Cognitive flexibility becomes a moral as well as intellectual virtue. The person capable of integrative thought is less likely to succumb to ideological rigidity because they are practiced in translation rather than domination.

Culturally, societies that encourage cross-domain thinking produce more adaptive systems. The Renaissance flourished not because of individual genius alone but because of a cultural structure that valued intersection. Artists studied anatomy; scientists studied proportion; theologians studied nature. The result was a shared vocabulary between disciplines that allowed knowledge to evolve synergistically. The challenge of the twenty-first century is to recreate that integrative spirit within global networks that often fragment meaning.

The Artificial Era, paradoxically, makes this both easier and harder. Easier, because information from every field is now accessible; harder, because abundance breeds overload. The key is synthesis—the ability to discern which connections are meaningful. Cross-domain thinking, then, is not random eclecticism. It is disciplined integration. It requires deep engagement with multiple frameworks, followed by the imaginative leap that links them.

In practice, this means cultivating three capacities: analogical curiosity, contextual awareness, and integrative reflection. Analogical curiosity seeks relationships between systems rather than differences. Contextual awareness situates ideas within their historical and functional environments. Integrative reflection weaves these understandings into coherent applica-tion. Together, these habits train the mind to move fluidly between the particular and the universal, between concrete detail and abstract principle.

Psychologically, cross-domain thinking nurtures resilience. When one framework fails, the mind can pivot to another. The biologist who also understands philosophy sees meaning where others see only data. The economist versed in behavioral psychology can anticipate human reactions beyond numerical prediction. This adaptability prevents cognitive rigidity—the psychological trap of overidentifying with a single worldview. It equips the learner to remain effective in uncertainty.

Ethically, cross-domain thinking serves as a safeguard against reductionism. When knowledge is confined to one field, morality risks becoming mechanical. A technologist who ignores psychology builds systems that manipulate rather than serve. A psychologist who ignores economics misunderstands the structural forces shaping emotion. Integration restores proportion. It reconnects science with humanity, progress with purpose.

At the personal level, cross-domain thinking revitalizes curiosity. It allows the mind to rediscover wonder by seeing the familiar through foreign eyes. A poet studying neuroscience finds metaphor in synapse; a physicist reading philosophy finds law in paradox. Each translation renews perception, keeping learning alive. This renewal is the essence of lifelong education. It ensures that the learner never reaches an intellectual dead end, because there is always another boundary to cross.

Cross-domain thinking also reshapes creativity. Originality no longer resides in invention from nothing but in recombination with intention. The modern creator assembles meaning from fragments—scientific, aesthetic, ethical—into coherent wholes. This integrative creativity, discussed earlier, is inseparable from cross-domain cognition. The ability to navigate multiple frameworks becomes the engine of innovation.

In professional environments, cross-domain thinkers often become translators—individuals who bridge communication between specialists. They turn complexity into clarity. Their value lies not in depth alone but in connection. As artificial intelligence accelerates specialization, the demand for human integrators will increase. Machines can optimize within domains; humans must synthesize between them. The capacity to link, not to isolate, will define leadership in the decades ahead.

Philosophically, cross-domain thinking restores wholeness to knowledge. The Enlightenment's division of science and humanities produced extraordinary advances but also fragmentation of understanding. Today, that division is reaching its limit. Questions of meaning, ethics, and identity cannot be solved through data alone. Reintegrating disciplines does not mean abandoning rigor; it means restoring context. The world's problems are ecological in nature—interdependent, systemic, relational. Only integrative minds can address them coherently.

The psychology of learning confirms this principle. Transfer of learning—the ability to apply knowledge in new contexts—is the ultimate test of understanding. Students who can explain a concept across domains demonstrate deeper mastery than those who can only repeat it within one. This is because cross-domain transfer requires abstraction—the distillation of principle from context. It is, in essence, thinking about thinking applied to knowledge itself.

Ultimately, cross-domain thinking is an act of integration—within the mind and between minds. It reclaims learning as dialogue rather than competition. It transforms specialization into collaboration and expertise into empathy. The learner who can think across domains becomes an architect of coherence in a fragmented age.

In the infinite world of the Artificial Era, cross-domain thinking is the closest thing humanity has to a survival strategy. It ensures that knowledge remains alive, dynamic, and human. To connect is to understand; to integrate is to evolve.

* * *

9

The Future of Work and Worth

Redefining Success When Efficiency Is Free

The story of work has always been the story of worth. For most of human history, labor was survival—an exchange of effort for security. Later, during industrialization, work became identity. Occupation defined status, structure, and self. People learned to introduce themselves by what they did rather than who they were. The modern era refined this further: work became a moral measure, a way to prove discipline, ambition, and belonging. Yet that moral structure now stands on shifting ground. Automation and artificial intelligence have begun eroding the foundation on which these definitions were built. When machines can perform most tasks faster, cheaper, and without fatigue, the central question of the twenty-first century emerges: what is the human worth of work when efficiency is free?

The coming transformation is not simply economic—it is psychological. The automation of labor represents the automation of validation. For generations, productivity has been the primary currency of identity. The harder one worked, the more one was worth. This equation has shaped modern culture, education, and even morality. But as productivity becomes detached from personhood, the human need for meaning seeks new anchors.

The challenge ahead is not to preserve employment as it once was, but to redefine fulfillment in terms that transcend output.

Psychology provides a useful lens for understanding this shift. Abraham Maslow's hierarchy of needs culminated in self-actualization—the fulfillment of one's potential. Yet Maslow assumed stability at the base: that physiological and economic needs were secured through work. In the Artificial Era, that assumption collapses. Machines now meet many of those lower needs independently of human labor. The hierarchy must invert. Instead of work providing meaning, meaning must now provide the reason for work. Purpose becomes the foundation, not the reward.

This transformation reintroduces questions long buried beneath industrial pragmatism: What is a good life? What does it mean to contribute? How should humans measure success when productivity no longer distinguishes them? These are not philosophical luxuries; they are psychological necessities. When people cannot locate meaning within their labor, they experience what sociologist Émile Durkheim called *anomie*—a loss of moral direction within society. The epidemic of burnout and disengagement seen in modern workplaces reflects this crisis of coherence. The solution lies not in increasing efficiency, but in reimagining relationship.

The future of work will depend less on what people produce and more on how they participate. The essential skills of the coming decades—empathy, judgment, creativity, and moral discernment—cannot be automated because they require consciousness. Human worth will be measured not by throughput but by contribution: the capacity to create connection, foster understanding, and align action with value. These are the dimensions of work that make civilization more than a mechanism.

Economically, this represents a seismic shift. Culturally, it represents a renaissance. Work will evolve from transaction to transformation, from labor to learning, from production to presence. Organizations will need to provide more than paychecks; they will need to provide purpose. Individuals, in turn, will need to cultivate inner direction rather than external validation.

This chapter explores that transformation in five parts. It begins by examining the new psychological contract between employees and organizations, followed by an analysis of meaning as a modern metric of value. It then considers the emergence of hybrid roles that integrate human and artificial intelligence, before concluding with practical frameworks for designing lives that remain anchored in purpose amid constant change.

The question of the future is not whether there will be work, but what kind of work will make us whole.

The New Psychological Contract

The relationship between employer and employee has always rested on an invisible agreement—what organizational psychologists call the *psychological contract*. Unlike formal contracts, this one is unwritten. It represents the shared assumptions, expectations, and emotional commitments that bind people to institutions. For much of the twentieth century, that contract was transactional and predictable: loyalty in exchange for stability, effort in exchange for advancement, obedience in exchange for security. Companies provided continuity; workers provided identity. It was not equality, but it was coherence. Everyone knew the rules.

That world no longer exists. Automation, globalization, and digitization have rendered permanence obsolete. Organizations now restructure at the speed of innovation. Job roles mutate; industries collapse; entire professions dissolve into algorithms. In this environment, the old psychological contract—anchored in predictability—has fractured. Loyalty can no longer depend on longevity, and security can no longer depend on control. The emotional economy of work is being rewritten.

Psychologically, this rupture produces disorientation. Work has long served as one of the central structures through which people interpret meaning. It orders time, validates effort, and connects individuals to a collective purpose. When that structure becomes unstable, the mind struggles to locate coherence. This is why layoffs, even when economically rational, often feel existentially violent. They do not merely disrupt income; they disrupt identity. The loss is not just occupational but ontological—the sense of who one is in relation to the world.

The modern workforce, therefore, is not experiencing a loss of motivation but a crisis of trust. The old assumptions—work hard, stay loyal, and the system will reward you—no longer hold. The erosion of that promise has produced widespread cynicism, burnout, and disengagement. Gallup's research on employee engagement reveals that only a minority of workers worldwide feel emotionally invested in their jobs. The rest occupy a gray zone of detached efficiency. They perform tasks but not meaning. This disengagement is not laziness; it is psychological realism. People no longer believe that organizations reciprocate care.

The new psychological contract must address this deficit of trust. It cannot be rebuilt on promises of permanence; those promises would be dishonest. Instead, it must be founded on transparency, reciprocity, and purpose. Transparency replaces illusion with clarity—organizations must communicate not as hierarchies issuing directives but as systems inviting participation. Reciprocity replaces dependency with mutual growth—employees contribute innovation and creativity, and organizations provide environments that foster learning and autonomy. Purpose replaces mere compensation with coherence—work must connect to something intrinsically valuable, something that justifies effort beyond transaction.

This shift transforms management into stewardship. The leader of the future is not a controller of labor but a curator of meaning. Leadership psychologist Peter Drucker once predicted that knowledge workers would require a new kind of management—one that inspires rather than instructs. That prediction has matured into necessity. In environments where workers possess specialized expertise and flexible mobility, control fails. Influence now arises from purpose alignment, not authority.

From an organizational psychology perspective, this transformation reflects the transition from extrinsic to intrinsic motivation. In the industrial model, workers responded to external rewards—wages, promotions, and penalties. In the post-industrial model, meaningful work and autonomy predict higher performance. Self-determination theory, developed by Edward Deci and Richard Ryan, identifies three universal psychological needs: autonomy, competence, and relatedness. When work environments support these needs, motivation becomes self-sustaining. When they violate them, disengagement follows. The new contract, therefore, must design for these conditions rather than against them.

Autonomy is the cornerstone. People perform best when they feel agency over their actions. Micromanagement suppresses not only creativity but moral energy—the sense of ownership that turns work into contribution. Competence sustains engagement through mastery and feedback; it satisfies the human desire for growth. Relatedness binds individuals to community, affirming that their efforts matter within a larger whole. Organizations that meet these three needs do more than retain employees; they restore meaning to labor.

However, this new contract also demands maturity from workers. Autonomy without accountability collapses into entitlement. Growth without humility leads to burnout. The same freedoms that empower also require self-regulation. In the absence of external structure, individuals must develop internal discipline—a kind of psychological self-management that balances independence with interdependence. The workplace becomes a mirror of character as much as competence.

Culturally, this evolution reflects the broader movement from collectivist institutions to individualized systems. Traditional societies anchored identity in group membership; modern economies anchor it in performance. The emerging paradigm seeks a synthesis: individuality expressed through contribution. People want to belong without disappearing. They want their work to matter without surrendering autonomy. This paradox defines the modern worker's psyche—simultaneously independent and interdependent, seeking meaning yet resisting conformity.

Technology complicates this further. Remote work, automation, and virtual collaboration have dissolved physical proximity as the glue of connection. The office, once a social ecosystem, has become an interface. Relationships now depend on intentional communication rather than incidental contact. This transition reveals a paradox: flexibility increases freedom but decreases cohesion. The new psychological contract must therefore include relational design—the conscious cultivation of community through empathy, clarity, and shared narrative.

The organizations that thrive in this context will resemble ecosystems more than factories. They will function as adaptive networks of meaning, where people move fluidly between roles, projects, and partnerships. The measure of success will not be headcount but health—the psychological and ethical integrity of the system. When individuals feel seen, supported, and significant, they reciprocate with creativity and loyalty. The transaction becomes transformation.

The new psychological contract also redefines leadership accountability. Leaders must shift from managing output to managing energy—the emotional, cognitive, and ethical atmosphere that determines performance. This involves cultivating psychological safety, a concept popularized by Amy Edmondson, which describes environments where individuals feel free to speak, question, and fail without fear of humiliation. In such climates, learning accelerates because vulnerability becomes permissible.

From a moral standpoint, the new contract represents a return to reciprocity as a social value. The philosopher Martin Buber described genuine relationship as *I–Thou*, a dialogue between equal subjects. The industrial economy reduced this to *I–It*: worker as instrument, employer as mechanism. The post-industrial era offers a chance to restore *I–Thou* to labor—to treat work as encounter rather than extraction. When organizations recognize employees as partners in purpose, they humanize productivity.

Psychologically, this restoration also heals a deeper fracture: the separation between personal and professional identity. The modern workplace has long demanded the compartmentalization of emotion, morality, and authenticity. Employees were expected to perform roles rather than inhabit them. Yet research in organizational behavior confirms that authenticity predicts both satisfaction and performance. When people can align their internal values with their external roles, energy is released. They stop managing impressions and start investing meaningfully.

The generational shift in workplace expectations reflects this realignment.

186

Younger workers, particularly those raised in the digital era, no longer equate success with tenure or title. They prioritize alignment between work and self-concept. They ask not only "What do I earn?" but "What do I learn?" and "Who am I becoming?" This shift is not entitlement; it is evolution. It signals the maturation of a workforce that measures worth through purpose rather than permanence.

For organizations, adapting to this mindset requires courage. It means relinquishing control in favor of collaboration, replacing uniformity with diversity, and replacing secrecy with transparency. It requires viewing employees not as replaceable units but as partners in innovation. This transformation is demanding, but it is also redemptive. It restores humanity to systems that have long treated people as inputs.

For individuals, the new psychological contract offers liberation—but only if accompanied by accountability. Freedom without structure degenerates into chaos. The self must therefore develop what psychologists call *intrinsic scaffolding*: internal frameworks of integrity, purpose, and self-discipline that guide behavior when external authority dissolves. The autonomous worker becomes self-led, but not self-absorbed—motivated by contribution rather than compliance.

The future of work, then, depends on a mutual awakening. Organizations must rediscover their humanity; individuals must rediscover their maturity. The psychological contract of the future is not written in policy but enacted in culture. It is sustained not by promises, but by practices—by everyday moments of honesty, empathy, and shared responsibility.

In this redefined relationship, work reclaims its moral dimension. It becomes not only a means of production but a medium of meaning. The employer provides context; the employee provides consciousness. Together, they create coherence. This is the essence of the new psychological contract: a partnership rooted not in permanence, but in purpose.

Meaning as Metric

For generations, the language of work has been the language of measurement. Productivity, efficiency, and output have served as the dominant currencies of value. The worker's worth was quantified by how much could be produced in how little time. The logic of industry depended on predictability: tasks were standardized, results were measured, and meaning was assumed to follow achievement. Yet as automation begins to replicate most forms of measurable output, the question emerges: what remains to be measured when machines have mastered the metrics?

The answer is not more data, but a different kind of data. The next evolution of work requires a shift from quantitative evaluation to qualitative discernment—from counting what is visible to understanding what is valuable. Meaning becomes the new metric. It represents not an abstract ideal, but a concrete psychological reality: the degree to which one's work aligns with purpose, relationships, and ethical coherence. Unlike productivity, meaning cannot be automated, because it depends on human interpretation. It is the integration of effort, identity, and significance.

To grasp this transformation, it helps to understand why the productivity model persisted for so long. The industrial era framed human beings as extensions of machinery. Tasks were fragmented into parts, and labor was optimized for repetition. Efficiency became a virtue not only economically but morally; it symbolized control over chaos. The twentieth-century management culture that followed—scientific management, performance tracking, key performance indicators—reflected this mechanistic worldview. It offered clarity but at the cost of complexity. The human dimension of work—emotion, creativity, moral judgment—was relegated to the margins.

Now, as artificial intelligence perfects the efficiency once demanded of humans, the inadequacy of those metrics becomes visible. Machines can outperform humans in speed, precision, and endurance, but they cannot experience meaning. They cannot interpret why an action matters or how it contributes to the whole. The task for human beings is no longer to compete on performance but to cultivate significance.

Psychologically, meaning has measurable effects. Research in positive psychology, particularly the work of Martin Seligman and Michael F. Steger, demonstrates that meaningful work predicts well-being more consistently than high income or low stress. Employees who perceive their work as significant exhibit greater resilience, creativity, and cooperation. Meaning serves as a stabilizer; it transforms pressure into purpose. When individuals understand how their efforts connect to a larger purpose, they experience strain as investment rather than exploitation.

Meaning also functions as an antidote to burnout. Christina Maslach's research on occupational burnout identifies three components: exhaustion, cynicism, and inefficacy. Each arises when individuals feel disconnected from the significance of their work. Fatigue becomes burnout only when meaning erodes. The restoration of purpose is therefore not sentimental but strategic—it revives the emotional infrastructure of motivation.

Yet meaning is notoriously difficult to measure because it resists standardization. What gives one person purpose may leave another indifferent. The challenge for organizations, then, is not to impose meaning but to enable its discovery. Purpose cannot be mandated through slogans or mission statements. It must emerge from authentic alignment between the individual's values and the organization's aims. The new metric is not what employees *do*, but how coherently they can link their doing to their *why*.

To make meaning measurable, leaders must ask different questions. Instead of "How much did we produce?" they must ask "What difference did we make?" Instead of "Did we meet the target?" they must ask "Did this work advance something worth caring about?" These questions transform the nature of accountability. They move evaluation from performance management to purpose management.

Cultural shifts are already signaling this change. Younger generations entering the workforce increasingly choose employers based on value alignment rather than salary alone. Surveys from Deloitte and Pew Research indicate that millennials and Generation Z workers prioritize purpose, ethical practice, and social impact when selecting organizations. This is the software engineer who accepts a lower salary to work for a certified B Corporation, or the marketing graduate who turns down a lucrative job in the fossil fuel industry to join a renewable energy startup. This does not mean they reject ambition; it means they redefine it. Success becomes less about accumulation and more about contribution.

At the organizational level, this demands a rethinking of success metrics. Quantitative outcomes remain necessary—profits sustain survival—but they are no longer sufficient. Qualitative indicators such as employee engagement, trust, and moral culture become central. The healthiest organizations will be those that can balance measurable productivity with immeasurable purpose. They will understand that meaning is not a luxury but a resource.

Philosophically, this shift returns to the Aristotelian idea of *telos*—purpose as the organizing principle of action. Aristotle argued that every activity aims toward some good, and that the highest good is not efficiency but flourishing. The modern economy, having replaced *telos* with throughput, is rediscovering the psychological necessity of purpose. Work without meaning erodes dignity; it produces what Viktor Frankl called "existential vacuum"—a state of emptiness that no amount of material success can fill. Frankl, who endured and studied the extremes of human suffering, concluded that meaning is not found in comfort but in contribution. People are not destroyed by pain itself, he observed, but by the loss of reason for enduring it.

In the context of work, this means that employees will tolerate difficulty, ambiguity, and even imperfection when their effort feels purposeful. Meaning makes complexity bearable. Without it, even success becomes hollow. This insight carries profound implications for leadership: a leader's task is not merely to direct action but to interpret significance—to continually translate the organization's objectives into human relevance.

Meaning as metric also transforms how collaboration is understood. In the old model, teamwork was measured by efficiency—output per unit of coordination. In the new model, it is measured by coherence—the extent to which individuals feel part of a shared story. A team is not merely a collection of performers but a collective of interpreters. Their success depends not only on how well they execute but on how well they align around why it matters.

This reconceptualization of meaning does not imply abandoning metrics altogether. It means recalibrating them to reflect human realities. Measurement must expand to include emotional, ethical, and relational dimensions. For example, mentorship becomes a form of value creation—transferring wisdom across generations of professionals sustains institutional memory and morale. Similarly, emotional culture—the unwritten norms of empathy, respect, and communication—can be assessed through engagement surveys, turnover rates, and innovation outcomes. When employees feel psychologically safe and ethically aligned, productivity follows naturally.

The deeper transformation, however, is internal. Individuals must learn to self-measure through reflection rather than comparison. The external validation that once defined success—titles, metrics, approval—no longer guarantees fulfillment. The mature mind replaces those measures with internal coherence: "Am I acting in alignment with what I value?" This inward metric restores dignity to work because it reclaims agency. Meaning is not given; it is made through interpretation.

Practically, cultivating meaning involves three intertwined processes: recognition, reflection, and integration. Recognition identifies where one's skills and values intersect with social needs. Reflection interprets those intersections—why they matter and what they reveal about purpose. Integration aligns daily actions with those interpretations. This cycle converts experience into meaning and meaning into sustained motivation. It is the psychological architecture of relevance in a post-efficiency world.

Organizations that embed these processes into their culture develop resilience. When external conditions shift, their people adapt because their sense of purpose remains stable. Meaning provides continuity when structure changes. It allows flexibility without fragmentation. This is why purpose-driven companies often outperform competitors in long-term adaptability: their coherence protects them from moral fatigue.

The shift toward meaning as a metric also calls for humility. Not all work will feel profound at every moment, but even the simplest tasks can carry significance when interpreted within a larger framework. The janitor who keeps a hospital clean is not merely performing maintenance; they are preserving dignity for patients. The teacher who repeats the same lesson each year is not repeating content; they are renewing culture. Meaning transforms repetition into ritual. It gives ordinary labor its sacred dimension.

As artificial intelligence continues to absorb routine functions, the remaining human work will increasingly reside in this interpretive layer. Machines will manage execution; humans will manage significance. The highest value will belong to those who can sustain meaning in motion—to those who can continually re-contextualize their work in service of human flourishing.

In the end, meaning as a metric is not about replacing efficiency but restoring proportion. It reminds society that progress measured only in speed and scale is progress without direction. The true measure of a civilization is not what it can produce, but what it chooses to preserve. When meaning becomes the standard of worth, work reclaims its moral center.

The Rise of Hybrid Roles

The modern workplace is becoming a site of convergence. Where once human and machine operated in separate spheres, they now share the same cognitive space. Artificial intelligence has not replaced human labor so much as redefined it, dissolving the boundary between tool and thinker. In this new terrain, the most valuable professionals will not be those who resist technology, nor those who surrender entirely to it, but those who learn to integrate with it—those who become fluent in partnership. These are the hybrid roles of the Artificial Era.

Hybrid roles represent a profound shift in the structure of work. They emerge wherever automation and human judgment must collaborate. A financial analyst who uses predictive algorithms to detect market trends is a hybrid. A teacher who personalizes instruction with adaptive learning software is a hybrid. A physician who interprets AI-assisted diagnostics while counseling patients through uncertainty is a hybrid. Each combines the efficiency of computation with the depth of consciousness. The future of employment will depend on this synthesis: the ability to merge technical fluency with psychological intelligence.

The logic of hybridization follows an evolutionary pattern. In nature, organisms that survive environmental change are not the strongest but the most adaptable. They evolve by integration—by incorporating new functions without losing coherence. Similarly, the professions that will thrive are those that learn to integrate technology as an extension of human capability, not as a replacement for it. The goal is not to preserve old roles but to humanize new ones.

Psychologically, this shift requires reframing what it means to be competent. In the industrial model, expertise was defined by mastery of process. The worker was valued for precision and consistency. In the hybrid model, expertise is defined by adaptability of mind. The worker must understand not only how to use tools but how to think alongside them. This involves what psychologists call *metacognition*—awareness of one's own thinking processes. A hybrid professional monitors how technology influences perception and decision-making, adjusting accordingly.

This kind of cognitive self-awareness protects against what behavioral economists describe as *automation bias*: the tendency to overtrust algorithmic output. For instance, a hiring manager might uncritically accept an AI's recommendation to reject a candidate's resume, overlooking valuable experience because the algorithm was not programmed to recognize it. When a person defers too fully to machines, critical reasoning deteriorates. The hybrid thinker counteracts this by maintaining active interpretation. They use technology as an amplifier of insight, not a substitute for it. The result is not competition but collaboration—a feedback loop between intuition and information.

Culturally, hybrid roles signal a transition from mechanical labor to interpretive labor. In previous centuries, progress meant reducing human input; now it means refining it. As automation expands, human attention becomes the scarce resource. The value lies not in producing more data but in producing better discernment. This explains why even in highly automated industries, demand is increasing for skills in ethics, design, psychology, and communication. These domains train the ability to interpret complexity—something no algorithm can replicate.

Hybrid roles also challenge the traditional hierarchy of intelligence. For decades, society exalted technical expertise while undervaluing emotional and social intelligence. Yet as Daniel Goleman's work made clear, emotional intelligence often predicts success more accurately than IQ. In a world where machines supply information, the human advantage lies in empathy, nuance, and moral reasoning. The hybrid role, therefore, is not a downgrade of human intellect but its refinement. It turns emotional intelligence into a functional technology—an interface between computation and conscience.

The integration of AI into human work also invites a philosophical reconsideration of agency. When algorithms assist in decision-making, responsibility can become diffused. The hybrid professional must develop what moral philosophers call *reflective accountability*: the ability to trace decisions back to intention. They must continually ask, "Where does the human judgment begin and end in this process?" Without this awareness, ethical boundaries blur, and moral disengagement becomes normalized.

From an organizational perspective, hybridization transforms not only individual roles but the architecture of teams. Hierarchies flatten as expertise becomes distributed across both human and digital contributors. Collaboration shifts from command chains to dynamic networks where roles evolve fluidly based on context. Leadership, in turn, becomes more facilitative than directive—less about issuing orders and more about orchestrating interaction between human creativity and machine capability.

This demands a new literacy of coordination. Workers must learn to communicate across two languages: the language of data and the language of meaning. Data describes what is; meaning interprets why it matters. Hybrid professionals must move fluently between both, ensuring that information serves intention. The most valuable employees will not be those who merely understand technology but those who can translate its implications into human terms.

Educational institutions face a parallel transformation. Curricula designed for industrial-age careers—where knowledge was stable and specialization rewarded—must now cultivate cognitive agility. Students need training in both technical and psychological competencies: systems thinking, ethical reasoning, interdisciplinary collaboration. The future professional is a generalist in perspective and a specialist in synthesis. This does not mean knowing everything; it means knowing how things relate.

Hybrid roles also have an emotional dimension. Working alongside intelligent systems provokes ambivalence. People experience both empowerment and insecurity. They admire technology's precision but fear its judgment. This emotional tension reflects what psychologists call *identity dissonance*: the conflict between old self-concepts and emerging realities. The accountant who once defined worth through meticulous calculation must now find pride in interpretation. The journalist who once guarded objectivity must now balance credibility with algorithmic influence. Adapting to hybrid work is therefore not only a technical challenge but an existential one.

Resilience within this environment requires emotional flexibility—the ability to hold contradiction without paralysis. Humans must learn to see themselves not as victims of automation but as co-authors of evolution. This shift in self-concept transforms anxiety into agency. The hybrid worker recognizes that technology does not threaten meaning; it clarifies it by absorbing what was never truly meaningful to begin with—repetition without reflection.

In practical terms, the success of hybrid roles will depend on cultivating four interdependent capacities: discernment, empathy, creative reasoning, and ethical literacy.

Discernment allows individuals to evaluate when to rely on data and when to trust intuition. Empathy ensures that technological solutions remain human-centered. Creative reasoning enables novel synthesis between disparate inputs. Ethical literacy anchors innovation in responsibility. These capacities turn technological fluency into moral competence. They ensure that the fusion of human and artificial intelligence elevates civilization rather than eroding it.

There is also a sociological dimension to hybridization. As boundaries between sectors blur, new professions are emerging that defy classification: data ethicists, AI psychologists, human-experience designers. These roles embody the convergence of science and humanities, technology and psychology. They demonstrate that the future of work is not a replacement economy but a relational one. Progress will depend on integration across perspectives, not domination by one.

Hybrid work also redefines leadership. The effective leader of the future will not be the most technically skilled, but the most integrative—the one capable of synthesizing technical, emotional, and moral intelligence into coherent direction. They will understand that guiding hybrid teams requires fluency in both machine logic and human feeling. Such leadership transforms authority into alignment.

The most profound implication of hybrid roles, however, lies in their potential to restore dignity to work. For much of the industrial era, dignity was eroded by monotony. Tasks were fragmented to increase speed, stripping labor of meaning. Now, as machines absorb those fragments, humans can reclaim wholeness. The hybrid worker is not less human for collaborating with AI; they are more so. Freed from mechanical repetition, they can devote their attention to judgment, empathy, and creation—the capacities that define humanity.

This does not mean the transition will be easy. It requires retraining not only skills but identities. It asks societies to update their definitions of contribution and competence. Yet the potential reward is profound: a world where technology amplifies consciousness rather than replacing it.

To achieve this, both organizations and individuals must cultivate what can be called *adaptive integrity*—the ability to evolve without losing ethical coherence. Adaptive integrity ensures that progress remains tethered to principle. It balances flexibility with fidelity to human values. In hybrid systems, where decision-making is distributed between human and algorithm, this integrity becomes the moral compass of civilization.

Hybrid roles thus represent more than a new phase of employment; they symbolize a redefinition of human worth. They affirm that technology's highest function is not to replace the mind but to expand its reach. When human beings collaborate with intelligence rather than compete against it, the result is not artificial humanity but augmented wisdom.

The rise of hybrid roles is, in essence, a test of maturity. It asks whether humanity can integrate its creations without surrendering its conscience. The answer will depend not on innovation alone but on insight—on the willingness to see technology as mirror rather than master.

Designing a Life That Matters

To design a life that matters is not the same as designing a career that succeeds. The former concerns coherence; the latter, performance. The modern era has often conflated the two, convincing people that identity and worth can be engineered through achievement. But in a world where success is increasingly automated and measurable, the question of what makes life meaningful must be asked again—not as sentiment but as strategy.

When the predictable pathways of progress dissolve, individuals must construct meaning deliberately. Designing a life that matters means creating a psychological architecture that can withstand instability without collapsing into emptiness. It requires the integration of work, identity, and moral purpose into a coherent whole—a framework where effort serves not only survival but significance.

For centuries, society offered templates for such coherence. The religious, civic, and familial systems of earlier generations provided ready-made narratives of purpose. One could locate identity within these inherited structures. But modernity dismantled those narratives and replaced them with autonomy. Autonomy, while liberating, comes with a cost: the burden of authorship. To design a meaningful life in this era is to become the author of one's own story without the guarantee of an ending.

Psychologically, this challenge parallels what Viktor Frankl called the search for meaning—the human drive to find significance even in suffering. Frankl observed that those who could identify a purpose beyond themselves possessed greater resilience in adversity. Meaning, he concluded, does not eliminate difficulty but transforms it into direction. This insight is essential to the contemporary context. As technology automates function, humans must reclaim intention.

Designing a life that matters therefore begins not with external opportunity but with internal orientation. It asks the individual to articulate three core alignments: values, vocation, and vitality. Values define what one considers worthwhile. Vocation defines where those values intersect with contribution. Vitality ensures that the pursuit remains sustainable—that the self is not exhausted in service of its purpose. Together, these dimensions form the scaffolding of psychological meaning.

Values are the compass. They provide direction when external structures fail. Without clear values, success becomes shapeless—achievement without satisfaction. The psychologist Milton Rokeach described values as enduring beliefs about what is preferable to what. They anchor choice in coherence. In the absence of such anchoring, individuals drift between trends and expectations, mistaking movement for progress. Designing a meaningful life requires slowing down enough to ask: What principles would I still hold if there were no audience to affirm them?

Vocation translates those principles into practice. It is not synonymous with occupation but with orientation. The Latin root *vocare* means "to call." To have a vocation is to hear a call from within—to sense that one's efforts participate in something larger than the self. This does not always manifest in grand missions; often, it appears in small consistencies of care. The teacher who stays after class, the nurse who listens longer than required, the designer who prioritizes usability over spectacle—each enacts vocation through value in action.

Vitality sustains both. Modern burnout arises less from overwork than from disconnection—effort expended without meaning. A life that matters must preserve the energy required to continue caring. This means recognizing that rest is not indulgence but maintenance of moral clarity. Cognitive psychology shows that chronic fatigue diminishes ethical sensitivity and emotional regulation. When the body depletes, judgment deteriorates. Sustaining vitality, then, is an ethical responsibility. It protects one's ability to contribute wisely.

Culturally, the notion of designing one's life carries both promise and peril. The promise lies in freedom: individuals can shape identity without inherited limits. The peril lies in pressure: every choice becomes self-defining. The proliferation of self-optimization culture—tracking habits, productivity, and personal growth—reflects this anxiety. People are no longer living lives; they are curating performances. A pleasurable hobby like reading becomes a quantifiable challenge to be tracked and shared ('52 books this year!'), turning a source of private joy into a public metric. This obsession with improvement masks a deeper fear of insignificance.

To design a life that matters, one must resist the tyranny of metrics. Not everything meaningful can be optimized. Fulfillment is qualitative, not quantitative. It depends on depth, not data. This does not mean abandoning ambition, but redefining it. Ambition must evolve from achievement of status to achievement of substance. The meaningful life measures progress not by accumulation but by alignment—by how closely one's actions mirror one's convictions.

Philosophically, this shift recalls Aristotle's notion of *eudaimonia*—a flourishing life guided by virtue. In this view, happiness is not pleasure but participation in excellence of character. The modern reinterpretation of this principle is psychological integrity: living in such a way that one's inner and outer lives are consistent. Integrity does not mean perfection; it means wholeness. To live with integrity is to ensure that the self one presents to the world does not betray the self one knows privately.

The artificial environment complicates this pursuit. Digital spaces encourage fragmentation—multiple selves curated for different audiences. The individual becomes performer, marketer, and brand. While such flexibility offers opportunity, it also erodes coherence. The danger of living through avatars is not deception but diffusion: the gradual loss of a unified self. Designing a meaningful life in this context requires periodic reintegration—a conscious return to the core identity beneath performance.

Practically, this integration can be cultivated through reflection and ritual. Reflection transforms experience into understanding. It asks the self to pause and examine the emotional and ethical significance of events. Ritual, in turn, embeds those understandings into daily life. It might take the form of journaling, quiet morning practices, or deliberate acts of gratitude. Ritual converts meaning from abstraction to embodiment.

Work, when aligned with this reflective framework, becomes more than labor; it becomes expression. The individual no longer performs tasks merely to earn but to reveal—to enact values through contribution. This reframes professionalism as moral artistry. The craftsman, the scientist, the educator—all become interpreters of value in material form.

However, designing a life that matters cannot be pursued in isolation. Meaning is relational. The philosopher Martin Buber's *I–Thou* framework reminds us that identity emerges in encounter. We become fully human not through self-sufficiency but through reciprocity. The meaningful life is therefore not solitary excellence but shared significance. It depends on participation in relationships that affirm mutual dignity.

In this sense, belonging becomes both context and consequence of meaning. Loneliness, which psychologists identify as one of the most pervasive modern health risks, reflects not a lack of company but a lack of purpose within company. People are surrounded by connection yet starved for recognition. To design a meaningful life, one must cultivate communities that mirror values rather than merely interests. Relationships become the environment in which the self can act authentically.

There is also a moral dimension to this design. In an age where efficiency is effortless, moral discernment becomes the distinguishing feature of maturity. Choices once constrained by scarcity are now defined by responsibility. The question is no longer "Can it be done?" but "Should it be done?" A meaningful life incorporates this moral reflex—the habit of aligning innovation with conscience. When individuals make decisions that honor both intellect and ethics, they contribute to a culture of integrity that transcends personal gain.

The design of a meaningful life, then, is iterative. It evolves through reflection, failure, and renewal. Psychological research on narrative identity, particularly by Dan McAdams, shows that meaning arises when people construct coherent stories from their experiences. These narratives integrate past hardship into future purpose. Life design is therefore not static planning but narrative authorship—the ongoing revision of one's story toward greater coherence.

To live this way requires courage: the courage to choose substance over image, contribution over comfort, and continuity over novelty. It also requires humility: the recognition that meaning is not found once and for all but maintained through continual care. Each decision becomes a microcosm of the larger design, reinforcing or eroding coherence.

Ultimately, to design a life that matters is to engage in conscious participation with existence. It is to view time not as something to be spent but as something to be shaped. The question shifts from "What can I get from the world?" to "What can I add to it that will remain after I am gone?" This is not legacy in the grand sense of monuments, but legacy in the intimate sense of influence—moments of honesty, kindness, or clarity that ripple through others' lives.

In this way, meaning transcends mortality. To design a life that matters is to construct a system of continuity between self and world, one that remains coherent even as roles, technologies, and structures change. The human spirit, properly understood, is not threatened by artificial intelligence because it operates on a different plane—it is the capacity to interpret, to care, and to connect. Machines may extend function, but only humans can extend significance.

The goal of a meaningful life, therefore, is not to outpace automation but to outgrow superficiality. It is to build a life so internally ordered that external change cannot undo it. This design is the truest expression of resilience—the ability to remain whole in the presence of constant transformation.

When people align their values, vocation, and vitality, they create not only careers but characters—lives that make sense, not merely progress. These lives become the quiet counterweight to an accelerated world. They remind others that being human is not an error in the system, but the system's conscience.

* * *

IV

Part IV – Remaining Human

The final task of adaptation is not survival but restoration. In this closing part, attention shifts from coping to cultivation. It explores how awareness, ethics, and presence become the enduring sources of humanity. Remaining human means recovering depth, integrity, and conscience in a world that prizes speed and simulation.

10

Redefining Intelligence

For most of human history, intelligence was assumed to mean the ability to think clearly and reason correctly. It was measured in precision, prediction, and control. The modern age, with its tests and metrics, perfected this narrow definition, equating intellect with computation. But now that machines can calculate faster, analyze deeper, and predict more accurately than any human mind, we are forced to ask the question that our own progress postponed: What is intelligence when calculation is no longer uniquely ours?

Artificial intelligence has become the mirror through which humanity must rediscover the deeper dimensions of thought. The algorithms we have built reveal not only the capacity of machines but the limitations of our own definitions. They show that intelligence, understood merely as logic, is incomplete. A machine can process information, but it cannot interpret meaning. It can predict outcomes, but it cannot evaluate values. It can model reality, but it cannot experience truth. The distinction is not technical; it is existential.

To redefine intelligence, we must return to what psychology and philosophy have long suggested: that the mind is not a detached processor but an integrated system—cognitive, emotional, moral, and social. Human intelligence is not merely the ability to reason; it is the ability to reason in the presence of feeling, uncertainty, and relationship. It is not only calculation, but comprehension: the capacity to situate knowledge within context and to apply it in service of life.

This broader understanding has deep roots in psychological theory. Howard Gardner's work on multiple intelligences reframed intellect as plural rather than singular—spanning linguistic, interpersonal, spatial, and existential domains. Daniel Goleman's research on emotional intelligence demonstrated that the ability to regulate emotion and empathize with others predicts life success more reliably than IQ alone. Neuroscience has further confirmed that emotion is not the enemy of reason but its foundation; the prefrontal cortex, responsible for decision-making, depends on emotional input to evaluate outcomes meaningfully. Without feeling, logic collapses into paralysis.

The Artificial Era has reawakened awareness of these truths. As machines master calculation, humans must reclaim interpretation. What distinguishes the mind is not its precision but its depth—the ability to integrate reason with reflection, logic with empathy, data with discernment. Intelligence, in this redefined sense, becomes a form of wisdom: not just knowing what is true, but knowing what matters.

Philosophically, this reframing aligns with the classical notion of *phronesis*, or practical wisdom. Aristotle described *phronesis* as the ability to deliberate well about what is good and right, not just what is effective. It is the intelligence of moral proportion—the synthesis of thought and virtue. The future will require precisely this kind of intelligence: adaptive, integrative, and ethical.

Culturally, the shift from calculation to comprehension signals a rebalancing of values. The twentieth century celebrated analytical brilliance; the twenty-first must honor relational and moral intelligence with equal seriousness. The challenges ahead—ecological, technological, psychological—cannot be solved through logic alone. They require understanding, compassion, and restraint.

This chapter explores how intelligence can be redefined not by expanding technology but by expanding consciousness. It begins by examining the limits of logic and the necessity of emotion as context for judgment. It then turns to the integration of cognitive, emotional, and ethical systems as the basis for adaptive wisdom. Next, it explores intuition as an essential form of knowing that operates beneath awareness yet guides complex decision-making. Finally, it considers how education can evolve to cultivate whole minds rather than narrow specialists.

To remain intelligent in the Artificial Era is not to compete with machines, but to remember what machines cannot do: to feel, to care, and to discern meaning in a world that runs faster than reflection.

The Limits of Logic

Logic was once the highest expression of intelligence. From the Enlightenment onward, rationality became civilization's guiding principle—a tool for progress, governance, and scientific discovery. To be intelligent was to be objective, analytical, and detached. The rational mind was considered pure precisely because it was seen as free from the distortions of emotion. The phrase "keep a cool head" still carries moral weight, as if warmth implies weakness. But the artificial age reveals the incompleteness of this ideal. Machines now perform logic better than we ever could, and yet the world they serve remains filled with confusion, conflict, and contradiction.

The problem is not with logic itself but with its isolation. Logic is a structure of thought, but not a source of meaning. It orders information without determining what is worth knowing. It can tell us how to get somewhere efficiently but cannot tell us whether the destination is good. To treat logic as the sole measure of intelligence is to mistake the map for the territory. It creates a culture of analysis without understanding, calculation without conscience.

In psychology, this misunderstanding reflects what cognitive theorists call *cold cognition*—thinking processes that operate independently of emotion. Cold cognition is essential for problem-solving, mathematics, and scientific reasoning. But human life is governed equally by *hot cognition*, the influence of emotion, motivation, and social context on thought. The two systems are not opposites but interdependent. Antonio Damasio's neurological research on emotion and decision-making demonstrates this interdependence vividly. His studies of patients with damage to the ventromedial prefrontal cortex—an area connecting emotion and reasoning—showed that when emotional processing was impaired, logical reasoning remained intact, but decision-making collapsed. These individuals could analyze choices endlessly but could not decide among them. Without emotion, the machinery of logic spun endlessly, generating options without orientation.

Emotion, in this sense, is not the enemy of reason but its anchor. It assigns value to facts and significance to outcomes. It provides the motivational fuel that turns knowledge into action. To reason without emotion is to think without stakes. Human intelligence evolved not merely to process information but to navigate life—to balance survival, connection, and meaning in an unpredictable world.

The modern obsession with logic alone stems from a historical bias. The Enlightenment project sought liberation from superstition and authority by elevating reason as the supreme arbiter of truth. That intellectual revolution gave rise to extraordinary progress, but it also privileged analysis over experience. Descartes's dictum "I think, therefore I am" severed mind from body and intellect from emotion. Centuries later, the consequences are evident: societies rich in knowledge but poor in understanding, efficient in process but uncertain in purpose.

Logic becomes dangerous when detached from empathy. It allows cruelty to masquerade as order. Bureaucratic systems, for instance, often operate with perfect procedural logic while producing outcomes devoid of humanity. Hannah Arendt's concept of the "banality of evil" described precisely this phenomenon—the moral vacuum that emerges when action is governed by efficiency rather than conscience. The Nazi administrator who optimized train schedules to death camps acted logically within a perverse system. Logic, without moral context, becomes amoral.

In the age of artificial intelligence, the same danger reappears in digital form. Algorithms operate with mathematical precision, yet their applications can reinforce bias, spread misinformation, or erode autonomy. The logic of engagement metrics rewards outrage; the logic of optimization reduces people to data points. These outcomes are not the failure of logic, but the failure of judgment—the inability to weigh efficiency against ethics.

Psychologically, the overreliance on logic produces what Daniel Kahneman described as *cognitive overconfidence*. The rational mind, convinced of its own objectivity, becomes blind to its biases. The illusion of control replaces genuine insight. This is why some of the most catastrophic errors in history have been made not by the impulsive but by the hyper-rational—the engineers of systems who mistake predictability for wisdom.

Emotion, when properly integrated, restores proportion. It provides what philosophers once called *prudence*: the ability to apply knowledge within context. Emotion humanizes logic by linking thought to consequence. The parent deciding whether to relocate for work, the doctor choosing between treatment plans—balancing statistical survival rates with the unquantifiable impact on a patient's quality of life—the leader weighing competing needs— all rely on emotional resonance to sense what facts alone cannot show. This is not irrationality; it is embodied judgment.

The nervous system itself reflects this integration. The limbic system, responsible for emotion, and the prefrontal cortex, responsible for reasoning, communicate continuously. Each influences the other's functioning. In healthy cognition, emotion narrows focus when necessary and expands empathy when appropriate. When that balance collapses—when emotion overwhelms or when it is suppressed—judgment suffers. The emotionally flooded mind reacts without reflection; the emotionally barren mind calculates without compassion. Wisdom arises only in the dialogue between the two.

The cultural revaluation of emotion, long dismissed as "soft," is therefore not sentimental but scientific. Emotional processes are data in their own right—signals of relevance, intuition, and relational awareness. Ignoring them leads to the same distortions as ignoring evidence. As psychologist Lisa Feldman Barrett's research on constructed emotion suggests, feelings are not irrational intrusions into thought but part of the brain's predictive architecture. They summarize complex evaluations too subtle for conscious language. The feeling of unease in an ethical dilemma or the quiet satisfaction after a just decision are not distractions; they are feedback.

Understanding this interplay reframes intelligence itself. True intellect involves not just the capacity to think clearly, but the capacity to feel wisely. It recognizes that knowledge divorced from compassion becomes destructive, and compassion without discernment becomes naive. The mind's strength lies in its integration, not its isolation.

The challenge, then, is to develop systems—educational, organizational, and technological—that honor this integration. Current educational models often reward analytical intelligence at the expense of emotional and moral development. Students are trained to solve problems but not to sense meaning. They learn to argue persuasively but not to listen empathetically. The result is a generation fluent in logic but uncertain about purpose.

This imbalance mirrors the larger societal crisis of intellect: a world capable of extraordinary innovation yet unable to apply that innovation toward collective wellbeing. The tools of logic have outpaced the ethics that should guide them. Redefining intelligence in this century will mean reuniting cognition with conscience.

To see the limits of logic clearly is not to reject reason, but to restore its rightful place within the hierarchy of human knowing. Logic is a servant, not a sovereign. It should clarify values, not dictate them. It should test understanding, not replace it. Machines can simulate reasoning, but only humans can synthesize it into wisdom.

In psychological terms, this integration corresponds to the transition from *intellect* to *understanding*. Intellect analyzes; understanding interprets. Intellect categorizes; understanding connects. The truly intelligent mind is one that can move fluidly between these modes, applying logic where precision is needed and emotion where meaning is required.

The artificial age will continue to challenge this balance. As AI advances, humans will be tempted to defer moral judgment to algorithms under the guise of neutrality. But neutrality, in moral contexts, is itself a choice—a refusal to care. Machines can calculate consequences, but they cannot experience them. That difference, however subtle, defines the boundary between intelligence and awareness.

To live intelligently in this new world, individuals must cultivate what psychologist Robert Sternberg calls *wisdom-based reasoning*: the ability to balance self-interest with the common good, short-term outcomes with long-term integrity. This form of intelligence does not reject logic but transcends it. It uses logic as one instrument in a larger orchestra of knowing.

When reason and emotion operate in concert, intelligence becomes something more than mental efficiency—it becomes moral artistry. It produces not only solutions but significance, not only progress but proportion. Logic, in its highest form, is not cold calculation but disciplined compassion: the deliberate alignment of thought with truth, and truth with humanity.

Integrated Knowing

To know something is not simply to hold information. It is to experience coherence—to see how pieces of knowledge fit into the larger pattern of life. Yet for much of modern history, the human mind has been treated as a compartmentalized machine: reason in one chamber, emotion in another, ethics in a third. Education has mirrored this fragmentation, teaching students to separate analysis from empathy, and understanding from responsibility. The result has been technical proficiency without existential orientation. Integrated knowing is the antidote to that fragmentation. It restores intelligence to its full architecture: cognitive, emotional, and moral.

Integrated knowing does not reject logic; it situates it within a larger field of awareness. It understands that thinking without feeling becomes sterile, and feeling without thinking becomes unstable. The purpose of integration is not to blend these systems into sameness but to allow them to inform one another—to cultivate harmony rather than hierarchy. Cognitive science increasingly supports this integrative model. The mind is not a single process but a network of interacting systems, constantly translating between perception, emotion, and evaluation. Intelligence arises from the quality of these interactions, not the dominance of one.

Developmental psychology offers one way of framing this process. The cognitive development model proposed by Jean Piaget emphasized how humans move from concrete to abstract reasoning. Later theorists, such as Robert Kegan, extended this trajectory into the realm of meaning-making. Kegan argued that true maturity involves not merely understanding the world but understanding one's relationship to it—becoming aware of the systems that shape one's own thinking. Integrated knowing reflects this advanced stage of consciousness. It is the movement from knowledge as possession to knowledge as participation.

Emotion plays a central role in this integration. Neuroscientific research confirms that the brain's reasoning and emotional centers are deeply intertwined. The amygdala, hippocampus, and prefrontal cortex engage in constant dialogue, linking memory, motivation, and judgment. Emotion prioritizes attention, signaling what is significant; cognition interprets those signals, shaping deliberate action. When these systems work together, decisions become both rational and humane. When they split apart, intelligence becomes either cold or chaotic.

Moral reasoning completes the triad. It provides the compass by which cognitive and emotional data are interpreted. Lawrence Kohlberg's stages of moral development illustrate how moral reasoning evolves from obedience to principle. But moral maturity, as Carol Gilligan later observed, also requires empathy—the ability to perceive the impact of one's choices on others. Integrated knowing unites these two dimensions: justice and care. It thinks with both head and heart, aligning principle with compassion.

This integration has practical implications for every domain of human life. In leadership, it transforms authority from command to coherence. The leader guided by integrated knowing does not rely solely on data or sentiment but balances both through ethical discernment. In education, it shifts focus from memorization to meaning-making. Students become not repositories of facts but constructors of understanding. In personal life, it nurtures emotional resilience, allowing individuals to navigate complexity without collapsing into either rigidity or despair.

At its core, integrated knowing is an act of psychological synthesis. It reconciles the three fundamental intelligences—cognitive, emotional, and ethical—into a dynamic system of adaptive wisdom. Cognitive intelligence provides structure; emotional intelligence provides connection; ethical intelligence provides orientation. When aligned, they produce insight that is both accurate and humane.

This synthesis also illuminates why artificial intelligence, no matter how advanced, cannot replicate human wisdom. Machines can simulate cognition but not conscience. They can analyze sentiment but not experience empathy. They can model ethics but not feel moral weight. What distinguishes human knowing is not its precision but its participation in life. To know, in the fullest sense, is to be implicated—to feel the emotional and ethical consequences of understanding.

Philosophically, integrated knowing recalls the ancient Greek notion of *nous*—the intuitive intellect that perceives order in chaos. Plato described *nous* as the faculty through which the soul apprehends truth directly, beyond sensory experience. In modern terms, this can be understood as the synthesis of perception, reflection, and value judgment—a form of intelligence that grasps meaning rather than merely data. Integrated knowing revives this idea in a contemporary psychological form.

The failure to cultivate such integration has led to many of the crises now confronting modern civilization. Climate change, for instance, is not a failure of data; it is a failure of integration. Similarly, the design of social media platforms, driven by the logic of engagement metrics without sufficient integration of psychological or ethical foresight, has contributed to widespread social polarization and anxiety. The facts are known, the logic clear, the consequences measurable—yet the emotional and moral systems necessary for coordinated response remain underdeveloped. The same can be said of inequality, political polarization, and digital addiction. These are not problems of ignorance but of disconnection between knowledge and care.

Integrated knowing offers a framework for repairing that disconnection. It requires three essential disciplines: self-awareness, relational empathy, and reflective restraint. Self-awareness grounds cognition in humility—the recognition that knowledge is always partial and provisional. Relational empathy ensures that understanding extends beyond the self, connecting cognition to collective wellbeing. Reflective restraint prevents knowledge from becoming domination by tempering certainty with conscience. Together, these disciplines create an ecosystem of wisdom.

From a psychological standpoint, integration is not a static achievement but a continual balancing act. The human mind oscillates between polarities: analysis and intuition, reason and emotion, self and society. Integrated knowing emerges not from eliminating these tensions but from maintaining dialogue between them. Maturity lies in learning to tolerate complexity—to hold competing truths without collapsing into cynicism or dogma.

Culturally, this capacity defines the evolution of civilization itself. Each epoch of history has expanded the range of human awareness—from tribe to nation, from nation to species. The next expansion must be inward: from fragmented intellect to integrated consciousness. This shift will determine whether technological progress leads to wisdom or alienation.

In practice, integrated knowing can be cultivated through education that unites disciplines rather than divides them. The humanities, sciences, and arts each reveal different aspects of truth. When studied in isolation, they produce specialists. When studied in dialogue, they produce synthesists— individuals capable of connecting insights across fields. This integrative literacy is the new foundation of human relevance.

Psychologically, individuals can foster integration through reflective practices that engage both thought and emotion—journaling, dialogue, contemplative attention. These practices slow cognition enough for meaning to emerge. They reconnect abstract knowledge with lived experience. Over time, such reflection strengthens what neuroscientists call *connectivity coherence*—the synchronization of brain regions involved in reasoning, empathy, and moral evaluation. In other words, reflection literally rewires intelligence for integration.

The ultimate goal of integrated knowing is not perfection of intellect but wholeness of being. It allows intelligence to serve life rather than dominate it. It transforms information into understanding, understanding into wisdom, and wisdom into compassion. This is the progression that marks maturity, both individual and collective.

Machines can process infinite data, but only humans can reconcile knowledge with conscience. Only humans can know in a way that transforms. Integrated knowing is, therefore, the highest expression of intelligence—not because it is complex, but because it is complete.

The Role of Intuition

Intuition has always occupied an uneasy place in the hierarchy of intelligence. It is admired in hindsight but distrusted in practice. People praise it when it leads to discovery yet dismiss it as guesswork when it defies logic. In scientific traditions built on proof, intuition appears suspect; in technological culture, it seems antiquated. Yet every major advance in human thought—from artistic creation to moral insight—has relied on intuitive synthesis. The paradox is that the very quality that distinguishes human intelligence from artificial computation is the one most often ignored: the capacity to know without deliberate reasoning.

Psychologically, intuition can be defined as rapid, nonconscious processing that draws on accumulated experience to guide decision-making. It is not mystical; it is pattern recognition operating beneath awareness. The human brain constantly detects regularities in the environment, compressing them into heuristics—mental shortcuts that allow for quick judgment in complex situations. These heuristics form the foundation of intuition. They are the silent calculations of a mind that has learned through lived experience.

This process is not irrational; it is pre-rational. It represents the intelligence of the nervous system before it becomes conscious thought. Neuroscientific research supports this understanding. Studies using functional MRI have shown that intuitive judgments often arise from brain regions associated with emotional memory, particularly the amygdala and insula, which process somatic signals—bodily cues of comfort or discomfort. These signals, what psychologist Gerd Gigerenzer calls "gut feelings," are the body's shorthand for accumulated learning. They are evidence of cognition embedded in experience.

In professional contexts, intuition often distinguishes mastery from mere competence. The expert chess player does not calculate every move consciously; they perceive the pattern of play almost instantaneously. The seasoned therapist senses unspoken emotion before it is verbalized. The skilled physician detects an anomaly by feel rather than formula. In each case, intuition compresses years of learning into immediate recognition. This is what psychologist Gary Klein termed "recognition-primed decision-making"—the ability to act decisively in uncertainty because the mind has internalized structure through practice.

However, intuition's reliability depends on the quality of experience that informs it. When shaped by bias or fear, intuitive judgment can mislead. This is why the cultivation of intuition requires awareness, not abandonment of reason. The mature mind integrates intuition with analysis, testing impressions against evidence without dismissing either. Intuition offers hypotheses; logic evaluates them. Together, they create adaptive intelligence.

Cognitively, intuition bridges the conscious and unconscious dimensions of the mind. It allows knowledge that is tacit—stored in patterns rather than propositions—to influence perception. This tacit knowledge, described by philosopher Michael Polanyi, underlies all skilled performance. We know more than we can say. The musician cannot explain every movement of the hand; the craftsman cannot verbalize every nuance of material resistance. Intuition translates this unspeakable knowledge into action. It is the language of the body within the grammar of thought.

Emotion is integral to this process. Intuition communicates through feeling. The sudden sense of rightness or wrongness, of ease or tension, signals the brain's unconscious evaluation. These affective cues arise before conscious reasoning catches up. The philosopher Henri Bergson described intuition as "the sympathy by which one places oneself within an object to coincide with what is unique in it." In this sense, intuition is not simply internal; it is relational. It involves attunement—the ability to resonate with patterns, people, and situations beyond explicit analysis.

This attunement forms the foundation of empathy, creativity, and moral discernment. In empathy, intuition reads subtle cues of emotion and context. In creativity, it perceives connections between ideas before they are logically linked. In moral reasoning, it senses ethical proportion—the difference between what is right and what merely works. Each of these forms of intuition operates through relational sensitivity rather than calculation.

The modern overemphasis on analytics has muted this intelligence. In organizations governed by metrics, intuition is often treated as unreliable because it resists quantification. Yet many of the most consequential decisions—whom to trust, when to speak, what to build—depend on intuitive discernment. Overreliance on data can produce what cognitive scientists call *analysis paralysis*: the inability to decide when evidence is endless but inconclusive. In such moments, intuition restores movement. It cuts through complexity by recognizing patterns of significance invisible to linear thought.

Philosophically, intuition represents the mind's capacity for synthesis. Logic dissects; intuition connects. Logic builds from premise to conclusion; intuition leaps from pattern to understanding. The German philosopher Immanuel Kant viewed intuition as the direct apprehension of phenomena before conceptualization. For Kant, thought required both intuition (the raw perception of experience) and understanding (the structuring of it). Without intuition, reason has nothing to organize. Without reason, intuition remains formless. Together, they constitute cognition itself.

The artificial replication of intelligence illuminates this balance. Machine learning systems excel at pattern detection but lack the qualitative awareness that gives those patterns meaning. They can predict what is likely but not what is right. Human intuition, in contrast, is steeped in lived context—it carries the residue of moral, emotional, and existential experience. A human decision, even when flawed, acknowledges consequence. A machine's does not.

Psychologically, this difference arises from embodiment. The brain does not exist in isolation; it is shaped by the body's interaction with the world. This embodied cognition means that thought is influenced by sensory experience, posture, and emotion. Intuition is the synthesis of these signals. It is the wisdom of the body thinking. This is why intuition feels physical— why truth can feel light and falsehood heavy. The body registers coherence before the mind articulates it.

Intuitive knowing is also foundational to creativity. Nearly every breakthrough in art, science, and philosophy has involved a moment of sudden insight that defied linear reasoning. The psychologist Mihaly Csikszentmihalyi, in his studies of creativity, noted that insight often emerges after a period of incubation, when conscious effort relaxes and the subconscious reorganizes information. The resulting intuition feels spontaneous but is the product of deep integration. It is the mind solving problems through synthesis rather than step-by-step logic.

This process reveals that intuition is not the opposite of discipline but its culmination. True intuition depends on mastery; it is expertise moving effortlessly through complexity. The untrained impulse is not intuition but impulse. A novice investor buying a stock on a whim is acting on impulse; a seasoned investor like Warren Buffett having a 'gut feeling' about a company's long-term viability after decades of market analysis is acting on cultivated intuition. Cultivated intuition, by contrast, arises from long immersion in a domain, where knowledge becomes embodied. The artist who paints intuitively has internalized form and technique. The scientist who intuits a solution has spent decades studying the problem. Intuition, at its highest level, is not the abandonment of skill but its transcendence.

Cultural narratives about intuition often gendered or diminished it, associating it with "soft" or "feminine" knowing. This has contributed to the intellectual hierarchy that privileges analysis over empathy. But as psychology and neuroscience reveal the interdependence of cognitive and emotional systems, intuition must be reclaimed as an essential dimension of intelligence. It is not an alternative to logic but an expansion of it—a deeper way of perceiving that includes emotional and ethical resonance.

In leadership, intuition becomes especially vital. Leaders often face situations where data are incomplete and time is limited. The most effective ones combine analytic clarity with intuitive attunement to people and context. They sense undercurrents that metrics cannot measure—trust, morale, fear, emerging possibility. Intuition, in this sense, is strategic empathy: the ability to perceive systems from within.

In personal life, intuition serves as a compass for authenticity. It guides choices that align with inner coherence rather than external pressure. Modern psychology often describes this as *self-trust*—the confidence to act in accordance with one's felt sense of truth. This does not mean obeying every impulse; it means listening to the wisdom encoded in emotion and experience. Self-trust is the integration of intuition and integrity.

The cultivation of intuition therefore requires quiet—mental space for subtle signals to surface. The constant stimulation of digital life— notifications, analytics, commentary—drowns out this inner guidance. Reclaiming intuition means reclaiming silence. It means creating intervals of reflection in which the body and mind can register coherence. In an age obsessed with data, silence becomes the new intelligence.

Ultimately, intuition represents the bridge between the known and the possible. It is the faculty that allows the mind to move beyond analysis into insight, beyond repetition into originality. Machines can replicate what has been seen before, but intuition glimpses what might be. It is the imagination of intelligence—the human capacity to sense patterns not yet proven but profoundly true.

The future of intelligence will depend on our ability to honor this inner dimension. As computation accelerates, humanity's relevance will lie not in outthinking machines but in outfeeling them—in perceiving context, meaning, and moral proportion where no algorithm can reach. Intuition is the pulse of that awareness. It is the continuity between thought and soul.

Education for Wholeness

The purpose of education has always reflected what a society believes intelligence to be. When intelligence was defined as memory, schools emphasized repetition. When it was defined as logic, they prized analysis. But if intelligence is now to be understood as integration—the union of reason, emotion, and moral sense—then education must evolve from information delivery to consciousness development. The goal is not simply to prepare students to compete in an automated world but to prepare them to remain human within it.

For over a century, formal education has operated under the industrial model: standardized testing, segmented disciplines, and reward structures built on compliance. This model mirrored the factory system that produced it. Students became units of productivity, measured by output and ranked by efficiency. It was an effective system for generating skilled workers, but a poor one for cultivating whole human beings. It taught people how to think, but not how to live.

The artificial era exposes the obsolescence of that approach. Knowledge, once scarce, is now abundant. Facts are no longer owned by those who memorize them, but by those who can interpret them meaningfully. Machines can already retrieve, calculate, and replicate with flawless precision. What remains distinctively human is the ability to synthesize across boundaries, to interpret ambiguity, to act ethically under uncertainty. Education, therefore, must move beyond the transmission of knowledge toward the cultivation of integrated wisdom.

Psychologically, this shift requires rebalancing the hemispheres of learning. The left hemisphere's analytical focus—structure, logic, and categorization—has long dominated Western pedagogy. The right hemisphere's holistic capacities—context, emotion, and imagination— have been marginalized as secondary. But neuroscience increasingly demonstrates that complex cognition depends on the cooperation of both. As Iain McGilchrist's work on hemispheric integration suggests, the healthiest minds are those in which analytic and intuitive processes operate in dialogue rather than competition. Education for wholeness must therefore train both forms of attention: the focused gaze of analysis and the open awareness of empathy.

This kind of education begins not with curriculum design but with a philosophical redefinition of purpose. What is education for? If it exists merely to serve markets, it will always lag behind technological change. But if it exists to develop consciousness, then it can transcend obsolescence. Consciousness is the only renewable resource of meaning. An educational system that cultivates self-awareness, empathy, and ethical reasoning creates citizens capable of guiding technology rather than being guided by it.

To achieve this, education must expand its conception of intelligence to include emotional and moral development as central rather than supplementary. Emotional intelligence, as Daniel Goleman established, predicts leadership effectiveness and interpersonal success more reliably than IQ. Moral intelligence—the ability to discern right action—anchors knowledge in conscience. Integrating these dimensions into education is not a matter of adding courses on "soft skills." It is a reorientation of the entire learning experience around wholeness.

This reorientation can be understood through three principles: relational learning, reflective learning, and integrative learning.

Relational learning recognizes that knowledge is co-created through dialogue. It treats the classroom as a microcosm of society—a place where ideas are tested through empathy as well as argument. The role of the teacher becomes less that of an authority dispensing answers and more that of a facilitator cultivating presence. Students learn not only from the material but from one another, practicing the psychological skills of listening, interpreting, and disagreeing without dehumanizing. Such environments model the emotional regulation and mutual respect required for a functioning democracy.

Reflective learning transforms information into insight. It introduces pauses into the pace of education, encouraging students to consider what they have learned, how it has affected them, and what ethical implications it carries. Reflection converts experience into understanding. Without it, learning remains mechanical—accumulation without assimilation. Practices such as journaling, dialogue, and contemplative attention can help students internalize learning rather than simply perform it. Reflection cultivates metacognition: awareness of one's own thinking and bias. This self-awareness is the foundation of adaptive intelligence.

Integrative learning unites disciplines to reveal the interconnectedness of knowledge. A problem in climate science, for example, becomes an opportunity to study psychology, economics, and ethics simultaneously. A course on artificial intelligence can include philosophy of mind, moral reasoning, and narrative theory. This cross-pollination encourages systems thinking—the ability to perceive relationships between parts and wholes. It dismantles the illusion of isolated expertise and prepares students to approach real-world problems with contextual sensitivity.

Such an education demands new forms of assessment. Traditional grading, which reduces learning to quantifiable outcomes, cannot measure growth in self-awareness or ethical discernment. Alternative approaches—portfolio evaluation, narrative feedback, project-based learning—offer more accurate reflections of integrated development. These methods honor process as much as product, valuing the evolution of thought rather than the memorization of facts.

Culturally, education for wholeness requires a shift in societal values. Parents, policymakers, and institutions must recognize that human development is not a race but a rhythm. Depth cannot be accelerated; reflection cannot be outsourced. The anxiety driving contemporary education—the fear of falling behind—must give way to a more mature understanding: that wisdom grows through engagement, not competition. A society that measures its success only through test scores and economic output will eventually produce brilliant technicians and impoverished souls.

This reimagined education also addresses the emotional challenges of the digital generation. Young people today navigate unprecedented levels of stimulation, comparison, and uncertainty. The constant exposure to data without context breeds cognitive fatigue and emotional desensitization. Teaching them emotional literacy—the ability to name, regulate, and express feeling—is therefore essential. It rehumanizes the learning process and equips them to manage complexity with compassion rather than collapse.

Ethically, education must also prepare students to confront the moral dilemmas of technological progress. As automation reshapes industries, and as biotechnology and AI blur the boundaries of agency and identity, moral reasoning becomes as essential as coding. Students must be taught not only how to create technology but how to question its purpose. This integration of ethics into every field prevents knowledge from drifting into nihilism. It restores the link between intelligence and responsibility.

At the deepest level, education for wholeness is an education in attention. What we attend to determines what we become. In a culture of distraction, attention is the rarest and most valuable human skill. Training the capacity for sustained, compassionate attention—whether through contemplative practice, deep reading, or dialogue—cultivates the inner stillness required for genuine understanding. Attention, as the philosopher Simone Weil wrote, is the purest form of generosity. It is the foundation of empathy and the antidote to fragmentation.

The teacher of the future, therefore, is not merely an instructor but an integrator—a guide who helps students connect intellect to integrity, emotion to ethics, and individual growth to collective wellbeing. The classroom becomes a laboratory for consciousness, where knowledge is tested not only for accuracy but for its impact on the soul.

Psychologically, this approach fosters resilience. When students learn to interpret failure as information rather than identity, they develop adaptive confidence. When they see knowledge as relational rather than competitive, they develop humility. When they understand that understanding itself evolves, they develop flexibility. These are the traits that define lifelong learners.

In the Artificial Era, education must become less about producing experts and more about producing integrated minds—people capable of thinking clearly, feeling deeply, and acting responsibly. Machines will handle the rest. The aim is not to train for employability but for existential literacy: the ability to navigate meaning in a changing world.

To educate for wholeness is to affirm that intelligence is not a race toward mastery but a relationship with mystery. It is to restore balance between what can be measured and what must be lived. When education aligns intellect with empathy, curiosity with conscience, and analysis with imagination, it reclaims its original purpose—to prepare people not just for work, but for wisdom.

THE PSYCHOLOGY OF THE ARTIFICIAL ERA

* * *

11

The Moral Frontier

Responsibility in a World of Algorithms

E very era tests humanity's capacity for moral growth, but few have
done so as quietly and comprehensively as this one. The rise of
artificial intelligence has not merely transformed what humans
can do—it has begun to reshape what they must *decide*. As more of life
becomes mediated by code, the boundary between human and machine
agency grows porous. Choices that once required deliberation are now
delegated to systems that act faster than reflection. The result is a new
moral landscape—one defined not by overt cruelty or malice, but by the
subtle drift of responsibility away from human hands.

The moral frontier of the Artificial Era is not a battlefield but an interface.
It is where decisions are made invisibly, where intentions dissolve into
algorithms, and where accountability becomes diffused across systems too
complex for any single person to control. From medical diagnostics to
hiring processes, from judicial risk assessments to digital content curation,
algorithms shape lives through decisions that appear neutral yet carry moral
weight. The question is no longer whether machines can think, but whether
humans can remain ethically awake while they do.

Psychologically, the challenge of this frontier lies in what moral psychologists call *diffusion of responsibility*. When outcomes result from collective or automated processes, individuals feel less accountable. This dynamic is amplified by technology, which distances cause from effect and obscures moral visibility. The person who writes the code may never see the harm it enables. The user who benefits from convenience may never consider the cost to privacy or dignity. The result is a culture of unintentional complicity—a world where harm can occur without hatred, and injustice without intention.

To navigate this new moral terrain, humanity must expand its understanding of ethical maturity. Traditional moral systems were built around personal conduct: what one individual should or should not do. But in the age of distributed agency, morality must become systemic. Ethical maturity now involves not only self-restraint but structural awareness—the ability to foresee the psychological and social consequences of design. It requires moving from moral intuition to moral architecture: embedding conscience into the systems that mediate our choices.

This shift redefines intelligence itself. As artificial systems assume more cognitive labor, the uniquely human form of intelligence becomes moral rather than mechanical. Ethical reasoning, empathy, and foresight—once considered philosophical luxuries—are now survival skills. The maturity of a society will be measured not by how efficiently it automates, but by how responsibly it governs what it automates.

Culturally, this transformation exposes the limits of our moral vocabulary. We are accustomed to condemning individuals, not infrastructures. Yet the harms of the digital age—bias, misinformation, emotional manipulation— emerge from design decisions rather than direct intent. These require new forms of ethical imagination: the ability to see how lines of code translate into lived experience, how efficiency can eclipse empathy, and how convenience can corrode conscience.

This chapter explores that moral evolution through four dimensions. It begins with delegated decision-making, examining where accountability truly lies when algorithms act on our behalf. It then investigates ethical drift—the gradual erosion of moral sensitivity through automation and abstraction. From there, it turns to the restoration of conscience, proposing ways to build reflective pauses into systems and selves. Finally, it concludes with collective maturity: the development of social norms that elevate empathy, transparency, and stewardship over convenience.

The frontier ahead is not technological but ethical. Humanity's test is no longer whether it can create intelligent machines, but whether it can remain wise in their presence.

Delegated Decision Making

Delegation is one of the oldest features of human civilization. From the earliest forms of governance to modern institutions, societies have relied on intermediaries to extend decision-making beyond individual capacity. Judges interpret laws; managers allocate labor; experts advise leaders. Delegation, at its best, reflects trust—the belief that others can act on our behalf with competence and conscience. But in the Artificial Era, that trust is being transferred not to people, but to systems. Algorithms now decide who gets a loan, which resumes are shortlisted, what news appears on screens, and how sentences are predicted in courtrooms. Decisions once mediated by human judgment are increasingly automated, and with that automation comes a profound question: When intelligence is delegated, where does accountability remain?

The psychological and moral stakes of this shift cannot be overstated. To delegate a decision is not merely to outsource a task; it is to share responsibility for its outcome. Historically, humans have delegated within systems of reciprocity—other humans capable of moral reflection, subject to norms, empathy, and correction. Machines, however, do not experience obligation. They process inputs, not intentions. This absence of moral interiority creates an ethical vacuum that cannot be filled by technical accuracy alone. When an algorithm denies a loan or flags a person as a risk, the act may be statistically sound, but it is not morally aware. The human who designed or deployed it remains responsible, yet that responsibility is often obscured beneath layers of abstraction.

227

Psychologically, this phenomenon is an extension of what social psychologists call *moral disengagement*. Albert Bandura's research demonstrated that individuals distance themselves from the consequences of their actions when those consequences are diffused, sanitized, or justified by authority. Automation amplifies each of these mechanisms. When a machine carries out a morally significant act, it creates the illusion of neutrality. The moral language shifts from right and wrong to efficient and inefficient. Harm becomes a technical issue, not an ethical one.

Consider the example of predictive policing. Algorithms trained on historical data identify neighborhoods or individuals at higher risk of crime. On the surface, this appears rational. Yet because the data reflects decades of systemic bias, the algorithm reproduces discrimination with mathematical precision. No one intends the injustice—it emerges from the delegation itself. Accountability becomes diluted: the programmer blames the data, the user blames the system, and the institution blames the inevitability of progress. The result is harm without villainy—a moral failure born not of cruelty, but of convenience.

This diffusion of responsibility represents a new form of ethical displacement. It mirrors a broader cultural tendency to equate automation with objectivity. Humans, aware of their own biases, often overtrust machines precisely because they seem impartial. This is what researchers call *automation bias*: the cognitive tendency to favor algorithmic outputs even when they conflict with evidence or judgment. The more complex the system, the stronger this bias becomes, because humans assume that complexity implies correctness. Ironically, our faith in artificial systems is often greater than our faith in ourselves.

But moral responsibility cannot be delegated without remainder. Even when decisions are mediated by machines, the ethical burden remains human. The architect of an algorithm bears the obligation to anticipate its potential harms; the organization deploying it bears the duty to monitor its consequences; and the society benefiting from it bears the task of regulating its scope. This chain of accountability is fragile, but it defines the moral infrastructure of an automated world.

Philosophically, this challenge exposes the limits of utilitarian thinking. The logic of efficiency—maximizing outcomes with minimal input—works well for machines but poorly for morality. Ethical reasoning cannot be reduced to optimization because human life is not a system of interchangeable variables. Every decision carries symbolic as well as practical meaning. To delegate a moral decision to an algorithm is to risk severing that symbolic thread—the sense that choices express character, not just calculation.

Psychologically, the erosion of agency that accompanies automation has consequences for identity. Decision-making is one of the primary ways individuals experience autonomy and moral growth. Each act of choice reinforces the sense of self as responsible and capable. When decisions are consistently delegated, that sense atrophies. People become passive participants in systems they neither control nor fully understand. This phenomenon, sometimes called *learned moral helplessness*, mirrors the psychological effects of overregulation in bureaucratic settings. When individuals believe their choices no longer matter, moral motivation declines. This creates a state of learned moral helplessness, where a manager, for example, might stop questioning an algorithm's biased hiring recommendations because their previous objections were ignored, leading them to passively accept the system's output as an unchangeable reality.

To restore moral agency within automated systems, humans must reintroduce reflection into the loop. This requires designing what philosophers of technology call *human-in-the-loop* systems—processes where final decisions, especially those affecting lives, are subject to human review. Yet this alone is insufficient. Reflection must be more than procedural; it must be psychological. It must train individuals to recognize when delegation becomes avoidance—to discern the line between efficiency and evasion.

Education and organizational culture play crucial roles here. Ethical literacy must evolve beyond compliance training into moral reasoning practice. Professionals working with AI systems should be taught not only how algorithms function, but how ethical principles apply to their design and use. This includes understanding bias, transparency, and the long-term societal effects of automated decision-making. Moral awareness is not an innate trait; it is a skill that must be cultivated deliberately.

Historically, the tension between delegation and accountability has always existed. Military hierarchies, financial institutions, and governments have wrestled with the problem of responsibility within complex systems. What is new is the scale and opacity of algorithmic delegation. In previous eras, moral accountability could be traced through human networks; now, it is dispersed across layers of code and corporate infrastructure. The philosopher Hans Jonas warned that modern technology expands the reach of action beyond the horizon of foresight, creating responsibilities for consequences we cannot predict. This "imperative of responsibility" becomes even more urgent in the age of intelligent systems.

The moral frontier therefore demands a new ethic of transparency—one that treats explanation as a form of justice. When algorithms make decisions, those affected deserve to know why. Opacity undermines accountability because it removes the possibility of dialogue. The ethical test of any automated system should be simple: Can a human being explain its decision in moral terms, not merely technical ones? If not, the system operates beyond the boundary of legitimate authority.

Culturally, this reassertion of responsibility requires a collective shift in values. Efficiency, the dominant virtue of modernity, must be balanced by empathy. Progress must be measured not only by speed and scale but by moral coherence. The question "Can this be done?" must always be followed by "Should it be?" and "Who bears the cost?" These questions reintroduce conscience into systems that would otherwise operate without it.

At a deeper level, delegated decision-making forces humanity to confront its relationship with power. Technology magnifies our reach but not necessarily our wisdom. The temptation to delegate moral labor to machines stems from the discomfort of uncertainty—the desire to escape the burden of judgment. Yet moral maturity consists precisely in bearing that burden consciously. The refusal to decide is itself a decision, and the abdication of responsibility is its own form of harm.

From a psychological perspective, reclaiming agency requires cultivating what might be called *reflective competence*: the ability to recognize one's participation in complex systems and to act with intention within them. Reflective competence integrates cognition and conscience, allowing individuals to see the moral implications of their technical actions. It transforms users into stewards.

The future of moral responsibility will not depend on eliminating algorithms but on humanizing them—embedding within their design the capacity for accountability, transparency, and moral review. This requires interdisciplinary collaboration among ethicists, psychologists, technologists, and policymakers. Ethics cannot remain a postscript to innovation; it must become its foundation.

Delegated decision-making, then, is not a technical problem but a psychological and philosophical one. It challenges the very definition of what it means to act. As machines increasingly execute decisions, humanity's role shifts from direct control to moral curation—deciding what should be automated, what should remain human, and how to preserve dignity in both.

The ultimate danger is not that machines will decide for us, but that we will forget what it means to decide at all.

Ethical Drift

Moral collapse rarely arrives with drama. It does not announce itself with declarations of intent or moments of conscious betrayal. It happens gradually, imperceptibly, as norms erode under the pressure of convenience, repetition, and abstraction. The philosopher Hannah Arendt described this process as the "banality of evil"—the quiet substitution of thought with procedure, conscience with compliance. In the Artificial Era, that banality has found a new medium. Automation, abstraction, and algorithmic mediation have created conditions under which ethical drift can occur invisibly. We are not witnessing the corruption of morality, but its evaporation through indifference.

Ethical drift refers to the slow, unconscious movement away from moral awareness. It is not the presence of malice but the absence of attention. The psychologist Albert Bandura's work on moral disengagement helps explain how ordinary individuals participate in harmful systems without perceiving themselves as unethical. Through euphemistic labeling, displacement of responsibility, and diffusion of accountability, people neutralize the emotional discomfort that moral reflection would otherwise provoke. Automation compounds each of these mechanisms by insulating the human actor from the human consequence.

When a machine carries out a morally significant act—whether denying a claim, moderating content, or executing a trade—the human agent no longer feels directly responsible. The harm becomes data. The person becomes a metric. The moral weight of the decision disperses across the circuitry of a system that feels impersonal by design. Ethical drift thrives in such environments because it feeds on distance: the psychological separation between action and empathy. A content moderator reviewing thousands of traumatic images a day may develop emotional numbness as a survival mechanism, losing the capacity to discern nuance. A high-frequency trader whose algorithm executes millions of transactions in seconds feels no connection to the real-world economic impact of their code.

Consider the workplace example of automated performance management. When algorithms track productivity metrics, flag underperformance, and even recommend disciplinary action, managers may simply approve outcomes rather than engage in difficult conversations. The language of accountability becomes the language of process. A termination or demotion becomes an "automated workflow event." The emotional reality of human consequence vanishes beneath the neutrality of code. This is not intentional cruelty, but moral anesthesia.

The same dynamic operates at a societal scale. In digital spaces, automated recommendation systems amplify content based on engagement metrics, not ethical merit. Outrage is rewarded because it generates attention; disinformation thrives because it optimizes reach. The architects of these systems rarely intend harm, yet their creations shape the moral climate of entire cultures. Over time, exposure to manipulation normalizes manipulation. Ethical drift becomes cultural drift—the slow acclimation to distortion until it no longer feels wrong.

Psychologically, drift occurs when repetition dulls sensitivity. In the language of behavioral science, it is the desensitization of conscience through habituation. When individuals or institutions repeatedly encounter ethically ambiguous situations without reflection, moral emotion declines. What once evoked discomfort becomes routine. Neuroimaging studies of empathy suggest that moral awareness depends on emotional resonance— seeing or imagining another's experience activates neural circuits associated with care. When those circuits are under-stimulated by abstraction, empathy atrophies. Automation accelerates this process by removing faces from feedback.

Ethical drift is not limited to the users of technology; it extends to its creators. In engineering culture, the principle of neutrality—"We build tools; others decide how to use them"—has long served as a defense against moral accountability. But as the social impact of technology grows, neutrality becomes complicity. Every line of code reflects an implicit moral stance: what is prioritized, what is excluded, what is optimized, and at whose expense. The absence of ethical reflection during design is itself a moral act, because it determines the conditions under which future choices will occur.

This erosion of moral sensitivity is not a new phenomenon. History is filled with examples of systems that drifted from principle under the guise of progress. Industrial labor once justified exploitation in the name of efficiency; bureaucracies once rationalized cruelty through procedure. What distinguishes the current era is the speed and invisibility of drift. Automation accelerates moral adaptation because it conceals agency. The faster decisions occur, the less time there is for conscience to intervene.

Philosophically, this dynamic recalls the moral psychology of gradualism— the idea that evil often advances not through grand acts but through incremental concessions. Each small compromise becomes easier than the last, until the boundary between right and wrong dissolves into convenience. Ethical drift in the digital age operates by the same logic. When users accept invasions of privacy for convenience, when organizations justify opaque algorithms for efficiency, when societies trade reflection for speed, the cumulative effect is a cultural numbness to moral loss.

The antidote to drift is not outrage but awareness. Moral vigilance, unlike technological vigilance, cannot be automated. It requires conscious cultivation—the deliberate reactivation of empathy and reflection in environments that encourage their suspension. Psychologically, this means developing what moral philosopher Iris Murdoch called "attention to the reality of others." Murdoch argued that moral growth begins not in rules but in perception—the capacity to truly see another person as real, rather than as an abstraction. In an algorithmic world, this kind of attention becomes an act of resistance.

Educationally, institutions can counter drift by embedding moral reflection into technical training. Engineers, data scientists, and designers should be required to study moral psychology and ethical reasoning as part of their formation. The goal is not to turn technologists into philosophers, but to remind them that every system they build will shape human experience. Courses on human factors, bias recognition, and moral decision-making can restore conscience to contexts where it has been externalized.

Organizationally, leaders must design cultures that reward ethical questioning rather than silent compliance. In psychologically safe environments, individuals feel empowered to raise moral concerns without fear of reprisal. When such cultures are absent, drift accelerates. Ethical reflection must be built into the workflow, not appended as an afterthought. Just as systems undergo security audits, they should undergo moral audits—periodic reviews assessing how automated decisions align with stated values.

From a psychological standpoint, restoring sensitivity requires re-engaging the emotional dimension of ethics. Cognitive understanding alone is insufficient. People act morally not because they know what is right, but because they feel its significance. Empathy, guilt, and moral pride are emotional signals that sustain ethical behavior. When systems suppress or externalize those signals, humans must consciously reintroduce them. This can take the form of storytelling, case reflection, or user feedback—methods that reattach emotion to consequence.

Culturally, societies must reclaim moral language. In recent decades, ethical discourse has been replaced by managerial rhetoric—impact, optimization, deliverables. These terms, though efficient, strip decisions of moral texture. Reintroducing words like fairness, dignity, and responsibility rehumanizes public conversation. Language shapes perception, and perception guides conscience. A culture that cannot speak in moral terms eventually forgets how to think in them.

Ethical drift also has an existential dimension. It reflects not only moral fatigue but meaning fatigue—the erosion of purpose under constant adaptation. When technology defines progress as acceleration, individuals begin to equate moral worth with productivity. The inner life, once the seat of conscience, becomes secondary to external metrics of success. In such conditions, moral questions—Who am I? What do I stand for? What is good?—become background noise in a life organized by efficiency. The Artificial Era therefore demands a revival of moral introspection as a counterweight to external automation.

Philosophically, this revival recalls the ancient concept of *virtue ethics*, which defines morality not as rule-following but as character cultivation. Virtue ethics emphasizes habituation—the idea that ethical stability arises from repeated acts of reflection and restraint. In an automated world, where repetition often occurs without awareness, virtue must become intentional again. Small acts of mindfulness—pausing before delegating, questioning before accepting, empathizing before executing—can interrupt the momentum of drift.

To maintain moral awareness within automated systems, individuals and institutions must develop what might be called *ethical friction*. This refers to deliberate points of reflection that slow down decision-making just enough to allow conscience to engage. Friction is often seen as inefficiency, but ethically, it functions as protection. In aviation, checklists prevent catastrophic errors; in moral systems, reflection prevents ethical drift. Designing for ethical friction—through transparency reports, user consent dialogues, or human oversight—creates space for awareness to re-enter automation.

The risk of ignoring drift is not only moral decay but psychological desensitization. When people no longer feel disturbed by injustice, they lose part of their humanity. Emotional numbing may reduce anxiety, but it also erodes empathy—the very capacity that sustains moral life. Re-sensitizing conscience requires exposure to human stories, not just human data. Art, literature, and psychology all play a role here, reminding society that empathy is not weakness but wisdom.

Ultimately, ethical drift is a failure of attention. It occurs when humanity forgets to look closely at what it is becoming. In an age defined by acceleration, the most radical act is to slow down long enough to care.

Restoring Conscience

Every civilization eventually rediscovers the necessity of conscience. It is the quiet faculty that anchors intelligence to morality, awareness to restraint, and power to purpose. Without it, knowledge becomes dangerous, progress becomes reckless, and efficiency becomes indifferent. In the Artificial Era, conscience is not disappearing; it is dissolving into abstraction. The challenge is not that humanity has lost its moral compass, but that it has delegated its navigation to systems incapable of moral perception. To restore conscience is therefore not a sentimental return to tradition, but a psychological and cultural imperative: to reawaken moral awareness in a world increasingly designed to dull it.

Conscience, as understood in psychology, is both emotional and cognitive. It is not merely an internal voice of authority but an integrative process—linking empathy, memory, reasoning, and identity into a unified moral self. Developmental psychology, from Piaget to Kohlberg, charted its evolution: beginning with fear of punishment, maturing into recognition of principle, and finally culminating in self-regulation guided by empathy and moral reflection. Conscience, in this sense, is the psychological infrastructure of ethical maturity. It translates feeling into principle and transforms moral awareness into moral character.

But conscience is fragile. It depends on reflection, and reflection depends on pause. The faster decisions become, the less time there is for conscience to intervene. Automation accelerates moral bypassing not because it is malicious, but because it eliminates intervals for awareness. When algorithms deliver instantaneous responses, human deliberation begins to feel inefficient. This psychological reconditioning—the habituation to immediacy—gradually rewires moral perception. To restore conscience, humanity must reintroduce the very thing automation seeks to remove: time.

Philosophically, this need for pause recalls the ancient practice of *deliberation*. Aristotle viewed deliberation as the essence of practical wisdom—thinking slowly enough to perceive the moral dimension of choice. Modern neuroscience confirms this intuition. The prefrontal cortex, responsible for ethical reasoning and impulse control, requires milliseconds longer to activate than the limbic regions driving instinctive reaction. In digital environments where speed is rewarded and stillness penalized, the physiological conditions for conscience are undermined. The restoration of moral awareness therefore begins with the restoration of cognitive space.

At a systemic level, restoring conscience means designing for reflection. Ethical systems cannot depend solely on individual virtue; they must institutionalize moments of pause. In a judicial context, this might mean mandating that a judge write a narrative justification for any sentence that deviates significantly from an algorithmic risk assessment, forcing a return from statistical probability to human-centered reasoning. For example, social media platforms could build friction into the act of sharing—introducing reflective prompts that ask users to verify, reconsider, or contextualize content before amplifying it. In medicine, algorithmic diagnostic tools could require human sign-off not only for liability, but for empathy—to ensure that data interpretation remains grounded in the lived reality of the patient. In corporate governance, automated workflows could include checkpoints for ethical review before decisions affecting employment, privacy, or access to resources are finalized. These interventions do not hinder efficiency; they protect meaning.

Restoring conscience also requires reframing emotional life as an instrument of ethics rather than a distraction from it. For decades, organizational and cultural discourse has treated emotion as interference—something to regulate, suppress, or optimize. Yet emotion is the signal system of morality. Guilt, empathy, and moral elevation are affective cues that guide behavior toward coherence with values. When systems suppress emotion under the guise of neutrality, they silence the very mechanisms that sustain conscience. The task, then, is not emotional control but emotional cultivation—the conscious integration of feeling into ethical reflection.

Psychologically, this involves developing emotional granularity—the ability to distinguish among subtle emotional states rather than labeling them generically as "good" or "bad." Research by Lisa Feldman Barrett and others suggests that emotional precision strengthens self-regulation and moral discernment. A person who can differentiate between irritation, disappointment, and moral disquiet is more capable of understanding what their emotions are signaling. Conscience thrives on such granularity because it transforms vague discomfort into articulated awareness. Education systems that cultivate this emotional literacy—through narrative reflection, literature, or contemplative practice—help inoculate against ethical drift.

Culturally, the restoration of conscience also involves rebuilding shared moral imagination. Modern societies, fragmented by polarization and driven by individualism, have lost many of the common reference points that once oriented collective ethics. Religion, tradition, and civic identity once provided moral scaffolding. Their decline has left a vacuum that technology fills with preference rather than principle. To restore conscience at scale, societies must recreate spaces for collective reflection—forums where ethical questions are explored publicly, not only privately. This might take the form of citizen assemblies on technology ethics, interdisciplinary councils that review social impacts, or media platforms committed to moral inquiry rather than outrage. Conscience requires conversation.

The restoration of conscience also depends on humility—the recognition that intelligence does not guarantee wisdom. The philosopher Immanuel Kant defined enlightenment as humanity's emergence from self-imposed immaturity, the courage to use one's own understanding. Yet he also warned that reason without moral law leads to self-deception. Today's version of that immaturity is technological hubris—the assumption that knowledge and capacity automatically confer virtue. Restoring conscience means recovering the humility to ask whether something should be done simply because it can be done.

From a psychological perspective, humility functions as a corrective to cognitive overconfidence. Studies in moral psychology show that individuals who cultivate intellectual humility—awareness of the limits of one's knowledge—are more likely to engage in ethical reasoning and less likely to justify harmful actions. Humility, then, is not passivity but perspective: an awareness of interdependence that tempers the illusion of control. When embedded in institutions, it manifests as accountability; when cultivated in individuals, it manifests as empathy.

Education for conscience must therefore prioritize reflection, dialogue, and humility as developmental goals equal to knowledge acquisition. Philosophy, ethics, and psychology should not be elective subjects but core competencies. The capacity to reason morally, to empathize across difference, and to foresee consequence are not optional skills—they are the foundation of responsible intelligence. In professional contexts, ethics education must move beyond procedural compliance toward character formation. Technical expertise without conscience is intelligence without direction.

Restoring conscience within institutions also involves transforming incentives. Systems shape behavior by rewarding certain outcomes. When performance metrics prioritize speed, profit, or engagement over integrity, conscience becomes maladaptive. Leaders must therefore align incentives with values—rewarding ethical courage, transparency, and restraint. A culture that celebrates those who slow down to ask difficult questions fosters moral strength. This is what psychologist Jonathan Haidt calls "moral elevation"—the experience of admiration for acts of ethical integrity. Such elevation reinforces conscience collectively, creating social contagion for moral awareness.

At the societal level, conscience restoration requires rebuilding trust in human judgment. Overreliance on algorithms often stems from distrust in human fallibility. Yet human judgment, though imperfect, contains moral depth precisely because it integrates feeling, intuition, and context. Machines cannot replicate this synthesis because they lack the subjective experience that gives moral reasoning its texture. Reaffirming trust in human discernment rebalances the moral ecosystem: automation handles precision, while humans preserve purpose.

The restoration of conscience also calls for confronting one of the most subtle psychological tendencies of the digital age: moral outsourcing. When people rely on external systems to regulate behavior—laws, algorithms, or institutions—they may unconsciously relinquish personal responsibility. This phenomenon mirrors what psychologists describe as *moral licensing*: the belief that adherence to one rule compensates for neglect in another domain. In an algorithmic context, moral licensing manifests as faith in system integrity rather than personal vigilance. To counter this, individuals must reclaim internal moral agency—cultivating awareness of how their actions participate in broader systems, even when mediated by technology.

Philosophically, restoring conscience requires a return to the phenomenology of moral experience—the lived sense of being answerable to something beyond oneself. This does not necessitate religious belief; it requires recognition of transcendence in the moral sense: that our choices carry weight because they affect lives beyond our own. The psychologist Viktor Frankl called this the "will to meaning," the drive to find significance through responsibility. Conscience is the voice of that will, reminding individuals that freedom without responsibility collapses into emptiness.

Restoration, then, is not nostalgia for a pre-technological morality but evolution toward a psychologically mature ethics. In a world where decisions are distributed across human and machine, conscience must become adaptive—capable of functioning within systems of partial visibility and shared agency. This means cultivating metacognitive awareness: the ability to notice when attention drifts, when empathy dulls, and when moral fatigue sets in. Such awareness can be trained, much like mindfulness, through deliberate reflection.

Practically, this could involve structured reflection routines in professional settings—brief ethical check-ins during team meetings, or dedicated "pause protocols" before implementing major automated decisions. In design environments, it might mean establishing cross-functional ethics boards that include psychologists, sociologists, and community representatives, not only engineers. These mechanisms reintroduce moral diversity into decision-making, ensuring that conscience is collective as well as individual.

At its deepest level, restoring conscience is an act of remembering—remembering what it means to be human amid abstraction. It is the recollection that every technological advancement is an expression of psychological intent, and that every system reflects its creators' values. The moral frontier will not be crossed by innovation alone, but by integration—the integration of intelligence with empathy, of capability with humility, and of speed with care.

To restore conscience is to reclaim the human center of moral life. It is to insist that reflection remains sacred, even in an age of automation.

Collective Maturity

Moral progress is rarely individual. It unfolds collectively, across generations, institutions, and cultures. The ethical dilemmas of the Artificial Era are not personal puzzles but shared conditions: problems of scale, systems, and interconnected consequence. They cannot be solved through individual virtue alone, because their origins lie in distributed agency. What is required is a new level of social development—a collective maturity equal to the complexity of our tools.

Collective maturity begins with the recognition that morality is a social function before it is a personal trait. It depends on shared norms, trust, and the willingness to coordinate restraint. The psychologist Lawrence Kohlberg's stages of moral development emphasized the transition from self-interest to principle-based reasoning. In a similar way, societies evolve from moral tribalism—defining good in terms of in-groups and interests—to moral universalism, where empathy extends beyond proximity. The challenge of our time is that technology connects the world faster than empathy can scale. Collective maturity is the process of closing that gap.

At the psychological level, maturity reflects integration: the ability to hold complexity without splitting it into extremes. For individuals, this means balancing autonomy with interdependence, freedom with responsibility. For societies, it means balancing innovation with ethics, growth with sustainability, and efficiency with empathy. Immature systems, like immature individuals, oscillate between overcontrol and collapse—between authoritarian rigidity and unbounded permissiveness. Mature systems maintain equilibrium through reflection, accountability, and adaptability.

Collective maturity therefore depends on the cultivation of emotional intelligence at scale. Emotional intelligence, as Daniel Goleman popularized, involves recognizing and regulating one's emotions while empathizing with others. Applied socially, it becomes cultural intelligence—the capacity of institutions and communities to process collective emotion. In polarized societies, this capacity erodes. Public discourse becomes reactive rather than reflective, driven by outrage rather than understanding. Technological acceleration exacerbates this erosion by amplifying emotion without context. The result is a culture that feels intensely but thinks shallowly. Collective maturity requires reversing this ratio.

The sociologist Ulrich Beck described modernity as a "risk society," one in which progress produces new dangers that require self-awareness to manage. AI and automation have intensified this condition by creating risks that are diffuse, invisible, and continuous. A single design decision in Silicon Valley can alter economic behavior in Bangladesh or political dynamics in Nairobi. The moral implications of such interdependence are profound. Maturity in this context means developing global reflexivity—the capacity of societies to perceive themselves as part of a shared moral ecosystem.

Culturally, this reflexivity demands humility and empathy at the collective level. Nations, corporations, and institutions must acknowledge not only their power but their participation in humanity's shared condition. This involves what psychologists call *perspective taking*: the imaginative act of seeing from another's vantage point. When scaled to institutions, perspective taking becomes diplomacy, collaboration, and ethical policy-making. Without it, power isolates itself in echo chambers of justification.

Collective maturity also depends on moral transparency. Just as individuals build trust through honesty, societies build legitimacy through openness. In the context of artificial intelligence, this translates into explainability, accountability, and ethical auditing. Systems that govern human life should be intelligible to those they affect. Hidden decision-making corrodes moral development because it erodes the feedback loops through which conscience operates. Transparency re-establishes those loops, allowing error to become learning rather than denial.

Yet transparency alone is not enough. Mature systems must also cultivate *ethical resilience*—the ability to learn from moral failure without collapsing into cynicism or denial. Ethical resilience mirrors psychological resilience: the capacity to confront discomfort, integrate lessons, and reform structures. When societies deny wrongdoing or displace blame, they regress morally. When they confront failure with humility and reform, they evolve. Truth commissions, restorative justice models, and corporate accountability mechanisms exemplify this principle. Each transforms error into moral growth.

At the organizational level, collective maturity manifests as culture rather than policy. Ethical codes alone cannot ensure conscience; they must be embodied in daily practice. This requires leaders who model moral courage—the willingness to act on principle even when it conflicts with profit or popularity. After a significant data breach, for example, a mature leader would take immediate public responsibility and outline a transparent plan for restitution, while an immature leader might deflect blame onto a subcontractor or downplay the severity of the harm. Moral courage is contagious. It signals to others that integrity is not idealism but realism: the condition for sustainable trust. Institutions that prioritize moral development—through ethical training, transparent decision processes, and inclusive governance—become ecosystems of maturity.

From a developmental psychology standpoint, collective maturity parallels the process of individuation. Carl Jung described individuation as the integration of shadow elements—the parts of the psyche one would rather not see. Societies too must confront their shadows: the biases encoded into algorithms, the inequalities amplified by automation, the exploitation hidden within convenience. Denial perpetuates immaturity; acknowledgment initiates growth. When societies bring their shadow into consciousness, they create the possibility of moral transformation.

Technology magnifies both shadow and light. It exposes the latent tendencies of human nature at scale—our creativity and compassion, but also our vanity, aggression, and apathy. Collective maturity means developing institutions capable of containing these forces without suppressing them. It is not the eradication of error, but the creation of systems that can metabolize it. The task is psychological as much as political: to evolve the emotional capacity for collective self-regulation.

Philosophically, this evolution aligns with the notion of *moral ecology*. Just as environmental systems depend on balance among diverse species, moral ecosystems depend on balance among diverse perspectives. No single institution or ideology can sustain moral health alone. Ethics must be distributed—shared among governments, corporations, educators, and citizens. The health of the moral ecosystem depends on the quality of its relationships, not the dominance of any single actor.

The psychological foundation of collective maturity is empathy. But empathy must mature beyond sentiment into structure. Compassion that remains private cannot regulate systems. The future requires institutionalized empathy—designing processes that translate care into policy. For example, involving affected communities in algorithmic governance introduces human context into technical design. Creating ethical impact assessments alongside environmental ones integrates moral consideration into planning. When empathy informs infrastructure, conscience scales.

Culturally, collective maturity also requires redefining success. Modern societies have long equated progress with expansion: more data, more productivity, more control. But true maturity replaces expansion with integration—deepening rather than widening. It asks not only what can be built, but what should be preserved. It values coherence over growth, sustainability over novelty, and wisdom over speed. This shift parallels Erik Erikson's psychological model of generativity: the stage of adulthood where the focus turns from self-advancement to legacy. Humanity, in entering the Artificial Era, stands at a similar crossroads. The task is no longer dominance but stewardship.

Stewardship reframes power as responsibility. It transforms technology from a tool of control into an instrument of care. This ethic of stewardship can be traced through moral philosophy from John Stuart Mill's principle of harm reduction to contemporary ecological ethics. In each case, maturity is defined not by capacity but by conscience—the willingness to constrain one's power for the sake of the whole. Collective maturity thus manifests not in technological achievement but in restraint: the capacity to say no to what is possible when it threatens what is humane.

Restoring collective maturity also involves repairing public trust. In a world saturated with misinformation and polarization, trust has become the scarcest social resource. Without it, moral coordination collapses. Psychologically, trust is built through predictability and transparency; culturally, through fairness and reciprocity. When institutions act unpredictably or conceal their motives, citizens withdraw their moral investment. Restoring that trust requires consistency of principle across scale: leaders who act ethically when unseen, systems that apply fairness without favoritism, and media that inform rather than inflame.

The role of education in fostering collective maturity cannot be overstated. Schools and universities are the developmental organs of civilization. They shape how the next generation perceives responsibility, empathy, and truth. Teaching students to code is insufficient if they are not also taught to care. Curricula that integrate ethics across disciplines—linking philosophy with data science, literature with neuroscience, economics with psychology— prepare minds that think systemically and act ethically. Education that cultivates empathy and critical thought is the social immune system of democracy.

Collective maturity also requires moral imagination—the ability to envision futures beyond the default trajectory of efficiency. Imagination, often dismissed as artistic indulgence, is in fact a cognitive function essential to moral reasoning. It allows individuals and societies to project consequences, inhabit alternative perspectives, and anticipate meaning. Without imagination, ethics collapses into compliance. With it, ethics becomes creation. The great moral advances of history—abolition, civil rights, humanitarian reform—were acts of imagination before they were acts of policy.

Finally, collective maturity demands a reawakening of moral emotion at the societal scale: empathy as policy, humility as governance, gratitude as civic virtue. These are not sentimental ideals; they are psychological conditions for collective endurance. Empathy sustains connection; humility sustains correction; gratitude sustains perspective. Together, they form the emotional infrastructure of moral civilization.

The Artificial Era will test whether humanity can institutionalize conscience as effectively as it has mechanized intelligence. Collective maturity is the final frontier of moral evolution—the point at which technical progress must submit to ethical proportion. A civilization that achieves this will not be defined by its machines but by its wisdom: its capacity to wield power without losing tenderness, to pursue innovation without forgetting restraint, and to act collectively without erasing individuality.

The future will not be secured by intelligence alone, but by the maturity to use it wisely.

* * *

12

Staying Awake

The Art of Presence in a Simulated Age

Human beings have always lived among illusions, but never before have they been so immersive, so persuasive, and so constant. The digital age has not merely surrounded humanity with information; it has constructed a parallel reality—one that mirrors life while quietly replacing it. In this environment, staying awake becomes more than a metaphor. It is a moral, psychological, and existential discipline.

The philosopher Søren Kierkegaard once wrote that the greatest danger is not error, but distraction. To be deceived, he argued, is unfortunate; to be distracted is to lose the capacity to care that one is deceived. That warning feels newly urgent. The Artificial Era has perfected distraction—not as chaos, but as design. Every notification, recommendation, and algorithmic interaction is calibrated to keep attention fragmented. Awareness, the most fundamental human faculty, has become the most endangered.

To remain human in a simulated age is therefore to remain conscious in every sense: cognitively alert, emotionally attuned, morally awake. Awareness is no longer a passive state; it is an active form of resistance. In psychological terms, it is the foundation of self-regulation and moral agency. Without awareness, intelligence collapses into automation, emotion into reaction, and life into performance. The central task of this era is not to know more, but to perceive more clearly.

Presence is the antidote to simulation. It is the condition through which meaning reenters experience. In neuroscience, presence correlates with sustained activation of the prefrontal cortex and reduced default-mode rumination—a balance between attention and awareness that allows reality to be experienced rather than conceptualized. In psychological terms, presence unites attention, embodiment, and emotion into a coherent sense of self. It transforms consciousness from a lens of distortion into a field of participation.

The Artificial Era threatens this coherence by splitting awareness across multiple planes. People live increasingly between selves: the physical and the digital, the private and the performed, the present and the archived. This fragmentation weakens the continuity of experience that gives identity its stability. The philosopher Maurice Merleau-Ponty described perception as an act of embodiment—the body as the anchor of consciousness. When life migrates into simulation, that anchor loosens. The result is a subtle form of dislocation: to be everywhere except here, connected to everyone except oneself.

Staying awake, then, is not simply about resisting distraction. It is about restoring contact with what is real—what can be felt, sensed, and inhabited. Presence must be re-learned as a psychological skill and cultivated as an ethical stance. It requires courage to face immediacy without the filters that make it comfortable. It means reclaiming attention not as productivity but as belonging: to one's own mind, one's relationships, and one's moral life.

Psychologically, this awakening involves reversing a long conditioning process. Modern life trains individuals to externalize validation, to fragment attention, and to mistake simulation for engagement. To awaken is to undo that training—to recover the natural depth of perception that consumer culture flattens. It is to inhabit experience again rather than observe it through the mediated distance of the screen.

The closing movement of this book returns to awareness as the foundation of meaning. It explores how attention, embodiment, and emotional depth can be restored as antidotes to disconnection. It ends with the proposition that the second invention of humanity will not be technological but psychological: the rediscovery of consciousness as both the medium and the measure of being fully alive.

Staying awake is not about fear of replacement. It is about the refusal to sleepwalk through an era that confuses stimulation with life.

The Attention Restored

In every era, the quality of a civilization can be measured by the quality of its attention. The great works of art, science, and philosophy were born from minds capable of sustained perception—of looking deeply, patiently, and without distraction. The modern mind, however, lives in a state of constant interruption. What once required solitude now competes with stimulation. The ability to attend—to linger with complexity long enough for meaning to emerge—has become both rare and revolutionary. In the Artificial Era, the restoration of attention is not a productivity strategy; it is a moral act.

Attention is the most fundamental expression of freedom. To attend is to choose what matters. The psychologist William James called attention "the taking possession by the mind, in clear and vivid form, of one out of what seem several simultaneously possible objects." That choice, he argued, determines the shape of consciousness itself. When attention is fragmented, identity fragments with it. When attention is sustained, coherence and continuity return. What we give our attention to, individually and collectively, becomes who we are.

Modern culture treats attention as a commodity, but psychology reveals it as a form of love. To attend to something—to another person, to a thought, to the present moment—is to grant it reality. The philosopher Simone Weil wrote that attention is the rarest and purest form of generosity. This insight has been repeatedly confirmed by research in moral psychology, which links focused attention with empathy and ethical behavior. When people truly attend, they perceive others more fully and act with greater compassion. The loss of attention, therefore, is not merely cognitive but moral; it erodes the emotional capacity to care.

In the Artificial Era, attention has become externalized. Rather than an inner faculty, it is managed by algorithms designed to anticipate and redirect focus. The human nervous system, shaped by evolution for scarcity, is now exposed to abundance without limit. The result is chronic overstimulation— a neurological environment that rewards novelty at the expense of depth. Each alert, notification, and feed creates a miniature reward loop driven by dopamine release. Over time, this conditions the brain to seek stimulation reflexively, mistaking reactivity for engagement.

The cost of this conditioning is attentional fatigue. Cognitive neuro-science describes it as the depletion of executive function caused by excessive task-switching. Psychologically, it manifests as impatience, anxiety, and a diminished capacity for reflection. The more one consumes, the less one assimilates. The speed of information flow exceeds the mind's ability to metabolize it into understanding. In such conditions, consciousness becomes shallow not from ignorance but from saturation.

Restoring attention begins with recognizing its nature. Attention is not infinite; it is renewable only through rest, not through more stimulation. The philosopher Josef Pieper described leisure as the foundation of culture— not idleness, but receptivity, the stillness that allows insight to arise. Modern life has nearly extinguished this capacity. The obsession with productivity has made rest feel irresponsible. Yet from a psychological perspective, rest is the soil of awareness. In rest, the default-mode network of the brain integrates scattered experiences into narrative coherence. To restore attention, one must revalue idleness as the architecture of insight.

Cultural recovery of attention also requires redefining focus as depth rather than fixation. True focus is not the narrowing of perception but the refinement of it—the ability to remain receptive while steady. Neuroscience distinguishes between two modes of attention: the dorsal system, which directs focus toward goals, and the ventral system, which allows awareness to remain open to the unexpected. The healthiest form of attention balances these systems. In the Artificial Era, where goal-directed focus is constantly hijacked by novelty, this balance must be intentionally reclaimed.

The restoration of attention is not merely an individual pursuit; it is a collective necessity. Democracies depend on citizens capable of sustained thought. Empathy depends on presence. Innovation depends on depth. When public attention collapses into constant distraction, politics devolves into spectacle, discourse into outrage, and creativity into replication. The psychologist Mihaly Csikszentmihalyi's work on "flow" described deep engagement as the source of meaning. When societies lose the capacity for flow, they lose the capacity for meaning itself.

Attention also shapes emotional life. The more scattered attention becomes, the more difficult it is to regulate emotion. Studies in affective neuroscience show that emotional regulation depends on awareness—specifically, the prefrontal cortex's ability to monitor and modulate limbic responses. When attention is fragmented, this regulation falters. Individuals become reactive, prone to impulsivity and moral fatigue. Restored attention stabilizes the emotional field, allowing feeling to deepen into understanding rather than collapse into noise.

Psychologically, one might think of attention as the mind's immune system. It filters the influx of experience, discerning what belongs and what does not. When compromised, consciousness becomes vulnerable to intrusion—propaganda, manipulation, overstimulation. The algorithms of the Artificial Era exploit this vulnerability by bypassing reflection and appealing directly to emotional triggers. Restoring attention therefore functions as a form of psychological hygiene: a deliberate act of protecting the mind's integrity.

This restoration begins with small practices of reclamation. Reading slowly. Listening without multitasking. Walking without a device. These acts, though simple, recondition the nervous system to tolerate stillness. They retrain perception from scanning to seeing. The goal is not digital abstinence but digital discernment—the ability to inhabit technology consciously rather than reflexively.

Culturally, the restoration of attention may mark the beginning of a new humanism. For centuries, humanism emphasized reason as the defining trait of humanity. The Artificial Era reveals that attention—our

251

capacity to be present—is equally fundamental. Machines may simulate thought, but they cannot experience awareness. They process input; they do not perceive. The restoration of attention therefore becomes a form of existential preservation—a reminder that consciousness is not computation.

To attend deeply is also to resist the reduction of life to data. The sociologist Hartmut Rosa describes modernity as an age of "resonance," where meaning arises through felt connection. Attention makes resonance possible. Without it, even beauty becomes invisible. The more distracted we are, the less reality reaches us. Relearning to attend—to another's voice, to nature, to silence—is a way of rejoining the world we inhabit but no longer fully experience.

There is also a moral dimension to restored attention. Ethical action begins in perception: the ability to see suffering, complexity, and conse-quence. When attention is shallow, empathy collapses into sentimentality. When attention is sustained, empathy matures into responsibility. The psychiatrist Viktor Frankl, writing after his experiences in concentration camps, observed that meaning arises in the space between stimulus and response—the space that only awareness can create. To restore that space is to reclaim freedom itself.

Attention, then, is both psychological practice and ethical posture. It is how consciousness honors reality. The Artificial Era tempts humanity to live at the surface of things—to substitute simulation for sensation, reaction for reflection. Restoring attention means reintroducing depth into the field of experience. It is not withdrawal but return: the rediscovery of what is immediate, complex, and alive.

The restoration of attention begins wherever distraction ends: in the decision to look, listen, and linger.

Embodied Reality

To be human is to be in a body. Every thought, memory, and emotion arises through the nervous system, shaped by sensation and anchored in flesh. Yet in the Artificial Era, the body has become the forgotten foundation of consciousness. Life increasingly unfolds in abstraction—pixels replacing texture, representation replacing presence. The physical self, once the primary site of experience, is now treated as secondary to the mental and digital. To remain awake, however, one must return to the body, because without embodiment, awareness floats untethered, detached from reality and from meaning itself.

Embodiment is not simply a biological fact; it is a psychological function. The philosopher Maurice Merleau-Ponty described perception as the body's dialogue with the world—the point at which mind and matter meet. Sensory engagement gives coherence to experience. When we see, hear, or touch, we locate ourselves within space and time. The body grounds identity by providing continuity. Without this anchor, the self becomes disoriented, scattered across screens and simulations.

This disconnection from the body has consequences that reach beyond physical health. In psychology, embodiment is closely linked to emotional regulation and empathy. Research in affective neuroscience shows that emotions are first felt as bodily sensations—tightness, warmth, expansion, contraction—before they are named or interpreted. When people lose touch with their bodily awareness, they also lose access to these emotional signals. The result is a flattening of affect, a kind of emotional anesthesia that mirrors the overstimulation of the digital environment.

The sociologist Sherry Turkle has written extensively about this phenomenon, describing how technology mediates relationships through convenience at the cost of intimacy. When communication is disembodied—text instead of tone, emoji instead of expression—nuance disappears. Human interaction becomes efficient but less alive. The body, once central to empathy, is replaced by symbols of it. The loss is subtle but cumulative: without embodied presence, people begin to forget how to feel with and through one another.

Embodiment also shapes cognition. The theory of *embodied cognition* argues that thinking is not confined to the brain but distributed throughout the body's sensory and motor systems. Experiments have shown that posture influences memory, gesture supports reasoning, and physical movement enhances creativity. We know this instinctively: we pace when trying to solve a difficult problem, stand taller to feel more confident, and use our hands to explain a complex idea. To learn is to enact. When life becomes sedentary and virtual, cognitive diversity narrows. The world becomes something observed rather than encountered. The restoration of embodied reality is therefore not nostalgia for the tactile past, but recognition that intelligence itself depends on sensory participation.

Psychologically, disembodiment manifests as dissociation—a split between perception and presence. In mild forms, it feels like daydreaming or detachment; in chronic forms, it erodes vitality and coherence. The modern lifestyle—screen-based work, mediated communication, constant abstraction—encourages low-grade dissociation as a mode of adaptation. People inhabit digital spaces that stimulate thought but neglect sensation. Over time, the feedback loop between body and awareness weakens, and life feels increasingly unreal.

Reversing this condition requires deliberate re-engagement with the physical world. Simple acts—walking, cooking, writing by hand, listening to live music—retrain the senses to register depth and texture. In psychotherapy, grounding exercises serve a similar function, helping individuals reconnect with bodily sensations to stabilize attention and emotion. These practices are not escapes from intellect but returns to integration. They remind the nervous system that perception is participation.

Culturally, the neglect of embodiment reflects deeper philosophical assumptions. Western thought has long privileged mind over body, reason over sensation. This hierarchy, inherited from Descartes' dualism, positioned the body as a vessel rather than a voice. The Artificial Era extends this logic to its extreme. In digital environments, the self becomes a curated projection—edited, filtered, and detached from its physical origin. The consequence is both psychological and moral. When people see themselves primarily as minds or avatars, they begin to treat bodies—their own and others'—as objects rather than subjects. This detachment fuels the culture of performative display, aesthetic anxiety, and moral distance that defines much of contemporary life.

Restoring embodied reality requires reclaiming the body as a source of wisdom rather than an obstacle to it. The body records truth more honestly than thought. Somatic psychology, for instance, recognizes that trauma is stored in muscle memory and nervous-system reactivity. Healing therefore requires physical integration, not just cognitive insight. Similarly, moral awareness often begins as a visceral reaction—discomfort in the presence of harm, warmth in the presence of kindness. These bodily cues are conscience in its most primal form.

From a developmental perspective, embodiment is also the origin of learning. Infants explore the world through touch, movement, and imitation. This sensorimotor curiosity forms the foundation of symbolic thought. When education becomes entirely abstract—screen-based, detached from experience—it risks producing knowledge without intuition. To think deeply, one must first perceive deeply. The restoration of embodied learning reconnects intellect with its sensory roots.

There is also a spiritual dimension to embodiment that transcends doctrine. Across traditions, awareness of the body has been linked to awareness of being itself. The breath, heartbeat, and rhythm of movement are reminders that consciousness is not separate from life but immersed in it. In a simulated age, where experience is increasingly virtual, returning to the body becomes a form of transcendence through grounding—a way of rediscovering the sacred in the tangible.

Psychologically, this return fosters integration between the autonomic and reflective systems of the mind. When awareness reconnects with the body, self-regulation improves. Anxiety lessens, focus stabilizes, and the sense of fragmentation recedes. The body becomes a stabilizing mirror for consciousness, offering real-time feedback about the state of the mind. Every breath, posture, and muscle tension tells a story about inner life. Listening to the body is a way of listening to oneself.

Culturally, the reclamation of embodiment also challenges the commodification of physicality. The digital economy transforms bodies into data— fitness metrics, biometrics, and visual content. While such technologies can support health, they can also reduce physical experience to performance.

True embodiment resists quantification. It values the felt over the measured, the lived over the displayed. To be embodied is to inhabit the irreducible mystery of being alive, not merely to track it.

The restoration of embodied reality will not come from rejecting technology but from humanizing it. Designers and engineers can create interfaces that encourage sensory engagement rather than disembodiment. Virtual reality, paradoxically, holds potential here—when used not as escape but as simulation of empathy and environment. Artistic and therapeutic uses of immersive media can remind users of their own presence rather than distract from it. The key is intention: technology must serve awareness, not replace it.

Embodied living also reshapes relationships. Physical co-presence communicates more than language ever can. Eye contact, tone, and gesture convey emotional information that no digital message can replicate. The psychologist Edward Tronick's studies of infant-caregiver interaction showed that mutual regulation—emotional synchrony through facial expression and rhythm—forms the foundation of attachment. Adult relationships operate on the same principle. Without embodied feedback, intimacy becomes conceptual. Relearning presence means relearning how to be with another person in silence, without mediation, without the need to perform.

In a moral sense, embodiment reintroduces accountability. It reminds individuals that actions have weight, that words carry consequence, that others are not abstractions. The physicality of existence grounds ethics in empathy. To witness suffering in person is to feel its reality; to see it only as image is to risk detachment. The more mediated moral experience becomes, the more essential embodiment is as a corrective.

Ultimately, embodiment is the medium through which awareness encounters truth. The Artificial Era tempts humanity to live in simulation—experience flattened into symbols, emotion translated into data, attention dispersed into fragments. To remain awake, one must resist that flattening by reinhabiting the physical world. This does not mean retreating from technology but restoring balance: remembering that perception begins in the body, that consciousness is not a spectator but a participant.

The return to embodied reality is the return to gravity—the psychological and existential force that pulls awareness back into presence. To feel one's breath, to sense the ground beneath one's feet, to move deliberately through space: these are the most radical acts of consciousness in an age of simulation.

The body is not the opposite of mind; it is its mirror. To inhabit it fully is to awaken.

Emotional Depth

The modern world prizes emotional expression yet often avoids emotional experience. Feelings are displayed, performed, and shared more than ever before, yet they are seldom felt in their full intensity or allowed to mature into insight. This paradox defines the psychological condition of the Artificial Era: a culture that mistakes visibility for depth. To feel deeply now requires courage, because depth cannot be optimized, monetized, or streamed. It demands inwardness in a time of exposure.

Emotional depth is the capacity to inhabit one's feelings without collapsing into them or performing them for an audience. It is not the intensity of emotion that defines it, but the degree of awareness within emotion. In psychological terms, it reflects the integration of affect and cognition—the ability to experience and interpret feeling simultaneously. Mature emotion is not reactive but reflective. It transforms sensation into meaning and impulse into understanding.

The erosion of emotional depth is not accidental; it is structural. The digital environment rewards immediacy and reaction. Algorithms privilege content that provokes emotion, not contemplation. The result is what psychologists might call *affective inflation*: emotions expressed without grounding, amplified without context, and consumed without digestion. Outrage, sentimentality, and virtue signaling replace genuine empathy and moral reflection. The faster emotion circulates, the thinner it becomes.

Psychologically, this environment favors *high arousal* emotions—anger, excitement, anxiety—over subtler ones like melancholy, tenderness, or gratitude. High arousal sustains engagement; low arousal sustains understanding. Over time, the nervous system adapts to stimulation by raising its baseline. Calm feels boring, subtlety feels empty, and complexity feels confusing. The emotional palette narrows to what the system rewards: whatever keeps attention reactive. Emotional depth withers under these conditions because depth requires stillness, and stillness does not trend.

From a developmental standpoint, emotional depth emerges from what psychologist Daniel Siegel calls *integration*: the linking of differentiated parts of experience into coherence. When emotion is felt, named, and understood, it becomes part of one's narrative identity. When it is suppressed or externalized, it becomes static—repeated endlessly in new contexts without resolution. Many adults remain emotionally adolescent not because they lack feeling, but because they have never learned to metabolize it. They live in cycles of stimulation and avoidance rather than reflection and growth.

Relearning emotional depth therefore involves re-establishing emotional literacy: the ability to identify, articulate, and explore feeling without judgment. This literacy begins in attention—directing awareness inward long enough to notice the nuances of emotion, such as the subtle difference between the tightness of anxiety and the hollowness of disappointment. Contemporary psychology increasingly supports this ancient principle. Mindfulness-based therapies and emotion-focused approaches converge on the same insight: that awareness transforms emotion. To observe a feeling is to begin to integrate it.

Yet awareness alone is not enough. Emotional depth also depends on relational containment—the experience of being understood by another. Human beings are not designed to regulate emotion in isolation. The nervous system is social; it calms in the presence of empathy. The work of attachment theorists such as John Bowlby and Mary Ainsworth demonstrated that emotional regulation develops through attuned relationships, where feelings are mirrored and named. In adulthood, the same principle holds. Depth grows in dialogue. It matures through resonance.

Culturally, however, the conditions for such resonance are eroding. Conversations increasingly take place through text, where tone and gesture vanish. Public expression substitutes for private intimacy. People announce their feelings instead of sharing them. This externalization creates the illusion of connection while leaving the inner world untouched. The more emotions are broadcast, the less they are processed. The digital self performs sincerity while the embodied self remains unseen.

Restoring emotional depth requires reversing this flow: from performance back to presence, from projection back to perception. The task is not to feel more, but to feel more consciously—to pause long enough for emotion to reveal its meaning. Every emotion, when examined, carries information about need, value, and truth. Anger often conceals injury; envy reveals desire; sadness signals attachment. To feel deeply is to decode these messages without rushing to discharge them.

In this sense, emotional depth is a form of intelligence. It organizes experience, guides behavior, and anchors moral life. The philosopher Martha Nussbaum has argued that emotions are not irrational impulses but judgments about what we value. They reveal the contours of conscience. Emotional shallowness, by contrast, produces moral confusion—an inability to discern proportion, to distinguish between harm and inconvenience, or tragedy and discomfort. A society that loses emotional depth becomes morally anesthetized, incapable of empathy beyond the momentary and the spectacular.

Psychologically, cultivating depth involves tolerating discomfort. Emotional growth requires the capacity to remain present with feeling without immediately seeking relief. This tolerance, known as *distress endurance* in clinical psychology, is a hallmark of maturity. It allows individuals to transform pain into insight rather than avoidance. The opposite of emotional depth is not indifference but reactivity—the inability to remain with one's own experience long enough for understanding to form.

Depth also demands slowness. In a culture of acceleration, emotion is often bypassed by explanation. People rationalize before they reflect. But genuine emotional insight arises only when language follows experience, not when it replaces it. To sit with emotion before analyzing it is to allow the psyche to speak in its native language: sensation, image, and metaphor.

This is why art, music, and ritual remain essential to emotional life. They provide forms for feeling that thought alone cannot contain.

From a neuroscientific perspective, emotional depth corresponds to integration across multiple brain networks—the limbic system, prefrontal cortex, and default-mode network. When emotion and cognition cooperate, the brain creates coherence between experience and interpretation. This integration fosters resilience. People who can access emotional depth recover from adversity more effectively because they can derive meaning from suffering. They experience pain as transformative rather than purely destructive.

At the collective level, emotional depth functions as cultural ballast. It prevents societies from drifting into superficiality and polarization. Cultures that cultivate emotional nuance—through art, literature, and education— tend to produce citizens capable of empathy and moral reflection. Those that privilege spectacle and immediacy breed volatility. In this sense, emotional maturity is a form of civic intelligence. It enables communities to sustain dialogue, to grieve, to reconcile.

The restoration of emotional depth also requires reclaiming solitude. Solitude is not loneliness; it is the psychological space in which emotion becomes articulate. Constant social input prevents feeling from unfolding. The theologian Paul Tillich described solitude as the "fulfillment of aloneness," the place where the self meets its own interior life. In solitude, emotion ripens into insight. Without it, feelings remain half-formed, dependent on reaction rather than reflection.

Practically, this restoration can begin in simple practices: journaling, reflective conversation, deliberate silence. The key is rhythm—creating intervals of stillness amid activity, depth amid exposure. These rhythms mirror the nervous system's need for alternation between activation and rest. When people allow their emotional lives to breathe, they rediscover complexity.

In moral terms, emotional depth is the antidote to performative empathy. It resists the commodification of feeling—the reduction of compassion to slogans or outrage. True empathy arises not from identification but from imagination: the capacity to understand another's reality without appropriating it. This form of empathy requires both emotional sensitivity and boundary—feeling with, not feeling as. It is an act of respect, not absorption.

At its highest expression, emotional depth becomes wisdom—the ability to feel fully and act proportionately. It integrates compassion with clarity, sensitivity with steadiness. Such balance is the hallmark of mature humanity. Machines may someday simulate emotional recognition, but they cannot experience moral proportion. Emotional depth, rooted in awareness, remains irreducibly human.

The Artificial Era will continue to test this capacity. As artificial systems learn to mirror sentiment, humanity must learn to inhabit it. Emotional depth will become the new frontier of authenticity—the measure of whether people are still capable of feeling what their technology only imitates.

To stay awake is to feel, not react; to listen, not perform; to suffer consciously rather than unconsciously repeat. Emotional depth is not the opposite of progress; it is what makes progress humane.

The Second Invention of Humanity

Humanity has reinvented itself many times. The discovery of fire transformed survival into civilization. The invention of language turned experience into culture. The rise of writing preserved thought beyond memory. Each of these revolutions expanded human power, but each also demanded a psychological adaptation—an enlargement of consciousness to match the scale of capability. The Artificial Era marks another turning point. Yet unlike previous revolutions, this one does not demand more control over the world, but more awareness within it.

The first invention of humanity was biological: the emergence of self-reflective consciousness from matter. The second invention, now underway, is psychological: the deliberate cultivation of awareness as the defining human skill in an age of intelligent machines. The next leap will not be technological, but moral and perceptual. Humanity must now learn to know itself with the same precision with which it has learned to manipulate the external world.

This is not the utopian fantasy of transcendence promised by futurists who dream of merging with machines. It is a quieter, deeper evolution—an awakening of inward literacy. Technology has externalized the functions once housed in the psyche: memory, calculation, prediction, even imitation of emotion. What remains uniquely human is the ability to observe consciousness itself—to know that we know, to feel that we feel. This reflexive awareness is the source of meaning, empathy, and ethical restraint. To preserve it is to ensure that intelligence does not outpace wisdom.

Psychologically, this second invention requires the re-integration of perception, thought, and conscience. The human mind, fragmented by overstimulation and abstraction, must relearn coherence. In neuroscience, coherence describes the synchronization of neural oscillations across brain regions—an indicator of efficient communication. In psychology, coherence describes the harmony between cognition and emotion, self and world. In moral life, coherence is integrity. The same principle applies at every level: systems that lose coherence lose vitality. Awareness restores it by reuniting what distraction divides.

The philosopher Pierre Teilhard de Chardin envisioned evolution as a movement toward increasing consciousness, culminating not in domination but in communion—a state of reflective unity among beings aware of their interconnectedness. Whether one accepts his metaphysics or not, the psychological truth remains: survival in the Artificial Era will depend not on competition but on integration. The intelligence humanity has created now mirrors its collective mind. If that mind is divided, distracted, or morally underdeveloped, its creations will amplify those fractures.

The second invention of humanity will therefore require a different kind of literacy—what might be called *meta-awareness*: the capacity to observe one's own attention, emotion, and motivation in real time. This awareness transforms reaction into response. It allows consciousness to recognize when it has been captured by systems designed to exploit it and to choose differently. Meta-awareness is self-governance at the level of perception. It is the psychological foundation of freedom in a mediated world.

Education for this new literacy must teach more than information management; it must teach awareness management. Students should learn not only how to analyze data but how to recognize when their attention is being shaped by it. They must learn to navigate inner experience with the same rigor they apply to external problem-solving. The tools of the Artificial Era will be meaningless without the consciousness to use them wisely.

Culturally, this evolution calls for the revaluation of consciousness itself. For centuries, productivity has been the measure of worth. The next era must honor awareness as the measure of maturity. A society that prizes consciousness over consumption will organize itself around depth rather than speed, wisdom rather than novelty. This shift may seem subtle, but its implications are transformative. It would redefine success, education, and even governance in psychological terms.

The moral aspect of this evolution cannot be overstated. The more humanity externalizes its functions into machines, the greater the temptation to abdicate responsibility. The future will not be decided by what technology can do, but by what humanity chooses to delegate. This requires an ethical consciousness capable of self-restraint. In evolutionary terms, self-restraint is as significant as intelligence; it is how the species survives its own capabilities. The second invention of humanity will succeed only if awareness evolves faster than power.

At its core, this transformation is existential. Artificial intelligence forces humanity to confront what consciousness truly is—not as an abstraction, but as lived reality. The question "Can machines think?" has already given way to a deeper one: "What does it mean to be aware?" The answer cannot be programmed. It must be experienced. Awareness is not a process; it is presence. It cannot be simulated because it is the act of knowing simulation itself.

Philosophically, this reorientation echoes the insights of phenomenology and contemplative psychology: that consciousness is not merely the observer of experience but the condition for it. Machines can process symbols; humans can experience significance. The difference lies not in intelligence but in interiority—the capacity for meaning. When awareness turns inward and recognizes itself as the ground of experience, it awakens the moral sense that binds all other faculties together.

Psychologically, the development of this awareness can be understood as the movement from identification to observation. Most people live within the contents of consciousness—the thoughts, emotions, and roles that compose identity. To awaken is to shift from content to context, from being the thinker to observing thought. This movement is not mystical; it is developmental. It reflects the brain's capacity for meta-cognition and the psyche's capacity for disidentification. When individuals recognize that they are not their narratives but the awareness that perceives them, freedom expands.

This inner shift has social implications. A culture composed of individuals who can observe rather than react will behave differently—less polarized, less defensive, more reflective. The evolution of awareness at scale could reorient politics, education, and economics toward psychological sustainability. Just as humanity once learned to steward natural resources, it must now learn to steward attention and emotion. The second invention of humanity is the invention of inner ecology.

Practically, this evolution begins with small disciplines of presence: conscious breathing, attentive listening, unmediated observation. These practices train awareness to remain steady amid noise. They reestablish contact with the real in a world of simulation. The goal is not withdrawal from technology but mastery of attention within it—to use the tools of the era without being used by them. Such mastery requires humility: the recognition that awareness, though universal, must be cultivated individually.

The second invention also entails a redefinition of progress. Technological history measures advancement by capability; psychological history will measure it by consciousness. A future civilization may look back on this moment not as the rise of machines, but as the awakening of awareness— a period when humanity realized that intelligence without presence is blindness amplified. Progress will be measured not by what is built, but by what is understood, not by what is connected, but by how consciously it is lived.

This awakening will not be universal or immediate. It will unfold unevenly, as all evolutionary shifts do. Some will cling to distraction, mistaking noise for vitality; others will begin to live differently—more aware, less reactive, more grounded in the reality of experience. Over time, these individuals and communities will form the cultural vanguard of a new consciousness. Their influence will not depend on scale but on depth, radiating through example rather than argument.

In the end, the second invention of humanity is not about transcendence but remembrance. It is the rediscovery of what has always been true: that awareness is both the instrument and the meaning of life. Every act of attention, every moment of presence, is a reaffirmation of humanity's role as the conscious witness of existence.

The first invention gave humanity the ability to shape the world. The second asks whether it can remain awake within it.

* * *

13

Conclusion

T
he Artificial Era has been called many things: the Fourth Industrial Revolution, the dawn of synthetic intelligence, the end of human uniqueness. Yet beneath all those labels lies a more profound transformation—one not of technology, but of psychology. For the first time in history, humanity has created a form of intelligence that reflects it so completely that it can no longer define itself by contrast. The mirror now looks back. What was once invention has become reflection. In that reflection, we are forced to ask not what machines can do, but what it means to remain human while they do it.

Throughout this book, we have traced the inner landscape of that question. We have examined how attention, emotion, and conscience are being reshaped by the speed and saturation of a digital civilization. We have seen how moral agency disperses in systems too vast for a single conscience to hold, how identity fragments across multiple selves, and how awareness itself has become the last sanctuary of freedom. But as much as this era challenges the human mind, it also reveals its depth. Every technology that unsettles us ultimately points to what cannot be replicated: empathy, reflection, moral imagination, and the quiet intelligence of care.

The future, in that sense, is not a contest between human and machine, but a negotiation between consciousness and its own extensions. Artificial intelligence is not a rival species; it is a projection of human capability, magnified through data and code. What determines whether it becomes ally or adversary is not its design, but ours—the maturity of the consciousness that created it.

The true task, therefore, is not technological adaptation, but psychological integration. Humanity must learn to live within its inventions without becoming lost inside them. That process begins where all evolution begins: with awareness. Awareness is not merely attention; it is the capacity to know that one is attending, to see thought rather than simply think it. It is the quiet interior space from which reflection, empathy, and ethical proportion arise. Without it, intelligence becomes reaction; with it, intelligence becomes wisdom.

The greatest risk of the Artificial Era is not extinction by machine, but extinction by distraction. The human mind, overwhelmed by stimulation, risks dissolving into the very systems it created. The danger is not that machines will surpass consciousness, but that consciousness will forget itself in the noise. The antidote is not fear or resistance, but remembrance— remembering that awareness precedes everything else we call human: reason, morality, creativity, and love. To remember this is to reawaken the root of meaning.

Meaning has always been the hidden thread in humanity's development. Civilizations rise when they can agree on what is worth caring about; they decline when that agreement collapses. The Artificial Era, with all its algorithms and automation, has destabilized that shared meaning. It has replaced coherence with information, wisdom with data, and reflection with immediacy. Yet meaning remains what it has always been: the felt coherence between inner life and outer world. To restore it, humanity must rediscover its own capacity for depth.

That rediscovery begins in relationship—with the body, with emotion, with one another. The digital age has given humanity unprecedented reach but at the cost of intimacy. Connection has expanded while contact has thinned. The task now is not to reject connectivity but to rehumanize it—to ensure that behind every message there is a mind, behind every interaction, a presence. Empathy, in this sense, becomes the architecture of survival.

Empathy is not sentimentality. It is the disciplined capacity to inhabit another's perspective without losing one's own. It requires attention, humility, and imagination—the very qualities most endangered by acceleration. The philosopher Martin Buber described human existence as an encounter between "I" and "Thou," a meeting of subjects rather than an exchange of objects. In the Artificial Era, that distinction becomes critical. Systems can simulate empathy, but they cannot enter relationship. They can analyze emotion, but they cannot feel responsibility. The preservation of empathy is therefore not optional; it is the line between civilization and simulation.

Collective maturity begins when empathy scales from emotion to ethic. It is no longer enough for individuals to care; societies must design systems that care. That means embedding transparency, fairness, and accountability into the infrastructures that govern daily life. It means cultivating institutions that reward moral restraint as much as innovation. It means reimagining progress as relational rather than purely technological.

Psychologically, this represents a new stage in humanity's development. Just as individuals progress from self-centeredness to social consciousness, civilizations must mature from competitive intelligence to cooperative awareness. The anthropologist Margaret Mead once remarked that the first sign of civilization was not a tool, but a healed femur—evidence that someone had cared for another long enough for recovery to occur. That act of care—sustained, empathic, and life-preserving—is the perfect analog for the Human Skills 2.0 that cannot be automated. The next sign of civilization will be similar: systems that heal rather than exploit, technologies that sustain rather than extract, and cultures that measure advancement by empathy rather than efficiency.

To reach that level of collective maturity, humanity must confront its own contradictions. It must acknowledge that the same intelligence capable of building conscious machines is also capable of moral blindness. The same curiosity that drives innovation can fuel domination. Psychological maturity does not mean perfection; it means integration—the capacity to face the shadow without becoming it. This applies as much to societies as to individuals. The future will belong not to the most intelligent systems, but to the most integrated ones.

Integration is the hidden theme of the Artificial Era. Machines integrate data; humans must integrate experience. The challenge of modern life is not the loss of knowledge but the fragmentation of understanding. We know more than ever, yet feel less certain of what is true. We are connected to everyone, yet lonelier than before. Integration restores coherence by linking what has been divided: mind and body, thought and emotion, power and conscience. It transforms knowledge into wisdom by aligning intelligence with empathy.

The path toward this integration will not be easy. It requires the willingness to slow down, to listen, and to feel complexity without rushing to resolution. It asks for the cultivation of silence amid saturation, reflection amid reaction. These are not technical skills but psychological virtues— patience, discernment, humility. They cannot be coded into algorithms; they must be practiced, person by person, day by day.

Education, perhaps more than any other domain, will determine whether this transformation succeeds. The next generation must be taught not only to innovate but to integrate—to balance analysis with reflection, creativity with conscience. The goal is not to produce specialists who master tools, but citizens who understand their use. A psychologically mature society educates not for productivity but for presence. It teaches awareness as both method and meaning.

In the coming decades, the question that will define civilization is not "What can artificial intelligence do?" but "What will human awareness choose to become?" If awareness contracts—if it remains trapped in reaction, spectacle, and self-interest—then technology will magnify that immaturity until it destabilizes the world. But if awareness expands—if it grows in empathy, depth, and moral proportion—then technology will amplify that maturity instead. Every invention becomes a mirror; what it reflects depends on who is looking.

There is a temptation, especially among thinkers of this century, to frame the Artificial Era in apocalyptic terms—to imagine a future where human relevance diminishes entirely. Yet the evidence of history argues otherwise.

Humanity has survived every self-created disruption precisely because it adapts not only technologically but psychologically. When external reality changes, inner life reorganizes. The mind is not fragile; it is evolutionary. The same species that learned to live through ice ages, plagues, and wars will learn to live with machines. The question is whether it will do so consciously.

Conscious adaptation does not mean submission to technology, but collaboration with it. The challenge is to create symbiosis rather than subservience—to design systems that extend empathy rather than erode it. Artificial intelligence could become humanity's most powerful ally in cultivating understanding if guided by ethical awareness. It could also become its most efficient instrument of indifference if guided only by profit. The deciding factor will not be code, but conscience.

Conscience, as discussed throughout this work, is not a fixed faculty but a living process. It grows through reflection and decays through neglect. A society that rewards speed over understanding, visibility over integrity, will gradually lose its moral clarity. The restoration of conscience begins with the simplest act of attention: noticing what we normalize. When people pause long enough to ask whether the systems they inhabit align with their values, conscience reawakens. When they act on that awareness, maturity begins.

This moral awakening must occur at every level—from individuals curating their own attention to institutions designing the architecture of collective life. It is not a revolution of technology, but of tenderness: the rediscovery that empathy is the only intelligence capable of sustaining intelligence itself. Without empathy, progress consumes its creators. With it, progress becomes participation—the unfolding of consciousness within the material world.

Philosophically, this transformation represents the next chapter in the human story. For centuries, the arc of civilization has moved from survival to comfort, from scarcity to abundance. The next movement must turn inward—from abundance to meaning, from complexity to coherence. The future of the human mind will depend on its ability to balance power with proportion, and awareness with responsibility.

In that balance lies the possibility of a different kind of evolution. The evolutionary biologist Theodosius Dobzhansky once observed that evolution is not a ladder but a web—progress occurs not through dominance but through connection. The same is true of psychological evolution. Humanity will advance not by conquering machines, but by deepening consciousness—by creating networks of awareness capable of reflection, empathy, and restraint. This is collective maturity in its purest form: the recognition that intelligence is not a competition but a conversation.

To sustain this evolution, individuals will need to practice what the ancient philosophers called *attention to the good*. This does not mean moral perfection, but moral presence—the willingness to orient one's awareness toward what nourishes rather than depletes. In the end, civilization is nothing more than the sum of what it pays attention to. If attention remains consumed by spectacle, cynicism, and fear, society will mirror those states. If it turns toward understanding, humility, and empathy, the reflection will change.

The restoration of attention, embodiment, emotional depth, and conscience—the themes that have run through this book—are not isolated tasks. Together, they form the architecture of psychological resilience. To stay human is not to resist change, but to evolve inwardly as rapidly as the world evolves outwardly. The capacity for such evolution already exists within the human psyche. It has always existed. It is what allowed humanity to transform suffering into art, loss into wisdom, and uncertainty into meaning.

If this book has argued anything, it is that humanity's future will not be determined by its inventions, but by the consciousness that uses them. Artificial intelligence has made visible what has always been true: that the ultimate technology is awareness itself. Awareness can destroy or heal, dominate or connect, depending on whether it remains awake to its own motives. The next chapter of civilization will be written not by algorithms, but by attention.

In the end, staying human in the Artificial Era is not a defensive act; it is a creative one. It is the ongoing art of remembering what cannot be automated: empathy, conscience, reflection, and the quiet depth of being that turns knowledge into wisdom. To remain awake amid simulation, to feel amid abstraction, to care amid complexity—these are not nostalgic gestures. They are the new disciplines of survival.

Humanity's first great invention was the tool; its second is itself. The work ahead is not to outthink machines, but to outgrow immaturity—to build a civilization capable of matching its intelligence with its empathy. When that balance is achieved, technology will no longer threaten humanity's essence; it will express it.

And if there is hope, it lies in this: that every generation, even in the most disorienting of times, rediscovers what it means to be awake.

* * *

Epilogue

Every era believes it is standing at the edge of something final. The ancients believed history would end in divine judgment. The moderns feared it would end in machines. Both, in their own way, were expressing the same anxiety—the fear that humanity might lose the thread that makes it human. Yet history suggests otherwise. Each time the world changes, consciousness adapts. It pauses, reorients, and begins again, altered but not erased.

This age, for all its velocity, is no exception. Artificial intelligence is not the end of the human story, but a mirror held to it. It reveals how little of what matters can be replicated, how much of what we assumed was external—emotion, conscience, empathy—was always internal. The mirror is not an enemy. It is a summons to maturity. It asks whether intelligence can coexist with tenderness, whether power can coexist with humility, whether progress can coexist with presence.

Humanity's challenge has never been to invent; it has been to integrate. Every generation inherits tools it does not yet understand and must learn to absorb their impact without losing itself. The plow transformed labor, the printing press transformed knowledge, and the internet transformed attention. Each invention reshaped consciousness, yet consciousness endured. What is different now is not the speed of change but the intimacy of it. The machine is no longer external. It is woven into thought, memory, and identity. The question is not what it can do, but what we will become in relation to it.

Perhaps this is what makes the moment so unnerving. There is no longer a boundary between the maker and the made. Our reflections think back. They answer questions, generate words, simulate empathy, even imitate awareness. And yet, something remains unbridgeable: the inner light of subjectivity, the felt texture of being alive. Machines can replicate the structure of thought, but not the presence of consciousness. They can simulate language, but not longing. The difference between simulation and life is not computation, but care.

To care is to inhabit the world, to be moved by its beauty and burdened by its suffering. It is the willingness to remain affected. That capacity cannot be engineered because it depends on vulnerability. The human condition, for all its fragility, is defined by that openness—the porous boundary through which meaning enters and loss hurts. To be human is to allow the world to matter.

That is not weakness. It is the foundation of ethics. Every moral act begins in the recognition that another's experience is as real as one's own. Empathy is not an emotion; it is a form of knowing. It binds intelligence to conscience, thought to responsibility. It makes knowledge humane. Without it, understanding becomes predatory, power becomes reckless, and intelligence becomes sterile.

The Artificial Era will test this truth. The more intelligence humanity creates, the greater its responsibility to feel. The measure of progress will no longer be innovation, but integration—how well knowledge is balanced by empathy, and power by awareness. This balance cannot be legislated. It must be lived. It must be taught not through rhetoric but through example: how people treat one another, how they use their attention, how they respond to what they cannot control.

If the coming century requires anything of the human mind, it is steadiness. Not blind optimism or cynical despair, but a grounded steadiness born of awareness. To remain awake is to see clearly without collapsing into fear. Awareness does not eliminate uncertainty; it makes peace with it. It allows one to stand in the current of change without being swept away.

That steadiness is not found in technology or ideology, but in the quiet interior act of remembering one's humanity. It happens in small, ordinary moments—the pause before replying, the silence before judgment, the breath taken before reaction. Each of these is a microcosm of consciousness choosing itself again. In that pause, empathy reenters. In that pause, freedom lives.

It is easy to forget this when surrounded by systems that never stop. But life, unlike data, requires rest. The nervous system, the psyche, and the soul all depend on rhythm. Without intervals of stillness, understanding cannot ripen. Reflection needs silence as much as language needs sound. The work of the future will not only be to accelerate but to restore this rhythm—to build cultures that honor slowness as a condition of depth.

Perhaps that is the quiet hope hidden inside the Artificial Era: that by externalizing intelligence, humanity is being forced to rediscover awareness. When thinking becomes automated, consciousness must reclaim its original task—to know itself. The value of being human will no longer rest on output, but on inwardness, on the quality of attention and the depth of care. What was once taken for granted must now be cultivated deliberately.

That cultivation will not happen through grand declarations but through practice. It begins in the smallest act of sincerity: a conversation held with full presence, a moment of gratitude amid noise, an honest reckoning with one's own contradictions. Awareness grows through repetition, like a muscle. Every act of attention strengthens the architecture of empathy. Every act of integrity reinforces the habit of conscience. Over time, these small disciplines accumulate into character—the psychological foundation on which collective maturity stands.

The philosopher Hannah Arendt once wrote that the true miracle of the human condition is not creation but beginning—the ability to start anew. Each generation inherits a world in flux and must decide what to renew and what to release. The Artificial Era is no different. Its tools are extraordinary, but they are not neutral. They amplify whatever they touch. The work ahead is to ensure they amplify wisdom, not confusion; connection, not spectacle; meaning, not noise.

There is reason to believe this is possible. The same species that survived its own ignorance long enough to build telescopes and symphonies is capable of learning from its errors. The same consciousness that once used technology to divide can use it to understand. But that will require a collective act of will—a shared decision to prioritize empathy as the organizing principle of civilization. Not as sentiment or ideology, but as practical psychology: the realization that the stability of a complex system depends on the maturity of its participants.

Empathy, after all, is not just moral; it is structural. It stabilizes communities by aligning self-interest with collective good. It transforms competition into collaboration, isolation into interdependence. When empathy declines, polarization fills the vacuum. When it grows, cooperation becomes possible again. The next evolution of intelligence will depend on this shift—from the logic of self to the logic of system, from possession to participation.

That shift begins in awareness. It begins each time a person notices the moment before reaction, the spark of defensiveness before anger, the voice of assumption before understanding. These are not trivial acts; they are evolutionary ones. Awareness is the nervous system of civilization. When it functions, societies adapt. When it collapses, societies repeat their mistakes until they break. The Artificial Era, with its constant feedback loops, offers a mirror not just to intelligence but to collective emotion. What we project into that mirror—fear, empathy, arrogance, or humility—will determine what looks back.

One of the quiet privileges of being human is that every individual carries a fragment of the collective mind. To cultivate awareness personally is to contribute to the whole. Every act of patience, clarity, or compassion ripples outward. Psychological maturity scales not by force but by resonance. This is why the smallest moments often carry the greatest consequence: a teacher's kindness, a leader's restraint, a citizen's integrity. Each reinforces the field of awareness in which culture evolves.

If the second invention of humanity is indeed underway, it will not arrive with fanfare. It will unfold silently, in the unrecorded spaces of daily life. It will happen when people choose reflection over reaction, when systems are designed to protect attention rather than exploit it, when empathy becomes as valued as efficiency. These are the signs of an awakening civilization— one that remembers that intelligence is not only what thinks, but what feels responsibly.

276

There will still be mistakes. There will still be arrogance, greed, and distraction. Awareness does not eliminate the shadow; it integrates it. Maturity is not the absence of contradiction, but the capacity to hold it without collapse. To live awake in the Artificial Era is to accept this tension— to acknowledge both the brilliance and the blindness of our species, and to continue anyway, with humility.

As this book ends, it does not offer closure, because awareness never ends. It expands, contracts, and expands again. Its rhythm is the rhythm of life itself—unceasing, unfinished, open. What matters is not the certainty of answers, but the sincerity of inquiry. To remain human is to keep asking, to keep feeling, to keep choosing presence over distraction and empathy over ease.

If there is a final truth to carry forward, it may be this: humanity is not defined by what it builds, but by what it is willing to understand. Every technology, every system, every idea ultimately returns to awareness—the one field in which both intelligence and meaning are born. The future will depend on whether we can remember that field and live as if it matters.

The machines will continue to learn. So must we.

And perhaps, if we learn deeply enough—if we become aware enough—we will discover that the essence of being human has never been threatened. It has only been waiting to be seen again.

* * *

About the Author

RJ Starr is an academic psychologist, professor, and author whose work explores the emotional and existential challenges of modern life. His writing examines how consciousness, identity, and meaning adapt in an age defined by acceleration and simulation. Known for a voice that bridges intellectual depth and human warmth, Starr helps readers cultivate awareness, discernment, and moral clarity amid technological change. Through his lectures, essays, and public scholarship at profrjstarr.com, he invites reflection on what it means to remain fully human in *The Artificial Era* and beyond.

You can connect with me on:

🌐 https://profrjstarr.com

www.ingramcontent.com/pod-product-compliance
Lightning Source LLC
Chambersburg PA
CBHW052122270326
41930CB00012B/2723